Charles Lee Feinberg

Dr. Feinberg was born in an orthodox Jewish home in Pittsburgh, Pennsylvania. He studied Hebrew and related subjects for fourteen years preparatory to becoming a rabbi. He received his A.B. degree from the University of Pittsburgh; his Th.B., Th.M., and Th.D. from Dallas Theological Seminary; his A.M. in Old Testament at Southern Methodist University; and his Ph.D. in Archaeology and Semitic Languages from the Johns Hopkins University.

At present he is Dean and Professor of Semitics and Old Testament at the Talbot Theological Seminary; a member of the Society of Biblical Literature and Exegesis; an associate member of the American School of Oriental Research at Jerusalem and Baghdad; a Fellow of the Philosophical Society of Great Britain; a Fellow by courtesy of the University of Southern California; formerly President of the Iran Interior Mission, Kermanshah, Iran. He has served as instructor in Church History; as Professor of Semitics and Old Testament; and now visiting Bible teacher at Dallas Theological Seminary; as pastor of the First Cumberland Presbyterian Church, Dallas, Texas and supply pastor in several other p   well-known Bible confere
United
ain, lis
and *W*
Feinbe
Comm
Bible.

Dr. Feinberg
Remembers, Premillennialism
lennialism? Israel in the Spotlight, and expository works on the minor prophets.

HABAKKUK:
PROBLEMS OF FAITH

ZEPHANIAH:
THE DAY OF THE LORD

HAGGAI:
REBUILDING THE TEMPLE

MALACHI:
FORMAL WORSHIP

By

CHARLES LEE FEINBERG, Th.D., Ph.D.
PROFESSOR OF OLD TESTAMENT
Los Angeles Bible Theological Seminary
Los Angeles, California

Published by

AMERICAN BOARD OF MISSIONS TO THE JEWS, INC.
236 West Seventy-second Street
NEW YORK 23, N. Y.

(Printed in U. S. A.)

To

The Revered Memory of

DR. LEOPOLD COHN,

Man of God,

Missionary Pioneer,

Personal Benefactor,

This Volume Is Gratefully Dedicated

AUTHOR'S PREFACE

THE present volume is the fourth in the series of five, projected for all the minor prophets. It is impossible for the author to express adequately his gratitude to God for the privilege of scrutinizing these pages of Sacred Writ, or to indicate fully the inexpressible blessing derived from such exercise of heart and mind. Similar and greater experiences of this nature are coveted for each reader.

The hour is later on God's clock than any one of us realizes. Prophecy should be studied, not for mental exercise alone, but to ascertain the will of God now for each life, and to move into the center of that place of blessing. May love for Israel result from such activity.

Grateful thanks are due to my wife; my son, Paul; my daughter, Lois; and my secretary, Mrs. Franceen Smith, for valuable assistance rendered in typing and proofreading the manuscript. The consideration and cooperation of Dr. J. Hoffman Cohn, worthy son of a worthy father to whom this book is dedicated, have been appreciated every step of the way from the publication of these studies in *The Chosen People* to their appearance in this final form.

May the Lord use these pages to His glory in Christ Jesus.

CHARLES L. FEINBERG.

Los Angeles, California

CONTENTS

HABAKKUK:

PROBLEMS OF FAITH

HABAKKUK:

PROBLEMS OF FAITH

Chapter I

THE PERPLEXITY OF THE PROPHET

The Prophet and His Times

NOTHING is known of the personal history of the prophet. Some have assumed on the basis of verse 19 of chapter 3 of this prophecy, that Habakkuk was of a priestly family, and so qualified to officiate in the temple service. No certainty attaches to this view. His name means "to embrace." Luther thus explained the name of the prophet: "Habakkuk signifies an embracer, or one who embraces another, takes him into his arms. He embraces his people, and takes them to his arms, i. e., he comforts them and holds them up, as one embraces a weeping child, to quiet it with the assurance that, if God wills, it shall soon be better."

There has been difference of opinion as to the time of the prophetic ministry of Habakkuk. Since the heading of the prophecy indicates nothing as to the reign in which he labored, the time of the prophet must be gleaned from the contents of the book itself. Some have referred the prophecy to Manasseh's or even Josiah's (with less reason, I think) days, but the best view is that which places it in the reign of

Jehoiakim. This is arrived at from the nature of the sins prevalent in Israel pictured in this book, and from the manner in which Habakkuk speaks of the Chaldeans. If this be true, then he was a contemporary of the prophet Jeremiah before the Babylonian invasion. At this time sin was indeed rife in Israel and the hour of the Babylonian invasion was not far off.

The book of Habakkuk differs from the regular addresses of the prophets who ministered to Israel. His is a record of his own experience of soul with God. Prophets spoke for God to men; he expostulates with God about His dealings with men. We are reminded in this regard of Jonah among the prophets and of Job among the poetic books. Primarily and essentially he is the prophet of faith. The keystone of the whole book is 2:4. His main theme (like Psalm 73 and other passages in the Old Testament) was the affliction of the godly and the prosperity of the ungodly. He dwells on the perfect dealings of God and the development of faith in His own. All concede to Habakkuk a very high place among the Hebrew prophets. The poetry of chapter 3 has been rightly praised on every hand as the most magnificent Hebrew poetry. The language of the book is very beautiful. The message for the most part is couched in the form of communion with God. Chapter 1 dwells on the invasion of the Chaldeans; chapter 2 predicts the judgment of God upon the Chaldeans; and chapter 3 pictures the coming of the Lord and the destruction of the hostile world powers. Though the book is short in compass, it is quoted from a number of times in the New Testament. Compare Habakkuk 1:5 with Acts 13:40, 41; Habakkuk 2:4

with Romans 1 : 17; Galatians 3 : 11; and Hebrews 10 : 38. See also Habakkuk 3 : 17, 18 and Philippians 4 : 4, 10-19.

The Complaint of the Prophet

The prophecy is entitled a burden because it predicts judgments upon Israel and her enemies. Habakkuk laments over the sin of his people and then over those of her foes. The first verse gives no clue as to the time of the prophecy which must be gathered, as we have indicated, from other details of the book. The man of God has been crying unto the Lord concerning the wickedness and violence in the land, yet the Lord has done nothing about it. He is jealous for God's glory. This is not a personal complaint, but he voices the desire and longing of the godly in the nation. Here we have unveiled for us at the very outset the exercised heart of the prophet of God. Everything is awry and God is apparently not intervening in the matter. In verses 9 and 13 of this chapter we have similar language to that of verses 2 and 3. The reign of Jehoiakim was full of injustice and bloodshed. Note Jeremiah 22 : 3, 13-17; for the same inquiry see Jeremiah 12 : 1; 20 : 8; and Job 19 : 7. Since the prophet is powerless to alter conditions and the Lord has not, he asks why he is permitted to see such iniquity on every hand and violence and strife rearing their ugly heads. What troubles the prophet is that the Lord seems to look on these heart-breaking conditions with indifference. The silence of God in human affairs, then as now, has ever been difficult to understand. But this does not mean that there is not an answer, and that divine wisdom is incapable of coping with the situation. All is under His seeing eye and everything is under the control of His mighty hand. But in the meantime the law was slacked (lit. chilled), rendered ineffective, paralyzed. It came to be looked upon as being without force or authority. Because of unrighteous judges the law was set at nought. Since the forms of judgment were corrupted, both life and property were insecure. Justice could not prevail because the wicked knew how to hem the righteous in on all sides, so that he could not receive his just due. Miscarriage of justice was the order of the day. Ensnaring the righteous by fraud the ungodly perverted all right and honesty. Because God did not punish sin immediately, men thought they could sin on with impunity. See Ecclesiastes 8: 11.

The Answer of God

God is far from being an unconcerned spectator in earth's affairs. We can always be certain that, if our hearts are stirred over the prevalence of sin and ungodliness, God is all the more deeply concerned. He addresses Habakkuk and the people of Judah, directing them to look out on the scene of world history among the nations. The Lord points them to the events transpiring among the surrounding nations: the Assyrian empire destroyed by Nabopolassar; the founding of the Chaldean rule; and the victory of Nabopolassar (with his son, Nebuchadnezzar) over the Egyptians at Carchemish. As they look they will wonder marvellously, a most emphatic expression. This power of Babylonia was to be used of God to chastise Israel. He may use others, but He claims it as His own work. Thus, instead of God's being inactive and indifferent, He is emphatically at work, in a way which men will scarcely believe. It will be of such unusual character. (In Acts 13:41 Paul warns the despisers of the gospel with judgment using this verse.) It has been suggested that probably at this time the Babylonian nation was still friendly. 2 Kings 20:12-19. Soon they were to invade the land in three sieges in the time of Jehoiakim, Jehoiachin, and Zedekiah. Our prophet has these invasions in view.

The statement that God will raise up the Chaldeans has reference to their invasion of Judah, because they had already been on the scene of political history for some score of years. Compare Isaiah 23:13. The Chaldeans were the inhabitants of Babylonia and were of Semitic origin from Kesed, son of Nahor, brother of Abraham (Genesis 22:22). They are mentioned in Isaiah 43:14; 47:1; 48:14, 20; Jeremiah 21:9; 32:4, 24; Ezekiel 23:23; their invasion is described in Jeremiah 5:15-18. The indication is clear that Habakkuk ministered at a time when the Chaldeans were coming to the fore in world politics. The prophet gives a threefold picture of the enemy of Israel: they are cruel, quick and impetuous in their ways, and bent on far-flung campaigns, such as were conducted under Nebuchadnezzar.

The Rod of God's Anger

Now the text describes at greater length what was touched upon in the message of verse 6, which is the classic passage for the characteristics of the Chaldeans, as Isaiah 5:26-30 is for the Assyrians. The

Chaldeans strike terror into the heart and are a
dreadful adversary. Their own desire is their only
law and standard of judgment. They make their own
rules of conduct. This is Babylon in its old character
(Genesis 11:4). Their dignity did proceed from
themselves, for they assumed the superior place in
the Babylonian empire on their own initiative. And
nothing is lacking in their preparation for military
campaigns. Their horses exceed leopards in their
swiftness, and in ferocity they surpass evening wolves.
Wolves, hungry from the lack of food during the day,
prey on the flock as night comes on. Jeremiah 5:6
and Zephaniah 3:3. The Chaldean horsemen are
irresistible in their attack, and swoop down as an
eagle intent on its prey. We have here the fulfilment
of the warning of Moses in Deuteronomy 28:49.
The purpose of the invaders is to perpetrate violence
in the land. This was Israel's sin (verses 2 and 3)
and it will be her punishment. The second part of
verse 9 has been variously interpreted and translated.
One translation would have it that the set of their
faces is forward; another is that their faces shall sup
up as the east wind. In either case the thought seems
to be clear that the enemy will be formidable and
irresistible in his advance. They will blast everything
before them as they go. The innumerable host of
their captives can only be compared to sand. The
Chaldean is fearless and confident of his power, for
he scoffs at kings and their helplessness in the face
of his attack. He runs roughshod over every obstacle and opposing fortress. He has been called a
hasty nation, and this is clearly seen in the manner
of his besieging a city. He needs only to cast up bul-

warks before fortified cities in order to lay siege to them, when they capitulate before him and he takes them captive. Verse 11 has received various treatments at the hands of translators and interpreters. It has been suggested that when the Chaldean is exulting in his victories, his mind will change (he will lose his reason) and he will pass over all restraints to his destruction. This passage would then be a prophecy of the disease that came upon Nebuchadnezzar when his reason was unseated. The language of Habakkuk has been likened to that of Daniel 4:16, 30-34 where an unforced harmony between the two books is said to exist. While this position is entirely within the range of the possible, it is not very probable. All that the prophet is stating here is that the successes of the Chaldean will be multiplied; he will carry all before him, as the wind sweeps over vast stretches of land. In doing so the Chaldean conqueror heaps up guilt before God because of his ungodly ambitions and his subjugation of many helpless peoples. God is given no glory in these successes, because the Babylonian victor praises his own strength. His own might and power are his god. The Assyrian did the same before him (Isaiah 10:13, 14) and multiplied others have followed this method since him. For one to make his own strength his god is to commit suicide of the soul. See Daniel 4:30. In this section of the prophecy we have had described for us in a remarkable pen portrait the Chaldean invader, his nature, his manner of operation, his purpose, his weapons, his attitude toward others, and the basic cause of his ultimate downfall. Blessed is the man that readeth and taketh heed.

The Deeper Perplexity of Habakkuk

Has the problem of the prophet been answered by the Lord? Or has the difficulty become worse in the mind of Habakkuk? The messenger of God is in greater perplexity now, for he remonstrates with God for inflicting punishment on Judah by a nation less righteous than they. The prophet directs his appeal to God whom the enemy has treated contemptuously. He speaks representatively for his people, and uses the well-known names for God as Jehovah, Holy One, and Rock. In addressing the everlasting God he declares by faith that God's people will not die. He knows the nature of the covenant-keeping God who will not allow His people to be wiped out. The ground of his confidence and hope is twofold: (1) God has been Israel's God from ancient times; and (2) He is so holy that He must punish ungodliness whether in His own nation or in the enemy. Since God does not desire the destruction of His people, it is manifest that He has only chosen the Chaldean to chasten and correct His chosen people. But the wound still aches in the heart of Habakkuk. How could the righteous God, who is so pure and cannot abide any form of iniquity, use such a wicked and treacherous people as the Chaldeans? And human life was so cheap to the Babylonians. They treated men as one would the fish of the sea who have no defenses or rights, and as worms of the earth who have no ruler to protect them. In a figurative manner the prophet shows how the Chaldean callously takes captives as a fisherman plies his trade. The angle, net, and drag represent the armies and weapons whereby the Chaldean carried on his military ambitions. His great successes gladdened and rejoiced his heart. But to whom did he give the glory? He worshipped his own military prowess. There is no indication that the Babylonians worshipped the sword as did some of the ancients. They did boast of their strength in war, however. How perverse man can be when he delights to worship the creature rather than the Creator, the gift rather than the Giver. In his distress and perplexity of soul the prophet asks the Lord whether this cruelty and idolatry of the Chaldean will go on without interruption. Will God not bring such rapacity to an end by His power? On this tense note our chapter concludes, but the answer of God will appear in the next chapter. There we shall see that the Lord hath set a bound to all which displeases Him. All is taken into account and the remedy is provided. We do well to bring our doubts and perplexities to the Lord, as did Habakkuk, and leave them with Him for final disposition and solution. He never fails.

"We Shall Not Die"

This is the glad and glorious testimony of any child of God who has been delivered from death in trespasses and sins through the work of the Lord Jesus Christ on Calvary. But it reminds us that those without Christ are dead spiritually and, if they continue thus, will die the second death which is eternal separation from God. The prophets of the Old Testament cried again and again to Israel that they should not die in their sins. We have the same blessed privilege to declare to every Jew that believing in the Messiah he may have life eternal and not die.

QUESTIONS ON CHAPTER I

1. Discuss the meaning of the prophet's name.

2. What are the opinions as to the time of Habakkuk's ministry? To which do you hold and why?

3. What is the nature of the book?

4. Indicate the theme of the prophecy.

5. With what events does each chapter deal?

6. Define clearly the perplexity of the prophet. Was he condemning God?

7. How does God meet the problem of Habakkuk?

8. Who were the Chaldeans? Describe them briefly.

9. What would be the manner of their attack upon Judah?

10. How do you explain verse 11?

11. Does the answer of God satisfy the prophet? If not, why not?

12. What is Israel's only hope for escape from the second death?

Chapter II

THE ANSWER OF GOD

The Answer of God 2:1

AT THE close of the first chapter we found the prophet distressed at the inscrutable dealings of God with His people, Israel. The prophet complained at first of the widespread iniquity in Judah, to which the Lord replied that He was aware of it all and would judge it at the hand of the Chaldean. When the prophet learns of the rod of God's anger, he is bowed down in greater mental agony that God should use a nation less righteous to afflict and chasten His people. With the problem still unsolved we come to the solution in this chapter. Since God has answered the first questionings of the prophet, he feels confident that God will do likewise with his greater problem. Just as a sentinel is set to keep an eye on that which occurs outside a fortified city, so the prophet stations himself in spirit to await God's answer to his inquiry. The thought is not that Habakkuk actually went to a watch-tower, but that he assumed such an attitude of heart, that of anticipation and watchfulness. The majority of interpreters understand the verse in a spiritual sense of inward preparation. The prophets are compared to watchmen. See Isaiah 21:8, 11; Jeremiah 6:17; and Ezekiel 3:17; 33:2, 3. In this spirit of alertness the prophet was ready to receive by revelation the response of God. The answer was first to his own

mind and heart, then to his people. The rendering
of the last part of the verse as "when I am reproved,"
is not preferable here. There is no indication that
any complaint was lodged against the prophet or that
he stood in need of reproof. He was expecting the
solution to his complaint.

And God did not disappoint His servant in his
need. The Lord commanded Habakkuk to write the
revelation given him upon tablets. These were the
customary ones for writing. Isaiah 8:1. It could
have been on such as were shown in the market-place
on which public notices were written (graven in clay)
in clear letters. The letters were to be large and legi-
ble enough to be easily read. The prophet was to
reduce the vision to writing so the people would have
it for the future. See Daniel 12:4 for similar wording. The one reading it was to run to tell it forth,
because it was such a message of joy to Israel, telling
them of the ruin of their enemy and their own deliverance. The deliverance was not to come immediately, but it was surely to come; the godly should
wait for it. Delay is only in the heart of man; God
is working the details according to His own plan.
Patience was needed. The purpose of God cannot be
hastened nor can it be delayed. It comes to fulfilment
at the appointed time. The vision hastes (not speaks,
but pants) on it its fulfilment. It seeks the accomplishment of the things it predicts. The end spoken
of here is not the end of the times of the Gentiles, as
has been suggested, but the realization of the prophecy in history. The vision will not deceive nor disappoint, but will assuredly come to pass. The latter
portion of verse 3 is quoted in Hebrews 10:37. The

passage in Hebrews is clear that the reference is ulti-
mately to the coming again of the Lord Jesus Christ.
The attitude of heart enjoined in our text of the
prophet is the normal one for the child of God today.
We are as men waiting for the return of their Lord.
Would that the hour were here!

Basic Divine Principles

In verse 4 we have the content of the vision given
the prophet which is the answer to his perplexity set
forth in 1:12-17. This text, which later became the
watchword of Christianity, is the key to the whole
Book of Habakkuk and is the central theme of all the
Scriptures. It is not treating of two classes in Israel:
those who would reject the prophetic message in
their pride and those who would humbly believe it.
The reference is undoubtedly to the proud Chaldean,
but since we have here basic divine principles these
truths can be applied in a secondary sense to any
individual who is in unbelief. The soul of the proud
Babylonian is puffed up and is not upright, but full
of deceit and dishonesty. This way is the path to destruction. On the other hand, the just or righteous
one (referring here primarily to the godly in Israel)
shall live by faith. There have been many attempts
to interpret the word "faith" as faithfulness or right
dealing, but the sense must be trust in God in this
context. See Genesis 15:6; 2 Chronicles 20:20;
and Isaiah 7:9. We have here the cause of life and
death. Pride leads to death because it will not receive by faith the grace of God. Habakkuk now has
his answer to his complaint. He is not to doubt that
the pride of the Chaldean will be his destruction,

while the godly is to continue looking to the Lord unto life. The second clause of verse 4 is quoted in Romans 1:17; Galatians 3:11; and Hebrews 10:38. The Talmud with insight declares that here all 613 precepts given by God to Moses on Sinai are summarized.

Moreover, the proud Chaldean has given himself over to the treachery of wine. Ancient writers confirm this statement that the Babylonians were very much addicted to wine. Note the disaster it brought in Daniel 5:1ff. A heathen writer said of them: "The Babylonians give themselves wholly to wine, and the things which follow upon drunkenness." What a scourge to any people is drunkenness! How well we do to heed the admonition in our own land. Filled with pride, drunken with wine, the Chaldean is also thirsty for power and conquest. His restless nature stirs him up to continuous conquests (1:16, 17), so his great desire is to go forth to destroy. Like Sheol (in the New Testament, Hades) his desire swallows up all and yet remains unsatisfied. Sheol was the place of the departed dead. The body was committed to the grave and the soul went to Sheol. From Luke 16 (especially verse 26) we learn that there were two divisions in Sheol before the death and resurrection of the Lord Jesus Christ: a section for the righteous (called also Abraham's bosom or Paradise) and one for the unrighteous. After the resurrection of Christ (Ephesians 4:8) He removed the righteous souls from Sheol to heaven where Paradise is to be found now. Compare carefully Luke 23:43; 2 Corinthians 5:1-10; and Philippians 1:23. In this day of grace the ungodly still go to Hades (Sheol), while the believer departs to be with the Lord in the third heaven. We have thus set before us the two ways, the way of life and the way of death. We note two types of character and the manner of God's dealing with each on the basis of fundamental divine principles. The proud, puffed up, dishonest, drunken, dissatisfied Chaldean will have death; the just, godly, righteous Israelite will have life through faith in the living God. God could not make the responsibilities and issues more clear than He has. And they hold good for all time.

The First Woe

Now follows a fivefold woe upon the wicked Chaldean oppressor. The five woes are presented symmetrically in five stanzas or strophes of three verses each. The woes are taken up and uttered by all the nations and peoples mentioned in verse 5 who have suffered at the hand of the cruel oppressor. In a taunt song they will heap woe on the Babylonian for his rapacious and plundering ways. He sought to heap up for himself that property which was not his. How long did he think he could go on thus with apparent impunity? Furthermore, he loaded himself with pledges (not thick clay as in some versions, which makes no sense here), that is, the wealth of the nations which he has plundered, as an exacting usurer accumulates pledges contrary to the Mosaic law (Deuteronomy 24 : 10), and which must be given up again. Suddenly he would be called upon to relinquish his ill-gotten gain. We know that the Medes and Persians struck unexpectedly at the Babylonians. The word "bite" forms a play on words with a simi-

lar word which means to exact usury. The thought
is that since the Chaldeans had spoiled so much
goods from others, they were in a sense indebted to
the nations: the surrounding peoples were their
creditors. The conquerors would not only be bitten
by the subject peoples, but would be shaken violently,
referring to the forceful seizure of a debtor by his
creditor. Matthew 18:28. The spoiler will be spoiled;
the plunderer will be plundered. All this will come
to him for his shedding of blood and violence in-
flicted upon the lands and cities of the nations.

The Second Woe

The second woe is pronounced upon the Chaldeans
for their covetousness and self-exaltation. The basic
meaning of "evil gain" is breaking off, as Orientals
do with pieces of silver and other metals in money
transactions, then it came to refer to those who
sought after ungodly gain. Like Edom, the Chaldean
set up his government on a basis where it was secure
from attack. The language is not literal, but is taken
from the imagery of an eagle. Job 39:27; Jeremiah
49:16; and Obadiah 4. The ungodly oppressor may
think his position an impregnable one, but because of
his many plunderings he has sinned against his own
soul and caused his own ruin. He has brought the
retribution of God upon himself. Even inanimate
things, the buildings he has erected to his own glory
and for the satisfaction of his own pride, will cry out
because of the injustices perpetrated in them. The
reference is not to the dissolution of the empire, as
though it were falling apart. But the stone and the
beam would cry out together to accuse of sin and

bloodshed. See Genesis 4:10, and by contrast note Luke 19:40 and Psalm 29:9 (A.S.V.).

The Third Woe

For tyrannical oppression of captive peoples a third woe is called down upon the Chaldean conqueror. Their cities were built with blood, for the wealth by which the king of Babylon built his magnificent buildings was gained from bloody wars. Captive labor was used to build the grand structures of the empire. But, contrary to the purposes of the proud rulers of Babylon, the Lord had determined that the labor of these subject peoples would not stand. It would all be consumed in the fire that was to bring the Chaldean empire to an end. The work was for nought. Of old a kingdom had been set up in Babylon to usurp power and glory (Genesis 10: 10; 11:4), but it must pass away and be replaced by God's kingdom. Revelation 11:15. The Babylonian kingdom must give way to the kingdom of the Lord and of His Christ. In order for the earth to be filled with the knowledge of the glory of the Lord, as the waters cover the sea, the kingdoms and rules of this world must be judged and destroyed. The purpose of God in creating the earth at all was that it might reflect His glory. Numbers 14:21; Isaiah 11:9.

The Fourth Woe

The next woe upon the Chaldean takes into account his shameful treatment of weaker or neighboring nations. Verses 15 and 16 are probably to be taken figuratively. Otherwise, they speak of shameful and immoral corruption. The condition of a

drunken man represents in Scripture the overthrow
of a conquered nation. Compare Nahum 3: 11. The
thought is that the Chaldeans with their lust for
power and conquest enticed other nations into campaigns for spoil and finally left them to suffer loss
and shame. For this, foul shame will be upon those
who allured the peoples and they will be as the un-
circumcised, which indicated to the Hebrews the
height of contempt. The cup of retribution in God's
wrath will come round in due time to the Babylonian. Jeremiah 25: 15ff. Judgment is determined
against her because of the desolation wrought in the
land of Palestine. They had denuded the forests for
their military campaigns and in their building enter-
prises, and had killed the beasts hiding there. From
earliest days conquerors cut down the forest of Leba-
non and killed its beasts, as is recorded by different
kings both of Babylonia and Assyria. The verse also
indicates a climax in wickedness from the destruction
of the forests and beasts to the desolation of the cities.
The land and city of verse 8 refer to all the nations;
in verse 17 the reference is to Judah and Jerusalem.

The Fifth Woe

The last woe is uttered upon the greatest sin of all,
idolatry. To bring out forcefully the utter worthless-
ness of idols the prophet asks of what profit it is. It
is of no use. See Isaiah 44: 9, 10 and Jeremiah 2: 11.
The teacher of lies is the idol because of the false
oracles connected with its worship. How senseless
of the idolater to cry for help to the dumb idol to
awake to help him. Ironically and scornfully, the
prophet questions whether such can teach. The idol

may be overlaid with gold and silver, showing earthly splendor, but there is no life within it. The prophets of the Old Testament are at their best when they expose the delusion and senselessness of idol worship. Idols are nothing, but there is a living, all-seeing, ruling God in the heavens. He is not hidden under gold and silver, but alive in heaven, ready and willing to help His people. He is the invisible God inhabiting His heavenly temple and all-powerful, therefore it behooves all nations to be solemnly and humbly reverent before Him. Psalm 76: 8, 9; Zephaniah 1: 7; and Zechariah 2: 13 dwell on the same majestic theme. The nations do well, as well as individuals, to submit silently to Him waiting for His judgment. Blessed be our God!

"The Just Shall Live By Faith"

How Israel needs to hear and heed his word of priceless counsel. The just does not live by works or the merits of the fathers. It is by faith alone in the sacrifice of the Messiah, the Lord Jesus Christ. The Jews are beloved for the fathers' sake (Romans 11: 29), but they are not saved for their sake, but for Jesus' sake who died for them. Let us tell them!

QUESTIONS ON CHAPTER II

1. How did the first chapter form the background for this one?

2. What preparation did Habakkuk have for the reception of God's answer to his problem?

3. What features are indicated as to the importance and nature of the message?

4. Discuss fully the meaning and significance of verse 4.

5. What is the connection between verses 4 and 5?

6. Indicate the Scriptural teaching on the subject of Sheol. Cite passages.

7. What is the subject of the first woe pronounced on the Chaldean?

8. What is in view in the second woe?

9. Why is the third woe announced against the Chaldean?

10. What sin called forth the fourth woe? Explain.

11. Explain the fifth woe.

12. How does the message of "the just shall live by faith" meet the need of Israel now?

Chapter III

THE TRIUMPHANT FAITH OF THE PROPHET

Poem of Prayer and Praise 3: 1

AFTER hearing the promises and warnings of chapters 1 and 2 the prophet concludes his book with prayer and praise. He recalls past manifestations of God's power and grace; he prays for the speedy deliverance of God's people; and he expresses a firm confidence in God which is unchangeable. Parallels to this poem are to be found in Deuteronomy 33:2-5; Judges 5:4, 5; Psalm 68:7, 8; 77:13-20; 114; and Isaiah 63:11-14. This ode was designed for public worship as is seen from the inscription, subscription, and the musical notation "Selah" in verses 3, 9, 13. It is admittedly one of the most majestic and sublime portions of the Word of God. The chapter is entitled a prayer, a designation used for "psalm" in Psalm 102:1. It was used in referring to devotional portions in general. The poem was set to shigionoth which is found (in the singular) in Psalm 7 also. We are certain that it refers to the kind of music which accompanied the song, although the translations of the word have been varied, such as "after the manner of elegies"; "a song"; "a reeling"; or "a triumphal song." Since the word comes from a verb meaning to err, the thought is one of a song sung in great excitement, a triumphal song.

[31]

It is interesting to note how Habakkuk lays bare his heart at the beginning of each chapter of his prophecy. He was no passive spectator of the sad spiritual decline of Judah, nor was he a passive recipient of the telling solution of God as he waited on his watch. These disclosures stirred him deeply, as they should do for all of us. What God had revealed of the Chaldean attack on Judah and God's retribution on Chaldea, that is, the answer of God in chapter 2 especially, had disturbed the prophet and filled his heart with terror and awe. He finds his outlet in prayer and calls upon God to revive His work in the midst of the years. The prophet of God would have Him manifest His grace to Israel and judgment upon their enemies by renewing the displays of His mighty power as of old in intervening on behalf of His people. While the years yet run their course and Israel still undergoes suffering, God is supplicated to make known by experimental proof the reenactment of His deeds of power. In God's wrath upon both Judah and the Chaldeans, He is besought to remember mercy. Judgment is to be tempered with mercy. In this verse we have before us the theme of the psalm and the heart of the prayer. In short, Habakkuk prays that God will do for His people as He has in the past, and while inflicting punishment will remember to deliver also.

God in His Majesty

In a sublime manner the prophet now pictures a future redemption under figures taken from past events. The background here is the memory of the events of the Exodus and Sinai. Just as the Lord

manifested Himself when He redeemed Israel from
Egypt, He will appear again to deliver the godly
among His people from their oppressors among the
nations and will judge their foes as He did the land
of Egypt. Some critics of this passage have shown
a lack of spiritual insight when they see in this section only a description of a storm sweeping from the
desert, instead of a glorious appearance of God, a
Theophany. The first verb of verse 3 (and so all the
verbs through verse 15) should not be translated as
a past, as though Habakkuk were placing himself
back at the time of the events of Israel's deliverance
from Egypt. It should rather be rendered "cometh"
with a future sense, for as the Lord once came to His
people at Sinai to do wonders among them and for
them and establish a covenant, so He will come again
to liberate them from their enemies. Teman was one
of the great cities of Edom; it was probably the
capital of the country and was the southernmost large
city of Edom. Here it is used representatively for all
Idumea. Paran was opposite Teman and only separated from it by the valley of the Ghor. 1 Kings 11:
18 indicates it was between Midian and Egypt. Selah
indicates a heightening of the musical accompaniment, the musical *forte*. It would allow for a pause
and meditation. This notation occurs 70 times in the
Psalms and three times in this chapter. The manifested excellence of the Lord covers the heavens and
His praise filled the earth. Verse 3 deals with the
extent of God's coming; verse 4 with its effects.
All creation reflects His splendor; light is His garment. Psalm 104:2. His brightness is as the light
of the sun and rays of light encircle Him. The word

"rays" means "horns" by comparison of the rays of
the rising sun above the horizon to the horns or ant-
lers of the gazelle, found also in Arabic poetry. And
there, in the brightness, is the hiding of His power.
The splendor actually conceals the glorious, invisible
God. Our God is a God that hideth Himself (Isaiah
45:15, but how gloriously revealed in Christ, John
1:18 and 2 Corinthians 4:6), but it is with excess
of light. Glorious God is ours!

God in His Power

As plagues were visited upon Israel's enemies and
burning pestilence went before the Lord in the desert,
so the Lord will accomplish in His future manifestations. According to Revelation 6 definite plagues
and visitations will precede the coming of the Lord
visibly to earth. Now Habakkuk pictures the Lord as
stopping in His march and causing great upheavals
in the earth. The Lord stood and measured the earth
with His all-seeing glance. With irresistible power
His hand drove asunder the nations and overpowered
them. Even the mountains, those lofty objects of
God's creative power, were scattered as dust, and
the ancient hills bowed as though in reverence and
submission. All was leveled before His august presence. His ways are everlasting: He works in time
and in all creation but transcends all. His goings are
ever accompanied with power as of old.

The Fear of the Nations

When God accompanied Israel's entrance into
Canaan, the nations were struck with fear. This
same pattern of events will obtain in prophetic times.

The people of Cushan were thrown into consterna-
tion. Calvin refers the name to Cushan-rishathaim,
king of Mesopotamia, of Judges 3:8, 10, but undoubtedly the reference is to the people of Cush or
the Ethiopians. Trembling seized the land of Midian,
those of the Arabian coast of the Red Sea opposite
the Ethiopians. Tents and curtains indicate their
nomadic life and stand for the people of these lands.
The prophet at this place addresses God directly for
vividness and emphasis. When God marches forth,
the rivers and the sea retreat. The Red Sea and the
Jordan were dried up to allow Israel to pass over
dryshod. What God has done to one river and one
sea, He can do to all. The poetic questions reveal
how powerful were the ways of the Lord with the sea
as with the land. The horses and chariots of salvation
upon which the Lord is pictured as riding are not
the angels, but the elements—the clouds and the
winds. See Psalm 104:4. The bow of the Lord was
drawn from its cover and the arrows fell fast upon
the heads and penetrated far into the hearts of the
Lord's adversaries. By an emphatic expression Habakkuk shows how completely unsheathed was the
bow of the Lord to accomplish His purpose. As it
was then, so it shall be again. Just as clear as the
first clause of verse 9 is, so obscure is the second.
There are but three words in the Hebrew, but as yet
they have not been explained satisfactorily. One
eminent Old Testament scholar counted more than
one hundred translations of these words. With such
diversity of opinion it were foolhardy to be dogmatic
at this point. We can only suggest a preference and
leave it with that. If we take the rendering of the

American Standard Version, the thought is that
God's supernatural interventions for His people are
not for one period alone, but His oaths secure them
for Israel in the future. Such a statement is true,
although it does make an abrupt change from the description of God's chastisements upon the enemies of
Israel. The marginal rendering of this same version
may be somewhat better. "Sworn were the chastisements of thy word" would convey the meaning that
according to God's solemn oath He had foretold
vengeance upon His enemies. Compare Deuteronomy
32:40-42. The earth itself in consequence of the
wrath of God trembles and waters gush forth from
beneath, or at the quaking of the earth the sea emp-
ties its waters on the land into rivers. Verse 10 continues the thought of an earthquake caused by the
mighty advance of the Lord of Hosts. The prophet
repeats in different form what was stated in verse 6,
because the mountains are so prominent on the
earth. The loud roarings of the waters of the deep
are likened to the utterances of a voice. The waves
of the sea are spoken of as the lifting up of its hands.
In this power-mad age we do well to remember that
power belongeth only to God.

God's Intervention for His People

The miracle at Gibeon is referred to in verse 11
when the sun and moon stood still in their respective
places in the heavens. Joshua 10:12. God wrought
wonders on earth, among the nations, in the seas, and
in the heavens as well. The arrows spoken of may
well refer to lightnings, instruments of the wrath of
God as the bow of verse 9. The Lord marched

through the land in His indignation and threshed the
nations in His anger. For a similar figure see Isaiah
63 : 1-6. Lest by this time anyone be in doubt as to
the purpose of these manifestations of the power and
wrath of God, Habakkuk states expressly that God
had in mind the salvation of His own people. There
are two interpretations of "thine anointed." One
sees here a reference to Israel, thus paralleling the
thought of "thy people." The other holds that the
anointed is God's King, the Messiah, through whose
instrumentality and agency God effects salvation for
His people. Many passages confirm this latter position, while the first view finds support in Psalm
105 : 15. If the reference be to a past event (as a
pattern) in the head out of the house of the wicked
man, then allusion may be to one of the kings of
Canaan. However, if the prophet is speaking of the
future, and this is the more probable, then the king
of the Chaldeans is meant. The description of laying
bare the foundations up to the neck is allegorical, the
house standing for the Chaldean dynasty. Habakkuk
identifies himself with Israel in verse 14 and depicts
the treatment God offers the invaders of His land.
By mutual destruction (as in the cases of 1 Samuel
14 : 20 and 2 Chronicles 20 : 23, 24) the enemy will
fall by their own weapons, those who like robbers delight to prey upon the defenseless. The poor here are
Israel. Bringing his recital of God's marvellous acts
to a close the prophet recalls the crossing of the Red
Sea (Exodus 14) when the Lord trod the seas and
mighty waters. Is there a God like our God? I know
not any.

The Terror and Trust of Habakkuk

A cycle of thought is completed in verse 16 which reverts to the subject of verse 2. He is still filled with fear and dread at the coming anguish for his people. He knows his homeland is to be overrun by the Chaldean invaders and he feels it deeply. It is hard indeed to stand by and see the inevitable stroke fall upon God's people. But his communion and meditation upon God and His ways, as well as His promises, have wrought in him trust as well as terror. It has not been a fruitless spiritual exercise, this looking to God for His own answer to the knotty problems of life. Out of it has come unswerving trust in spite of coming trouble. Though the enemy come in and destroy the fig-tree, the vines, the olive trees, mar the fields, and carry off the flock from the fold and the herd from the stalls, yet Habakkuk will rejoice in the Lord and joy in the God of His salvation. The Lord God Himself will be his strength and sustaining power, enabling him to surmount all obstacles with abundance of vitality as he freely moves about in his own land. What desolations the Chaldeans were to carry out, but what consolations God grants His servant to carry him through. Not only will he have calm in the hour of trial, but joy in spite of all desolations of the land. This is one of the most forceful manifestations of faith's power recorded in the Bible. With renewed and joyous strength the prophet will be as the gazelle which is so swift that greyhounds are in danger of dropping from over-exertion in the chase. The musical signs suggest that the psalm was used in the liturgy in the temple; it is not so certain from the use of "my" in the subscription that Habakkuk performed this Levitical function himself. Note what a contrast the conclusion of this prophecy is to the perplexity that overwhelmed the prophet at the beginning of the book. He finds the all-sufficient answer to all his problems in God Himself. He will trust God though all blessings fail. What a word for the times in which we now live.

"For the Salvation of Thy People"

How full of meaning are these words and how well they summarize God's purpose in His dealings with Israel, His chosen. God has done so much for this purpose in past ages—out of Egypt, through the wilderness, in the land, out of captivities, in the midst of persecutions—but above all at Calvary when the Messiah of Israel, the Lord Jesus Christ, gave Himself for their sins. Shall we not carry the message for the salvation of God's people?

QUESTIONS ON CHAPTER III

1. Outline this chapter briefly.

2. Point out the parallels to this chapter in the Scripture.

3. Indicate the nature of the style of the passage.

4. What was Habakkuk's reaction to the revelation he received in chapter 2?

5. For what does he make supplication?

6. What is the method of interpretation of this poem?

7. Describe the majestic picture given of God.

8. How is the power of God set forth by the prophet?

9. What will be the reaction of the nations to God's display of power in behalf of Israel?

10. Discuss verse 9. Which interpretation do you hold? Why?

11. Why does God intervene for the sake of His people?

12. As the prophet views the future what feelings fill his heart?

13. Point out specifically the definiteness of the prophet's faith in God.

14. How would you summarize God's purpose in Israel?

15. How could you help to further it?

ZEPHANIAH:
THE DAY OF THE LORD

ZEPHANIAH:

THE DAY OF THE LORD

Chapter I

GLOBAL JUDGMENT

The Man and the Message   *1:1*

THE name "Zephaniah" means "the Lord hides" or "he whom the Lord hides." Nothing beyond 1:1 is definitely known of the prophet's life. The genealogy in the superscription of the prophecy is given for four generations. No other prophet has his pedigree carried back so far. It is not usual in Old Testament usage to note a man's ancestry beyond his grandfather unless for special purpose. He was of royal blood and was the great-great-grandson of the godly King Hezekiah. The arguments that have been advanced against this view are not convincing. Our prophet ministered about a half century after Nahum, in the reign of Josiah. Manasseh and Amon had been godless kings, but Josiah was a God-fearing ruler. 2 Kings 22 and 23. Most students of the book think the reformation of Josiah had already begun. See 2 Chronicles 34:3-7. The reformation in Judah in 621 B. C. (the ten tribes were already in captivity for a century) touched only the small remnant; the mass in Israel were in the condition pictured here in chapter 1 and in Jeremiah's prophecy. With the latter group all was outward and external, and a strong reaction followed the reformation. The people were ripe for judgment. It is strange that Zephaniah does not mention Josiah's reforms.

Our prophet has been considered as one of the most difficult in the prophetic canon, but his message has a definite focal point, namely, the Day of the Lord. He uses the expression more often than any other prophet of the Old Testament. In the first chapter he announces his word of judgment, centering particularly upon Judah; in the second chapter he predicts judgment on several peoples after an exhortation to repentance; in the last chapter, after a short word concerning judgment on Jerusalem, he promises future glory for Israel's restored remnant in the latter days. His prophecies of world judgment and final salvation for God's own people are comprehensive. A sixteenth century writer indicated: "If any one wishes all the secret oracles of the prophets to be given in a brief compendium, let him read through this brief Zephaniah." He has affinities in his prophecy with the message of earlier prophets. Similar expressions are found between Isaiah and Zephaniah and even more between Jeremiah and Zephaniah. In the time of Zephaniah the enemy of Israel was the Chaldean, rather than the Assyrian as with Nahum and others.

Universal Judgment

The prophet begins his book with a declaration of universal destruction. God will consume and destroy everything on the face of the earth, whether man or beast. The birds of the heavens and the fishes of the sea will be included in the same visitation. Beasts, birds, and fishes have common interests with man and suffer with him. The detailed enumeration is intended to express both the terror and universality of the punishment. God will utterly destroy all. Universal destruction because of man's sin has occurred before in the history of the world. Note Genesis 6 : 7. Especially will the Lord punish the wicked with their stumblingblocks, the objects and rites of their idolatrous worship. See Ezekiel 14 : 3, 4, 7. Thus far the pronouncement of judgment has been of a universal nature, now it is restricted to favored Judah and Jerusalem, who had the revelation of the will of God. The judgment on the whole earth will fall ultimately on Judah and Jerusalem. Verses 4 to 6 show an advance from crude, external to developed, internal idolatry. When the Lord predicts that He will stretch out His hand upon Judah and Jerusalem, He is indicating some special work of chastisement. Isaiah 5 : 25; 9 : 12, 17, 21. Baal worship will be uprooted and destroyed. Baal was the god of the Canaanites, already worshipped by Israel in their apostasy in the time of the Judges (2 : 13). Manasseh's reign was notorious for this worship. 2 Kings 21 : 3, 5, 7; 2 Chronicles 33 : 3, 7. The godly Josiah destroyed them. 2 Chronicles 34 : 4. The feminine deity usually associated with Baal was Ashtoreth. It was a nature worship and full of immoral practices. The remnant of Baal has reference to all that was left of Baal and idolatry generally. It has been inferred from this verse that the reformation of Josiah had already begun, and a curb had been imposed upon the flagrant idolatries of the nation. To the very last

trace the godless worship of Baal was to be extir-
pated. This was fulfilled in Judah after the Babylonian Captivity. The very name of the Chemarim
would disappear also. They were the idol priests
(Hosea 10:5), whom Josiah put down. 2 Kings 23:
5. The Hebrew root means "black" (from the black
garments they wore) or "zealous" (for their fanati-
cism in idolatry). The other priests mentioned in
verse 4 are outwardly priests of God, but careless
about the spiritual laxity of the people.

Another class designated in Judah for judgment
were those that worshipped the host of heaven upon
the housetops. It was carried out on the flat housetops to afford a clearer view of the sky, and chiefly
by altars for burning incense. Compare Jeremiah
8:2; 19:13; and 32:29. This worship was called
Sabeanism, and prevailed quite early in the East.
Moses warned against it in Deuteronomy 4:19.
Nevertheless, it was widely practiced in Israel, thus
virtually making every home an idol sanctuary. See
2 Kings 21:3, 5; 23:5, 6; Jeremiah 7:17, 18; 44:
17-19, 25. Still others in Judah had a compromise
system of worship which included the worship of God
and of Malcam, the same as Moloch (Amos 5:26)
and Milcom, god of Ammon (1 Kings 11:33).
Finally, there are singled out those who at first
heeded the exhortation of Josiah to repentance and
then turned back, and those who were indifferent to
it all from the beginning. Such is the bill of particulars of the living God in His righteous wrath against
the wickedness of Judah. Every type of iniquity is
noted and set forth. All things are laid bare before
Him with whom we have to do.

Visitation upon Judah

Before the prophet elaborates upon the judgment just indicated, he calls all to silence before the Lord. See Habakkuk 2:20. He announces that the Day of the Lord, the day of judgment, is at hand. That final Day of the Lord is led up to by preliminary judgments as stages in the process. Zephaniah is speaking of the same ultimate Day of the Lord which Joel prophesied. Joel 1:15 and Obadiah 15. The particular sacrifice in view here is the judgment on God's people, Judah. The consecrated guests are the Chaldeans. Note Isaiah 13:3; 34:6; Jeremiah 46:10; and Ezekiel 39:17. The final picture is given in Revelation 19:17, 18. How galling must be the judgment when God sanctifies the heathen Babylonians as His priests to slay the sacrifices. The first punishment is set forth for the princes who follow the customs of the heathen. They should have been leaders in righteousness instead of evil. Judgment will fall on the royal family, because they followed after foreign customs and oppressed the people. By the king's sons are not meant the sons of Josiah. He could not have had sons old enough to have incurred such guilt. Those in view are either princes of the royal house or children of the king who would be ruling when the prophecy came to fulfilment. Compare 2 Kings 25:7 and Jeremiah 39:6 where Zedekiah's sons were slain and he was blinded. Josiah the king is not included because he was to be spared the judgment because of his godly life. Some think the reference to foreign apparel points to the strange vestments brought in from the pagan abroad in which the ungodly in Israel worshipped idols. With foreign dress came foreign manners and worship, especially idolatry.

Verse 9 points out judgment upon those who plunder and rob their fellow-citizens. According to 1 Samuel 5:5 it was a practice in Dagon worship at Ashdod to leap over the threshold, so some have thought the prophet is denouncing here an idolatrous rite. The end of the verse shows this view to be untenable. What is referred to is the zeal with which the servants of the rich hastened from their homes to plunder the property of others to enrich their masters. The homes of the poor were entered by force to spoil their goods. Thus the homes of the rich were filled with that which had been gained by violence and deceit. In verses 10 and 11 the dishonest merchants who have grown wealthy through their wicked practices are warned. The agony of Jerusalem in the invasion of Nebuchadnezzar is pictured for us. All parts of the city will be affected. The fish gate was on the north side of the city which was susceptible to attack. Nebuchadnezzar entered through this gate. It received its name from its proximity to the fish market where fish was brought from the Lake of Tiberias and the Jordan River. It answers to what is now called the Damascus Gate. The second quarter was the second district of the city on the hill Acra, where Huldah the prophetess lived. 2 Kings 22:14. Along with the crying from the fish gate and the wailing from the second quarter will be joined a crashing from the hills, Zion, Moriah, and Ophel, within the walls. The verse indicates the progress of the enemy until they occupy the prominent positions of the city. The word translated "Maktesh" is mor-

tar and is not a proper name. Recent atlases indicate
the place as unknown. It is thought to be a section
of Jerusalem located in the hollow—some make it the
Tyropoeon Valley in the city—where the merchants
carried on their business. The Lord will judge His
people as corn is pounded in a mortar. The people
of Canaan mentioned here are the merchants of
Judah who transacted their affairs like the Canaanites or Phoenicians. Hosea 12:7 uses the same
designation. Their riches will perish with them.

The wickedly indifferent ones among them are ar-
raigned next. The prophet predicts that the Lord
will search out very minutely, as a man does with
lamps, the most concealed wickedness. The punishment will fall after such a search upon those settled
on their lees, a figure which is proverbial for indifference and slothfulness. Jeremiah 48:11. Hard
crust forms on the surface of fermented liquors when
they are not disturbed over a period of time. Thus
settled in their carelessness, they deny God's governing providence in the universe, His activity and
agency in the world, as though He brought about
neither good nor calamity. For such wickedness and
impudence God will bring upon them the curses of
the law: they would enjoy neither their wealth, nor
their houses and vineyards. See Leviticus 26:32, 33;
Deuteronomy 28:30, 39; Amos 5:11; and Micah
6:15.

The Day of the Lord

Every calamity in the godless reigns of Josiah's
successors was one more step or prefiguring of the
final one in the Day of the Lord. For further details
on this day in the minor prophets the reader is re-

ferred to the Book of Joel. The day is called great because of its tremendous effects. Joel 2:11. So deadly would be the Chaldean attack that even the mighty would despair and give themselves over to hopeless grief. Isaiah 66:6. In verses 15 and 16 we have a most emphatic description of the gloominess and terror of the day. Thomas of Celano in 1250 wrote his famous judgment hymn from verse 15, "Dies irae, dies illa," meaning "That day is a day of wrath." The day is one of wrath, trouble, distress, wasteness, desolation (the Hebrew words for wasteness and desolation — sho'ah and umesho'ah — are alike in sound to convey the monotony of the destruction), darkness, gloominess, clouds, thick darkness, trumpet, alarm against fortified cities and high towers. Unable to find a way of escape out of their distressing calamity, the people of Judah will walk like blind men (Deuteronomy 28:29). As though worthless, their blood and flesh will be poured out as dust and refuse. In that hour of catastrophe neither silver nor gold will avail to preserve from the wrath of the holy God. God's fiery judgment will consume the whole land and bring to a sad end all who dwell in the land. The judgments of God are terrible, but how ineffably sweet is His grace which He has manifested to guilty sinners.

Those Who Seek Not the Lord

In the days of Josiah and the prophet Zephaniah there were those in Judah who sought not the Lord because of wicked indifference. But it is also possible not to seek the Lord because the message of His redeeming grace has not been plainly and lovingly given. Paul indicates in Romans 10 that there can be no seeking of the Lord until the Gospel message has been heard. How many, think you, have heard this word of life in Israel? All must hear it in order to believe on the name of their blessed Messiah, the Lord Jesus Christ. In these closing days of a fast-dying civilization it is our God-given, blood-bought privilege to make it possible for Israel to hear and live. May we all respond in the light of the coming judgment seat of Christ.

QUESTIONS ON CHAPTER I

1. Discuss the time of Zephaniah's ministry.

2. What is the central theme of this prophecy?

3. Indicate the subject treated in each of the three chapters.

4. What kind of judgment is pronounced by the prophet?

5. Why will punishment fall on Judah and Jerusalem?

6. Discuss Baal worship in Israel.

7. Who are the Chemarim?

8. How did the people worship the hosts of heaven?

9. Under what figure is the Day of the Lord set forth (verse 7)?

10. Upon whom does the stroke fall?

11. Discuss verse 9 with reference to leaping over the threshold.

12. Describe the agony of Jerusalem during the invasion of Nebuchadnezzar (verses 10 and 11).

13. What is meant by "settled on their lees"? (Verse 12.)

14. How does Zephaniah set forth the Day of the Lord?

15. For what reasons do men fail to seek the Lord?

16. Can we make it possible for Israel to seek the Lord?

Chapter II

THE STROKE FALLS ON ALL

Call To Repent   *2:1*

AFTER the fearful setting forth of judgment in
chapter one, the reader may be inclined to feel
that nothing more can be said, that the whole story
has been told out. God does not announce coming
judgment without indicating at the same time the
means of escape from the visitation. Thus we find
the second chapter opening with an urgent exhortation to God's people to repent. From this call to
repentance the prophet proceeds to foretell judgment
on the nations surrounding Israel, and especially
those who have afflicted her. Zephaniah calls upon
the nation to gather themselves together. The
thought is emphasized by the double use of the same
verb. The gathering together is not meant to en-
courage them to collect themselves together or to
collect their thoughts, as has been suggested, but to
come together to a religious assembly to entreat the
favor of the Lord in order that by prayer He may
turn away His judgment. See Joel 2:16. The word
translated "gather together" ordinarily means to
gather stubble or fuel for burning, here to crowd together. The nation is addressed in a derogatory
manner because of their sin and called a nation that
has no shame. They shrank not from continuous sinning. It is not that they were not desired, as some
suppose, or that there was nothing in the nation to

commend it to God, but that they were dead to shame. Sin ever hardens the sensibilities. But there is no time for delay, for the decree hastens nearer as though going on to a birth. The decree is that which God has determined, in this instance, to do with the sinners of the nation. The day of repentance is a glorious opportunity, but it passes away as rapidly as the chaff is suddenly blown away by a strong gust of wind. They must avail themselves of it immediately. After it comes the day of the Lord's fierce anger. Thrice over comes the call to seek the Lord, righteousness, and meekness. Apparently the remnant of the nation is now addressed, for they are called the meek of the earth (land) who have kept the ordinances of the Lord. It will be remembered that Nebuzaradan left the poor of the land to be vinedressers and husbandmen in the time of the captivity. Note 2 Kings 25:12. Though they are meek, they are to seek to grow in this blessed trait. Having diligently followed the requirements of the law of the Lord, they are encouraged to pursue righteousness further. If it please the Lord, they may be hid, preserved, in the day of the Lord's wrath. Isaiah 26:20. It has been suggested that we have a play on the name of the prophet Zephaniah in the word "hid." The door of repentance was even then wide open for any to enter.

Judgment on Philistia

If the anger of the Lord sweeps as a storm through the land of His people, we may be certain that He will not wink at sin elsewhere. God cannot overlook sin in His people, but He will not allow the nations to afflict them without punishment. Nations from the four points of the globe are included to indicate again the universality of the judgment. The God of Israel is and always has been the God of the universe, the God of the nations. Verse 4 begins with the reason why the ungodly should repent and the meek should take courage. The land of Philistia to the west comes first into view for judgment. Four of the five Philistine cities—Gaza, Ashkelon, Ashdod, and Ekron—are mentioned, while Gath is omitted. Amos 1:6-8 omits the fifth also. Uzziah and Hezekiah had kept Gath in subjection. 2 Kings 18:8 and 2 Chronicles 26:6. In English it is impossible to recapture the play on the Hebrew words for Gaza's forsaking and Ekron's uprooting. Ashdod will be driven out at a most unusual time, at noon-day. It is the hottest time of the day and is usually spent in sleep in the Orient, so not a likely time for an invasion to be attempted. When they least expect it, the blow will fall upon them. See 2 Samuel 4:5 and Jeremiah 6:4. Woe is pronounced against the Philistines who lived on the coast in the region of the sea. They are called Cherethites or people of the Cretans, because some of their number had come from Crete (Caphtor of Amos 9:7). David's body-guard was made up of Cherethites and Pelethites (2 Samuel 8:18; 1 Kings 1:38, 44), considered the twofold origin of the Philistine people. The name Philistine itself properly means emigrant. The name Canaan originally signified the flat coast-land. This portion of the land was to be left without inhabitant. Instead of being thickly populated the region will be fit only for pasture land for nomads. All this has been literally fulfilled upon Philistia. But it was not to remain in this uninhabited condition permanently: the remnant of the house of Judah (Israel had long been exiled as we saw in chapter one) were to inherit the land of Philistia when its people were dispossessed in judgment. God was to visit His people with mercy and return them from their captivity to enjoy the homes and land of Philistia. This portion was included in the original grant of the land by the Lord to Abraham. He will faithfully keep His covenant.

✝ Judgment on Moab and Ammon

The origin of the children of Moab and the children of Ammon is important and can be found in the account in Genesis 19: 30-38. Though of incestuous and shameful descent these peoples were characterized by great arrogance. Because of the fall of the northern kingdom and the decline of the southern monarchy, the pride of these nations east of Israel was increased greatly. They reproached and reviled the people of God. After each calamity of Israel these nations sought to profit for themselves by seizure of some of Israel's land. These peoples showed their enmity toward God's people on every opportunity. Read carefully Numbers 22; 24: 17; Judges 3: 12ff.; 10: 7ff.; 1 Samuel 11: 1-5; and 2 Samuel 12: 26-31. Thus their revilings were not restricted to the time of the captivity, but must cover many occasions when Israel was in distress. Their pride is condemned by the prophets Isaiah and Jeremiah. Compare Isaiah 16: 6; 25: 11; and Jeremiah 48: 29, 30. That the final fulfilment of these predictions is yet future to our day can be seen from the connec-

tion of verses 8 to 10 with verse 11. Moab and
Ammon will become like Sodom and Gomorrah.
Their own territory will suffer as the cities which
were destroyed in the days of their ancestor Lot. The
land of these nations will be converted into a possession of nettles and into salt-pits, indicating sterility and desolation. They have been desolate ever
since (Jeremiah 17:6) like the regions on the Dead
Sea. Salt is used in the Old Testament as a figure
for sterility and ruin. Job 39:6. This portion of
shame and reproach shall they have because of their
pride which led them to reproach Israel and magnify
themselves against the chosen of the Lord. The nations are exceedingly dull in learning how greatly
they displease the Lord when they deal in pride
against the nation whom He has chosen as His medium for world-wide blessing.

Universal Worship of the Lord

We cannot stress too strongly that God's ultimate
object and purpose are not to punish and destroy but
to overrule evil for good and to bring peace out of
hopeless chaos. In His wrath He will be terrible to
the sinning nations, thus dealing summarily with the
gods they worshipped. The Lord is said to famish
all the gods of the earth; that it, He will make lean,
diminish, or destroy them. The Lord is the De-
stroyer of their gods when He brings judgment on
the nations who worshipped them. Idols have no real
existence apart from the people who serve them.
1 Corinthians 8:4-6. Along with the complete destruction of the idolatrous nations will go idol worship from all the earth. Then will men worship the

one true God, each from his place, that is, each in the place where he lives, thus making the worship of the Lord universal. This Scripture is not fulfilled in our age when some worship the Lord from every nation. See John 4:21-24 and 1 Corinthians 1:2. The prophet is speaking of that time when the world of nations will be converted to the worship of the true and living God. A similar thought is strongly expressed in Malachi 1:11. The picture refers to the latter days of Israel's history and brings us directly into Messianic times and millennial conditions. Indeed, it is the other side of the picture given in some prophetic passages as Isaiah 2:2; Micah 4:1, 2; and Zechariah 8:22, 23; 14:16. These portions should be studied in their contexts to give the true chronological framework. After the second coming of the Lord Jesus Christ to the earth, these conditions will obtain. All nations in that day will be united, not to do their own wills nor to worship the works of their own wicked hands, but to worship and serve the only God. It is the hour for which the waiting believer devoutly hopes, and the one toward which he labors in his day.

Judgment on Ethiopia and Assyria

Thus far Zephaniah has foretold God's judgment upon nations east and west of Judah; now he directs our attention to Ethiopia and Assyria, nations to the south and north of the Holy Land. The Ethiopians are warned of slaughter by the sword of the Lord. Much is said in the prophetic books of the Old Testament concerning the sword of the Lord, and it is a subject which will repay study. Ethiopia (Cush) is south of the First Cataract of the Nile and ruled Egypt from about 720 to 654 B. C. Compare Isaiah 11:11 and 18:1. A fulfillment of this prophecy has been seen in Nebuchadnezzar's invasion and conquest of Egypt. The fortunes of Ethiopia were bound up with those of Egypt which was subject to Ethiopic dynasties. Note Jeremiah 46:9 and Ezekiel 30:5, 9. There is reason to believe that Egypt itself is meant under the term Ethiopians. From Ethiopia the word of judgment proceeds to Assyria. At the time of this prophecy the nation had not fallen. The recital of woe and judgment climaxes with Assyria which was the strongest political factor of the day. For a fuller treatment of the doom of Assyria the reader is referred to the prophecy of Nahum. Here it is briefly and pointedly stated that the Lord will destroy Assyria and desolate Nineveh, making her as dry as the wilderness. This is all the more remarkable when we realize that at the very time of the prophet's prediction, the plentiful irrigation of the mighty city was its great boast and joy.

Zephaniah now elaborates on the desolate condition of the ruined city. The once populous and renowned city will be fit only for beasts and herds. The pelican and porcupine (or hedgehog) will make their abode in the ruins of the city. These creatures are found in another picture of desolation given by Isaiah in 34:11. They will lodge in capitals which are the ornaments of magnificent buildings now thrown down and affording hiding and lodging place. The doleful singing of some lonely bird will be heard from the

windows of palaces and homes. The homes will be
deserted of man and none will pass over the thresh-
olds any more. The beautiful wainscoting and fine
carved work of the walls and ceilings of the houses
will be ripped apart and laid bare. The prophet in
concluding this message of doom takes up a satire
such as was sung over a defeated enemy. Nineveh
is characterized as the joyous city that had lived care-
lessly. The greatness and glory of Assyria were
known the world over. About 225 years before this
Israel felt the iron hand of Assyria in the Battle of
Karkar (854/3 B. C.). More than 100 years before
this her armies overran Palestine and for more than
half a century dominated Judah. Now she herself
was ripe for the most condign punishment. In her
godless self-sufficient boasting she had claimed that
there was none beside her. This was the claim of
Babylon also as recorded in Isaiah 47:8. See Laodi-
cea in Revelation 3:17. Such self-sufficiency is the
very attribute of God. Isaiah 45:21, 22. For this
arrogance she is brought down to the basest desolation, a place for beasts only. The magnitude and
suddenness of her destruction will make her the object of the scorn and contempt of all that pass by.
They will wag their hand, implying that she has
brought her jujdgment on herself. When the Greek
Xenophon passed the site of Nineveh in 401 B. C.,
he was only able to find out that a great city had once
stood on the site and had been destroyed because
Zeus had deprived her people of their wits. What
folly and insanity for puny man to arrogate to himself divine prerogatives and attributes!

The Lord Will Visit Them

The promise of the prophet foretold that the Lord would turn in mercy to His people and bring them back from captivity. All this will be accomplished for Israel in prophetic times. In the meantime we joyously have a message of surpassing importance for all Israel today. It is that God has already visited His people in grace by the coming of their Messiah in Jesus of Nazareth, foretold by the prophets. By simple faith in the sufficient work of the Redeemer the Spirit of God visits the willing heart to regenerate and impart new life forevermore. This is Israel's greatest need in the light of which all others pale into significance. Shall we deny them the light of life?

QUESTIONS ON CHAPTER II

1. What way of escape from judgment is indicated?

2. In what sense was the nation to gather together?

3. How long was the opportunity for repentance to last?

4. Describe the judgment on Philistia.

5. Who were the Cherethites?

6. What was the origin of Moab and Ammon?

7. How had they mistreated Israel?

8. What is their punishment?

9. How does God propose to destroy idolatry from the earth?

10. When will men universally worship the Lord? (Verse 12.) Cite Scripture.

11. What nations south and north of Palestine are pointed out for judgment?

12. Indicate the wrath of God on Ethiopia.

13. Why was the pronouncement of doom on Assyria remarkable?

14. Describe the desolation of Nineveh.

15. Show how fully these predictions were fulfilled.

16. How does God visit His people today?

Chapter III

WRATH AND BLESSING

Woe Upon Godless Jerusalem   *3:1,2*

AFTER the series of woes on the nations in chapter 2, the prophet returns in his message of denunciation to Jerusalem. Because she was so highly favored and privileged, much more was to be expected of her in the way of faith and obedience to the Lord. Although the city addressed in verse 1 is not named, it is abundantly clear from verse 2 that Jerusalem is meant. She is accused of rebellion, pollution, and oppression. She was rebellious because she would not submit to the known will of God; she was polluted because of long continuance in sin in spite of her outward ceremonial exactness; she was oppressing because she regarded not the rights of the poor, the orphans, and the widows. The nation seen corporately has four distinct charges laid against her. She obeyed not the voice of God in the law and by the mouth of the prophets; she received not correction—when God's chastisements were upon her, she did not learn the lessons intended; she trusted not in the Lord, but in herself, her idols, and her allies; and she drew not near to her God in faith, worship, and repentance, estranging herself from Him, though He sought to be nigh her (Deuteronomy 4:7). As the people, so were the leaders. Three classes in the nation—the princes, the prophets, and the priests— are singled out for special condemnation. There is

no denunciation of the godly king, Josiah. The
princes, however, were like roaring lions in the midst
of her. They were ever on the search for more prey.
Those who should have shepherded the flock were
devouring them. See 1:8, 9; Micah 2:2; Zechariah 11:4. The judges of the people were filled with
insatiable greed, devouring all at once in their raven-
ous hunger. They left nothing till the morning. In
verse 4 we have the only denunciation of the prophets
in this book. They were guilty of levity, trifling with
the weightiest matters. There was no gravity or
steadfastness in their life or teaching. They were
treacherous because unfaithful to Him whom they
claimed to represent, rather encouraging the people
in their apostasy from the Lord. By their unholy
deeds they profaned the sanctuary; they made the
sacred profane. They did violence to the law by dis-
torting its plain intent and meaning when they were
teaching the people. Compare for a similar charge
Ezekiel 22:26. Princes, prophets, and priests were
alike guilty of polluting the nation by their wicked
example and ways.

The Chastenings and Warnings of God

In spite of Jerusalem's iniquities and corruptions
the righteous Lord is in her midst. His presence in
their midst makes all the more certain their judgment for sin. He is never implicated with iniquity.
The morning is the time in the East for the admin-
istering of justice, so every morning the Lord brings
His justice to light. His righteous conduct is made
known through His true prophets who exhort to godliness, and through His judgments on the ungodly in

the nation. By chastisements and warnings He continues to manifest His justice. He does not fail or miss, but the ungodly have no shame such as would lead them to repentance. God had meant that by His judgments on other nations His own people would have been warned and turned to Him. During Josiah's reign Judea enjoyed peace though wars troubled other peoples. She was spared during the ravaging invasion of the Scythians into Western Asia. Even the fate of the ten tribes did not deter the southern kingdom from sin. Verse 6 describes the desolations the Lord wrought among the nations surrounding Judea, and these were meant as warnings to her. But she did not heed the example of other nations in their judgment. God intended by these visitations that Judah would learn to fear Him and receive correction, so that her dwelling-place would not be destroyed. Howsoever the Lord had marked them out for punishment because of their sins, yet if they had repented, He would pardon and not cut off the city. But they in defiance of the Lord and His displeasure, rose early, indicating the deliberateness of their sinning, and corrupted their ways. The early morning in the Orient is the best for doing business. With great zeal and earnestness they pursued their sinful course. Great is the enticement of sin and great is the penalty it incurs, but man rushes headlong into it, nevertheless.

Wrath upon the Nations

In order to complete the entire cycle of prophecies of God's wrath, Zephaniah reverts in verse 8 to the theme of chapter 1, the judgment of God upon all the nations. The godly among the Lord's people are exhorted to wait for Him, to trust Him. As the beast ready for plunder the Lord will yet rise up to the prey. The prey has been understood as those among the nations who will fall to Him as His portion in salvation. Compare Isaiah 53:12 with 52:15; 49:7. But there must be destruction and extermination before this can be realized. The godly are to await the judgment of God upon the nations, for it will ultimately issue in their redemption. The Lord is determined to gather the nations (Zechariah 14:2) and kingdoms to pour out upon them in one great act of judgment His indignation, His fierce anger, and the fire of His jealousy. The words are vivid and portray a scene of great prophetic importance. See also Joel 3:1-3 and 3:12-16. (According to the Massoretic scholars who labored faithfully on the text of the Old Testament, verse 8 is the only verse of the Old Testament in which all the letters of the Hebrew alphabet, even the final letters, occur.)

The Conversion of the Nations

The remainder of our chapter treats of Messianic times. In these verses we have glowing promises of blessing and restoration for God's people and the nations. Zephaniah now outlines what the results will be of God's judgments on the nations. After His wrath is poured out upon the ungodly among the nations, then in the program of His mercies He will bestow upon the Gentiles a pure language in order that they may call upon the name of the Lord and serve Him unitedly. The prophet is not predicting a universal language (some say Hebrew, as though we have here a reversal of Babel), but that the impure speech of the nations will be cleansed. It will be a purified, uncontaminated speech, rather than clear, easily understood speech. Note Isaiah 6: 5 for the opposite thought. The impurity of which they were formerly guilty arose from their swearing by and praying to false gods. The remnant of the nations is thus indicated as converted to the Lord. The nations learn righteousness through judgment. All will call upon the name of the Lord, a restoration of the conditions indicated in Genesis 4: 26. They will not only worship the Lord by word of mouth, but will also serve Him with one consent (literally, shoulder). The figure is taken from the yoke or burden borne by two, helping one another. Compare this expression with that found in 1 Kings 22: 13, "with one mouth." There is no basis here for teaching a restoration of Pentecostal gifts. The verse does not have this in view. In their converted condition the nations will show their willingness to be used of the Lord in behalf of Israel. From beyond the rivers of Ethiopia they shall bring the dispersed of Israel to their own land as an offering to the Lord. Isaiah 49: 22, 23; 60: 4-9; and 66: 20. The rivers of Ethiopia are the branches of the Nile: the Atbara, the Astasobas, the Blue Nile, and the White Nile. The land is Ethiopia itself. Isaiah 18: 1. There are some who suggest that the ones meant by the suppliants are Jews dispersed in Ethiopia. They point to the west of Abyssinia where the well-known Falashas (the word is from the same Semitic root as Philistine, meaning emigrant) live. They are said to trace their origin to Palestine and the Jewish religion. It is thought that the Abyssinian Christians were originally in part Hebrew believers. We prefer with others to understand the words "my suppliants, even the daughter of my dispersed" as the object of the verb and not the subject. In other words, the Lord's people dispersed in Ethiopia will be brought by the Gentiles to their homeland as an offering to the Lord. The passages from Isaiah indicated above amply attest this truth. Such is the meaning rather than that the dispersed ones bring an offering to the Lord. The effect of the conversion of the Gentiles will be to place them in alignment with the purpose of God for Israel in their restoration to Palestine.

The Remnant in Israel

Now the prophet describes for us the condition of Israel as cleansed, restored, and rejoicing in their land. When they are gathered out of the nations, they will have no cause for shame, because the Lord will have removed from her the ungodly and impious ones. Every shameful deed will have been cleansed. Former transgressions will be put away. Especially will pride be dealt with. Pharisaic pride will be a thing of the past. The temple mountain will not be subjected to the haughtiness that was found there at one time. Instead of proud ones the Lord will leave in the midst of the land such as are afflicted and poor, the meek and humble, those who truly find their refuge in the name of the Lord alone. Iniquity, falsehood, and deceit will be purged from the remnant of Israel. In that condition spiritually they will find physical prosperity and peace as well. Neither home nor foreign oppressor will then harass them.

They will enjoy the rich blessing of God unmolested and undisturbed. See parallel passages in Micah 4:4 and 7:14. They will fulfill their divine calling. Exodus 19:6.

Millennial Glory and Joy

But the full story of blessing and restoration has not been recounted. The prophet now describes it in fuller detail. In view of the glad day that is coming they are exhorted to sing, shout, be glad, and rejoice. God never multiplies words like these without intending an emphatic declaration. The reason for the rejoicing is given in verse 15. Israel's day of judgment and chastisement is past; every adversary has been cast out; and the Lord, the King of Israel, is in her midst. No wonder then that she has no further cause for fear. Slackness of hands from anxiety and fear will be an experience of the past. The promises seem to reach a climax with verse 17. The Lord's presence in her midst is repeated (v. 15); this is the source of all the blessedness. He is the mighty Savior. As the bridegroom rejoices over the bride, so the Lord rejoices over His people. The marriage contract between the Lord and Israel will be restored. Isaiah 62:5; 65:19; and Hosea 2:19, 20. Then He will rest (literally, be silent) in His love. This is one of the boldest statements in the Bible. It is stated that God will rest in silent ecstacy over His people, Israel. What assurance for Israel! The love is too great for words to express. The Lord will rest complacently in it. The idea that God will no longer have occasion to rebuke and denounce can only be a secondary one here. He has quiet joy in

His love. Then the silence is broken with singing. Read what the Word of God says of the voice of the Lord in Psalm 29: 3-9 and imagine, if you can, what that singing with joy will be.

Because they could not celebrate the feasts of the Lord in exile, the godly sorrowed for the solemn festal assembly. These the Lord will gather back to the land of their inheritance. They belonged to the land as its rightful citizens. They had felt keenly as a burden the reproach that had fallen upon God's people. Regathered and restored, the nation will be a source of blessing to all the world. At that time, in the millennial day, preceded first by the judgment on the enemies of Israel, the Lord will deal with those who afflicted Israel. He will recompense them as they have deserved. Those who are lame and those who were driven away stand for all in the dispersion; all will be redeemed and restored. God will give them a celebrated name in all the earth, whereas formerly they were the objects of shame and derision among all the nations. She will fulfill that which was her destiny from the beginning. See Deuteronomy 26: 19. The Lord will exercise His pastoral care over them by bringing them in and gathering them to Himself from captivity. It will be so wonderful that they will scarcely believe it, yet it will materialize in their sight. Blessed and glad day for tempest-tossed Israel!

The King of Israel in Her Midst

Zephaniah's message centers about judgment and especially that of the fearful Day of the Lord. No nation is exempt. But we do him an injustice if we think of him only in the light of chastisement. He concludes his prophecy with words of blessing and promise for the nations and Israel. But these promises to the nations can only be realized when the blessings of God are upon the nation Israel. The King of Israel in the midst of Israel is the Lord God Himself. Would God that were already fulfilled! It can only be hastened as we apply our every energy to the evangelization of this needy and oppressed people. They must be told of salvation in the crucified and risen and coming Messiah, the Lord Jesus Christ. Every day that the salvation of Israel draws nearer, that of the world's salvation draws nearer also. Psalm 67. Let us be up and doing.

QUESTIONS ON CHAPTER III

1. Who is denounced in verse 1? Why?

2. What classes in the nation are pointed out for special condemnation?

3. What was the guilt of each group?

4. How did God graciously warn His people? (Verse 6.)

5. In what way is verse 8 related to chapter 1?

6. Discuss God's judgment of the nations. Cite Scripture.

7. What is the theme of this chapter from verse 9 to the end?

8. What does Zephaniah mean by "a pure language"? (Verse 9.)

9. Is there ground here for teaching a restoration of Pentecostal gifts? Explain your position.

10. How do the nations reveal their converted condition?

11. Describe the restored condition of Israel. Point out parallel passages.

12. What will be the millennial glory and joy of Israel?

13. Does Zephaniah foretell only chastisement? Explain.

14. Indicate the manner in which we can hasten the hour when Israel's King is in her midst.

HAGGAI:
REBUILDING THE TEMPLE

HAGGAI:

REBUILDING THE TEMPLE

Chapter I

ARISE AND BUILD

The Prophet and His Times *1:1*

OUR prophet is the only person in the Old Testament with the name "Haggai." The name means "festal one" and it has been suggested that the name was given him because he was born on some feast. Haggai is one of the prophets whose personal history is unknown. He is mentioned in Ezra 5:1 and 6:14. He is the first of the post-captivity prophets, those who ministered after the return of Israel from Babylonian exile. Note Ezra 4 and 5 for the historical background. It is well to read Ezra, Nehemiah, and Esther in the study of Haggai, Zechariah, and Malachi. They refer to the same period in the history of Israel. The king is Darius Hystaspes and the time is 520 B.C. The prophecy covers the short space of but four months. 2:3 does not necessarily imply that Haggai lived in the time of the first temple. He was probably born in exile. The historical background may be summarized conveniently thus: the remnant had returned from Babylon; the feasts were reinstituted; the foundation of the new temple had been laid; then the work on the restoration temple was stopped because of the opposition of hostile neighbors and national indifference; Darius Hystaspes favored the work when he came to the Persian throne; Haggai and Zechariah exhorted the people to the work of rebuilding in their prophetic messages to the nation. The commission of Haggai from the Lord was to rouse the people to rebuild the temple destroyed by Nebuchadnezzar in 586 B. C. He begins with the rebuilding of the temple, but goes on to speak of the shaking of all nations, the coming of the Lord, and the glory of His millennial reign.

Some find four addresses in the prophecy while others find five. Probably the former position is the correct one, the divisions being 1:1-15; 2:1-9; 2:10-19; 2:20-23. The main sections of the book are indicated by dates. The ministry of Haggai preceded Zechariah's by about two months. He begins his message with reproof and warning and then passes on to the promise of God's presence with Israel in the renewed work. The next outlines the glory of the temple in the future. After setting forth clearly the principles of sin and holiness, he predicts God's continued protection and blessing upon His people. The style of Haggai is simple prose which is given force by frequent use of questions.

The Rebuke

The prophet dates all his messages, the first falling in the second year, the sixth month, the first day of the month of the reign of Darius. The first day of every month was the new moon when the people were gathered for worship. This was an appropriate time for the declaration of the message of Haggai. The

sixth month is Elul, about our September. Darius
began to reign in 521 B. C. and this word came in
the second year of his rule. The dating of the
prophecy (so Zechariah also) according to the reign
of a Gentile king reveals clearly that the times of the
Gentiles were in progress. See Luke 21 : 24. The
date of verse 1 harmonizes with Ezra 4 : 24. Because
of the enemies of the Jews the rebuilding of God's
house ceased till the second year of Darius of Persia.
The prophecy is addressed to Zerubbabel and Joshua,
civil and religious leaders of the day, but is intended
for the whole nation as the contents show. "Zerubbabel" means "begotten in Babylon." He is called
Sheshbazzar in Ezra 1 : 8 and 5 : 14, 16. He was the
grandson of Jehoiachin (1 Chronicles 3 : 17, 19) and
was appointed by Cyrus to be governor of Judah
(Ezra 5 : 14). Joshua was the son of Jehozadak who
was high-priest at the time of the Babylonian invasion (1 Chronicles 6 : 15).

Haggai begins with a rebuke of the people's indifference. He sets forth their excuse for not rebuilding the temple. They were saying it was just
not time to come and rebuild the house of the Lord.
It was a complaint that the time was not proper nor
auspicious. The root of the difficulty was coldness in
them toward the things of God. How easy it is to
camouflage that dread condition in any of us with an
abundance of excuses, evasions, and subterfuges. If
faith had been present, the decree of Artaxerxes
would have been no deterrent in the work. Since
Persian decrees could not be altered, it has been suggested that the decree of Cyrus could not have been
repealed by another. God speaks of Israel as "This

people" and not "My people," not so much in contempt as in displeasure. Note that they were not saying the building should not be done; only that it was not time yet to do it. And all this in the face of the fact that the work had been interrupted for fifteen years. To the dilatory plea of the people the Lord makes reply by the prophet, asking whether the hour was suitable for them to dwell in their ceiled houses while the Lord's temple lay waste. Their selfishness, indifference, and ingratitude are laid bare at once by the inquiry. They were moved by selfish interests only in all that they did. Ceiled houses indicate homes that were panelled, luxuriously fitted, not confined to the ceiling, but including the walls also, an overlaying with boards or panels. Wainscoting with cedar was common in the residences of the kings. Compare 1 Kings 7:7 and Jeremiah 22:14. They had shifted the most important thing out of the picture. First things must be placed first. It was not merely a physical building or structure that was the issue; all revolved around the question of the worship of the Lord. How blessed it is to have the clear vision given of God to place the preeminent things first. Note Paul's "first of all" in relation to the gospel. 1 Corinthians 15:3. The blameworthy attitude of Israel in this particular may well be compared with David's concern as given in 2 Samuel 7:2. The blessing of God rests upon an outlook such as his; only the displeasure of the Lord can be expected by the course taken by Israel.

The Calamity

The exhortation of the Lord to Israel in their sin was to consider (literally, set their heart) their ways.

This call is a favorite one with Haggai; he employs it again in verse 7 of this chapter and twice in 2:18. It is a command to self-judgment. They were to judge the nature of their deeds (or excuses) by the results which followed them. They sowed bountifully, but harvested little; they ate, but were never satisfied (Leviticus 26:26; Hosea 4:10; Micah 6:14); they drank, but did not have enough; they clothed themselves, but were not warm; they earned wages, but they were soon spent. God disappointed them in all their expectations. The visitations continued as long as the negligence lasted. All the while they were blind to the issues involved and to the chastening hand of God. Their self-seeking had gotten them nowhere. It had brought loss instead of gain. Their necessities were so expensive that their wages left no surplus. A selfish and self-centered people needed to be shown what loss it was to neglect the work of the Lord for their own material gain. There is no contradiction between verse 6 (also verses 9-11) which depicts conditions of poverty, with verse 4 which mentions their ceiled houses, because there were surely wealthy members of the nation as well as the poorer class. The principle of Matthew 6:33 still holds good for every age. He that labors without the Lord labors without benefit or profit. Zechariah 8:10.

The Charge

In view of what the prophet has disclosed of the displeasure of the Lord, Israel is again called upon to consider their ways. The repetition indicates greater urgency to do so. With verse 8 the people are informed of the remedy for their trouble. They

were to betake themselves to the mountains, any
wooded area, to fetch timber to build the house of
the Lord. Thus would the Lord be pleased and be
glorified. He had been displeased with the desolate
condition of His house, and had surely gotten no
glory from their lack of obedience and concern for
the things of God. The blessed results of obedience
are here noted. In short, Haggai is saying, "Give
God the supreme place in your life." God would
then be honored in the worship of His people. A
heart attitude of obedience would have shown worship and gratitude on their part, thus glorifying God.
God made it quite plain just how He could be glorified. The Babylonian Talmud indicated that five
things were lacking in the temple of Zerubbabel
which were present in the temple of Solomon:
(1) the ark of the covenant; (2) the holy fire; (3)
the Shechinah glory; (4) the spirit of prophecy (the
Holy Spirit); and (5) the Urim and Thummim.
Whatever may have been lacking, God promises His
blessing will be present.

God's Visitations

The prophet reverts to the thought of God's judgments on Israel because of their disobedience (see
verse 6). When they labored much and looked for
large harvests, there was little to repay their toil.
When that little was brought home, God blew upon
it. They were not to lay the unproductiveness of the
soil to the long neglect of the land during the period
of the exile. It was distinctly God's chastening hand
upon them. He tells them the reason for it all. It
could well have been that each year at the harvest

time, when the crops had been brought into the barns, that the Lord had sent strong winds which leveled the barns and scattered the grain. God scattered it and blighted it. How could God's action be explained? Why did He do it? The answer is simply that they allowed the Lord's house to lie in ruins, while each ran to his own house. The word "run" reveals the zeal they showed in pursuing their own affairs and interests, while they disregarded the work on the temple. There is a contrast between "my house" and "his own house." Because of their sin the heavens withheld the dew which replaces the rain in the dry summer months. There was no fruit from the earth. The Lord brought drought upon the land and the mountains that affected the grain, the new wine, the oil, all the produce of the ground, and all the labor of man and cattle. Famine is indicated in the Scriptures as an instrument of God's wrath. See 2 Kings 8:1 and Psalm 105:16. The grain, wine, and oil were the chief crops of the land. Compare Deuteronomy 11:14 and 18:4. The cattle are included here because they had to suffer the fortunes of man. The law had foretold such visitations for disobedience. Note Leviticus 26:19, 20; Deuteronomy 28:23, 24.

The Obedience of the People

The message and reasonings of Haggai with the people fell upon good soil. In verse 12 we have the effect of Haggai's first sermon. Zerubbabel, Joshua, and all the remnant who had returned from exile took the message to heart. There was no dissension nor division. The people recognized the word of Haggai

for what it really was—the message of God through
His servant. Their purpose to obey is stated in verse
12, just as the fulfilment is given in verse 14. Upon
their obedience the Lord grants them an all-sufficient
word of encouragement for the task that lay yet before them. Haggai is designated as the Lord's messenger in the Lord's message. Simply stated, the
words mean that the prophet was invested with divine authority. Our prophet is the only one in the
Bible who is called the "Lord's messenger," though
all the true prophets were also such. The word, in
fact, is not exclusively applied to prophets. It is used
of priests in Malachi 2:7. It does not have the
significance here of angel, as many of the Church
Fathers in the early Church held, although the Hebrew word legitimately has both meanings, as does
the corresponding Greek word in the New Testament. The word of encouragement was that the
Lord would be with them. Short message it was but
all that was needed for that hour or any other. What
more could any man need or hope for? The promise
indicates that their repentance was genuine. It guaranteed them the presence of the Lord for help, protection, and blessing. It was the greatest of all blessings, because it includes all others. This is the all-
sufficient assurance of their future success. See Romans 8:31. The favor of God was now to rest abundantly upon them in the place of His former displeasure.

The Resumption of the Building

It was the Lord who energized leaders and people
alike and inclined their hearts to the work. Philip-

pians 2:13. They were encouraged of God from
their previous discouragement. There was a lapse of
23 days between verse 15 and verse 1; the interval
had been spent, doubtless, in planning and preparing
for the work by way of removal of debris, gathering
of material, and the like. Blessed is the lot of that
people that yields to the leading of the Lord to do
His work in His appointed time. Blessing must
follow.

"It Is Not the Time"

How many times have we heard, and with increas-
ing weariness, the complaint that it is not the time to
bring the gospel of Christ's redeeming grace to the
lost sheep of the house of Israel? At one time the
excuse is that they have had their chance; at another time it is that the work is so fruitless; and yet
again it is that this is a Gentile age. There is not one
scintilla of truth in any of these statements. Why
use pretexts when God would have us spend ourselves in the evangelization of Israel? How long,
think you, dear reader, we have for the task? Time
is all but gone, and eternity draws near with startling
rapidity. Let us redeem the time and opportunity.

QUESTIONS ON CHAPTER I

1. Explain the name of the prophet.
2. To what group of prophets does Haggai belong?
3. In what age of Israel's history did he minister?
4. Discuss the historical background of the prophecy.
5. What was the aim of Haggai's ministry?
6. What are the main divisions of the prophecy?
What subjects are treated in them?

7. What were the time and occasion of the first message?

8. Why did Haggai rebuke the people? Elaborate.

9. Was the prophet interested only in the physical features of the nation's worship?

10. What were the consequences of the nation's disobedience to the will of God?

11. What was the remedy for their trouble?

12. What five things were said to be lacking in the temple of Zerubbabel?

13. What indications did Israel have of the Lord's displeasure upon them? (Verses 9 to 11.)

14. How did the people respond to the prophet's preaching?

15. How is indifference to Israel's lost condition often displayed?

Chapter II

THE COMING GLORY

The Encouragement of the Lord   2:1-3

HAGGAI dates his second message on the twenty-first day of the seventh month. Reference to Leviticus 23:39-44 will show that this was the seventh day of the Feast of Tabernacles, the final feast of ingathering. Work had now gone on for almost a month on the rebuilding of the temple. Many were making comparisons between this temple and Solomon's. The people needed hope and encouragement now to guard against despondency after they had resumed the work in answer to the exhortation of the Lord through the prophet. In the first chapter of this prophecy the nation needed a word directed to their consciences because of their coldness and indifference; now they stood in need of a word of cheer and comfort to strengthen their hands and purposes as they pursued the task in obedience to the Lord. Again the message is addressed to the civil and religious leaders of the nation and the remnant that had returned from captivity. The Lord Himself draws a contrast between the temple of Solomon and the one then in process of construction. He asks who among them remembers the glory of the first temple, and inquires whether they do not find this temple as nothing in comparison. Ezra 3:8-13 gives us the historical background for the question of the Lord. There it is recorded that at the time the second temple was founded, the priests accompanied the laying of the foundation with appropriate psalms of praise and with singing and blowing of trumpets. While the younger generation shouted with joy and exultation over the achievement, the older men who had seen the first temple in its glory wept because of the evident contrast between the two buildings. It is to this latter group especially that the words of our prophet are now directed. God speaks of the former glory of His (this) house. From God's viewpoint there was only one house of the Lord on Mt. Zion, whether it was the temple built by Solomon, Zerubbabel, or Herod later. Because of the limited means of the people (see 1 : 6, 9-11) and the absence of such treasures as the ark, the temple of Zerubbabel must truly have appeared as "nothing" in the estimation of many. Should this disparity be the occasion for discouragement and further stoppage of the work? No, there is a threefold word to be strong to Zerubbabel, Joshua, and all the people. The same God who draws the contrast in all its vividness is the one who offers the needed spiritual stimulus for the ongoing of the building. Thus the comparison of verse 3 was not introduced to dishearten them, but to urge them to rely heavily on their God. Moreover, God's estimates differ widely from ours. They are charged to continue the work with the repeated assurance (1 : 13) that the Lord will be with them. And they have ample reason to know that the Lord will keep His promise. He kept the word which He covenanted (literally, cut, with reference to the sacrificial victims cut to ratify a covenant) with His people when He brought them from Egypt. The covenant at Sinai is referred to here. See Exodus 6:7; 19:5; and especially 33:12-14. If the Lord kept His promise in this regard through all the intervening centuries, He can be depended upon now to maintain His promise. Yea, and His Spirit was still abiding (the participle is used signifying "abideth") with them at that very moment. Surely they have nothing to fear. God is for them; who can successfully be against them?

The Greater Glory

The next four verses of our chapter are distinctly Messianic with a blending, as in so many other passages like Zechariah 9:9, 10; Isaiah 61:1-3; and Daniel 9:24-27, of the first and second comings of the Lord Jesus Christ, Israel's King and Messiah. The Lord predicts that in a little while He would shake the heavens, the earth, the sea, and all the nations of the earth. There are some who see here only a startling display of God's power in the realm of nature. This is to see too little where much is intended. What is the connection of these statements with the promise of the Lord uttered in verses 4 and 5? It is after this manner: the Jews are encouraged to continue the work of the temple by the assurance that the Lord, who is God of the nations, would in a brief period of time manifest His infinite power to bring about an overturning in the kingdoms of the world in preparation for the setting up of Messiah's kingdom. The passage has been referred to the revolutions in the Persian and Greek empires. There were such shakings in these governments, but they can only be considered as initial and preparatory steps in the long process where the kingdoms are shaken from their position of rule, and finally the kingdom of the Lord Christ is realized upon earth. Note Revelation 11:15; also Hebrews 12:26, 27.

Much difference of opinion has centered about the interpretation of verse 7, especially the words translated "the desire of all nations" (Authorized Version) or "the precious things of all nations" (American Standard Version). Some of the translations offered are: "the precious possessions of the heathen" or "the Gentiles shall come with their delightful things" or "the choicest of all nations will come." The interpretation in these renderings is pretty much this: the lack in this temple by way of outward adornment would be more than compensated for by the precious gifts which all the nations would yet bring to make the temple of the Lord glorious. This they would do in homage to the true God. This interpretation is supposed to square with the fact that the feminine singular subject has a plural verb. It is suggested that reference is being made to "the good things to come" of the new covenant. We do well to remember that from earliest times the majority of Christian interpreters have referred this passage to the coming of Christ. Jewish tradition also referred it to the Messiah. Without being dogmatic we should like to point out that the desire of all nations can only refer to the longing of all nations for the Deliverer, whether they realize it or not. In Hebrew an abstract noun is often placed for the concrete, so this could refer to the Messiah. The plural verb is no argument against the Messianic interpretation, because the verb sometimes agrees with

the second of two nouns. The first temple was filled
with a cloud of glory (1 Kings 8:10, 11; 2 Chronicles 5:13, 14); this temple was yet to be filled with
the divine glory in Christ (John 1:14); but the
prophecy relates to the glory of His second coming
(Malachi 3:1). The Lord promises that the nations
will be shaken (not converted); that shaking began
preparatory to the first coming and it will be finished
at the second. See Daniel 2:35, 44 and Matthew
21:44. Thus will the Lord fill His house with glory
inexpressible. Says the prophet in verse 8: "Do not
be disturbed over the absence of the precious metals
(it has been estimated that in Solomon's temple over
$20,000,000 worth of gold went to overlay the Holy
of holies) in the temple now in building, for the Lord
could supply that easily (Psalm 50:12), but He intends to beautify it by the glory of His Son in His
first coming and second coming, first veiled, then
revealed." The poor remnant of that day had little
to ornament and decorate the rebuilt temple, but silver and gold are the Lord's. Moreover, the latter
glory of this house will excel the former and the Lord
will grant peace there. For "latter glory" see the
contrast of verse 3 with its statement "in its former
glory." The temple of the Lord in Jerusalem is conceived of as one existing under different forms.
Through the presence of Christ in the second temple
its glory would exceed even that of Solomon's temple. The opinion has been given that the latter glory
has reference to the millennial glory of the temple
described in Ezekiel 40 to 48. We have just noted
how Scripture sees a continuity between the temple
in its different stages, so this position cannot be ruled

out. Though Zerubbabel's temple was leveled to the
foundations by Herod when he renovated it, his
temple was considered still the second temple. The
peace noted here is not only that spiritual peace
which He wrought out in Jerusalem (Colossians 1:
20) and grants to believers now (Romans 5:1;
Philippians 4:7), but is that ultimate external peace
also which He will effect as the Prince of Peace
(Isaiah 9:6, 7). Thus we have the sufficient answer to the discouraging appearances of verse 3.
God has the best reserved for the future. The eye
of faith alone can discern it.

Cause and Effect

The second section of chapter 2 contains a message delivered some two months after the preceding
message. It seeks to show that since blessing was
withheld because of disobedience, now that they are
obedient, it will surely be granted. The cause and
effect can be stated thus: their former disobedience
was to their former chastisements and trials as their
present obedience is to their coming blessings. The
people are instructed by Haggai to seek legal counsel
from the priests of the day. The priests were the
teachers of the people in matters of the Mosaic law.
See Deuteronomy 17:8, 9. The priests perform their
function when they interpret the law (verses 11-13);
the prophet does his duty by applying it (verse 14).
Verses 11 to 13 describe the nation as they had been,
a condition not to be repeated. There were two distinct questions: (1) if a man were carrying sacrificial (holy) flesh and happened to touch another object, would the object touched thereby become holy

or set apart to the Lord? (2) if a man who was unclean by reason of contact with a corpse should touch
any such object, would the object become unclean
because of the man's uncleanness? The answer to
the first question is negative; to the second it is
affirmative. The passages bearing on the subject
should be read carefully. Note Leviticus 22:4-6;
Numbers 19:11; and Leviticus 6:18. Moral clean-
ness cannot be transmitted, said the Mosaic law, but
moral uncleanness can. Legal impurity is more easily
transmitted than legal purity. A healthy man cannot
communicate his health to his sick child, but the sick
child can communicate its disease to the father. In
spite of their poverty the people were still bringing
their offerings ("which they offer" of verse 14; it
was on the altar at Jerusalem probably in view of the
people, see Ezra 3:3), even though they had been
previously neglecting the work of the temple. These
offerings had not been acceptable, a fact clear from
the withholding of the divine blessing, and now the
prophet explains the•reason. Just as the one who
was ceremonially unclean polluted all he touched, so
they under the displeasure of the Lord for their long
disobedience, transmitted the results of their lack of
obedience to the work of their hands which made it
unprofitable. And since holy flesh of the sacrifices
could not communicate its consecration to anything
beyond those objects in the sacrificial service, so
their external good works, even their offerings on
God's altar, could not avail beyond the carrying out
of outward ceremonies, thus being unable to secure
the blessings of God and the joy of holiness. All
their former work partook of their spiritual unclean-

ness. They are not to return to their former diso-
bedient ways; they are warned to desist from their
past experience. Haggai is explaining cause and effect here from the angle of the Mosaic law, just as
he briefly explained it from the viewpoint of sowing
and reaping in 1:6, 9-11. That the same time past
is in view is clear from the use of "This people" in
1:2 and "this people . . . this nation" in 2:14.

Their condition when indifferent to the Lord's
house is reviewed in verses 15-19. They are asked
again to consider their plight while they had interrupted the work on the temple. In those trying days
when one came to a heap from which he expected
twenty measures, he found it yielded after threshing
only ten measures. The winevat that was supposed
to have fifty measures of wine had only twenty. God
dealt with them further in chastisement. As in the
time of Amos (4:9) the Lord smote them with
blasting, caused by excessive drought, and by mildew,
caused by excessive moisture. What was left was
smitten with hail. In spite of these evident tokens of
the Lord's displeasure the people did not turn to Him
in repentance and faith. The call of the prophet is
to consider and to consider. How little thought men
give to the vital and important relationships of life,
especially those which they sustain toward the Lord
of all. The proof of all the prophet has been stating
can be very easily found in an examination of the
barns and granaries. There was no seed in the barn,
and the vines and trees had not brought forth. But
from the day of their obedience the Lord promises to
bless them. He who withheld the blessing can as
sovereignly bestow it in answer to faith and obedience.

Zerubbabel and Messiah

The last message of Haggai is directed to Zerubbabel personally and is uttered on the same day as the message on the people's uncleanness and lack of blessing. The message of the prophet to the governor of the day merges with God's future judgments on the nations. The end time is in view and the Person of the Messiah is prefigured. The shaking referred to here and the overthrowing of rule in earth is the same as indicated in verses 6 and 7. The passage has been assigned to the time of the overthrow and revolt of peoples and provinces (Persians, Babylonians, Medes, Armenians, and others) who sought to destroy the Persian Empire when Darius began to reign in 521 B. C. We take it as definitely prophetic. Notice that it is "throne" in the singular and not the plural. There is one supreme rule over the earth, permitted of God and carried out by Satan, and it will be replaced by that of our Lord Jesus Christ. See Revelation 11 : 15. The strength of the nations will be destroyed when the Lord overthrows chariots, charioteers, horses and horsemen. Chariots and cavalry were the chief strength (Zechariah 10: 5) of the armies of the East. The destruction will be completed when each turns against his brother. Ezekiel 38 : 21 and Zechariah 14 : 13. This will take place in the Battle of Armageddon. But Zerubbabel is not appointed to wrath but for a special mission. God elevates and honors him. The promise actually applied to the office he held as ruler in Judah, because it could not have reference to Zerubbabel's own lifetime. In his day there were no such revolutions as indicated here. Also note "In that day" and not "in this day." The Messianic line was to come through Zerubbabel just as through David. David's throne is here in vivid contrast to the doomed dynasties of the world. Zerubbabel was honored by a place in both genealogies of the Messiah. Matthew 1 : 12 and Luke 3 : 27. Christ is truly the Son of Zerubbabel as well as Son of David. Jewish commentators have referred this passage to the Messiah also. The title of servant is one well known for the Messiah. Isaiah 42 : 1; 52 : 13; and others. God promises to make Zerubbabel as a signet for He has chosen him. The signet was a mark of honor and authority. It was the object of care and pleasure. See Song of Solomon 8 : 6 and Jeremiah 22 : 24. It was much valued and constantly in view. The signet was used by the owner to sign letters or documents, thus it represented him. The owner rarely parted with it but wore it (Genesis 38 : 18; Jeremiah 22 : 24) always. It came to stand for one's most prized possession. All this prefigures the precious Christ.

"From This Day Will I Bless You"

Yea, from the day, yes, from the very moment of obedience God does bless. Have you ever given Israel the Gospel in obedience to His command? From the day that you do, He will abundantly bless you and yours.

QUESTIONS ON CHAPTER II

1. After the work of rebuilding was begun, what was the great need of the people? Why?

2. Describe the scene at the laying of the foundation of the second temple.

3. Discuss the difference between Solomon's temple and that of Zerubbabel.

4. To what time do you refer verses 6 to 9 of this chapter? Cite Scripture proof.

5. What is the connection with the preceding verses?

6. Discuss clearly the words "the desire of all nations." Defend your position.

7. What will be the "latter glory" of the temple?

8. Why does Haggai introduce the questions in verses 11-13?

9. What do the questions mean and how are they to be answered?

10. What was the intended application to Haggai's contemporaries?

11. Describe the plight of the nation during the interruption of the work on the temple. (Verses 15-19.)

12. What was the final message to Zerubbabel personally?

13. Indicate Zerubbabel's relation to the Messiah.

14. What is meant by the figure of the signet?

15. Can we be assured of God's blessing in giving the Gospel to Israel?

MALACHI:
FORMAL WORSHIP

MALACHI:

FORMAL WORSHIP

Chapter I

THE POLLUTION OF THE PRIESTHOOD

Malachi and His Day   *3: 1*

MALACHI is the last of the great succession of prophets who foretold the coming of Messiah for over one thousand years. Nothing is known of the personal history of the prophet. Some think "Malachi," which means "my messenger," is not a proper name at all. Liberal critics generally claim that the book was originally anonymous. Because the Hebrew (so the Greek also) has one word for "messenger" and "angel," several Church Fathers took the prophet for an incarnate angel. Since the priesthood is prominent in the book, some have thought Malachi was a priest. The Aramaic Targum of Jonathan considers that Ezra the scribe was Malachi. It is claimed that nothing is said of the prophet's lineage or place of birth. The same holds true for Obadiah and Habakkuk. Jewish tradition makes Malachi (with Haggai and Zechariah) a member of the Great Synagogue. No prophetic book of the Old Testament has come down to us anonymously, so we can hold with assurance that Malachi was the name of the last prophet in Israel.

Our prophet ministered in the time of the governorship of Nehemiah. It is clear that he ministered after the captivity: the temple was rebuilt; the priestly worship was carried on; and the people had fallen into spiritual decline. He prophesied about a century after Haggai and Zechariah; he sustained the same relation to Nehemiah that they did to Zerubbabel and Joshua. The time would be near the end of the fifth century B. C.

Malachi's message is, for the most part, rebuke and condemnation. The spirit of the people manifested in his day developed later into the sects of the Pharisees and Sadducees. The moral and spiritual conditions of Israel in his day are those of professing Christendom today. The spiritual life of the remnant who had returned from Babylonian Captivity is fully portrayed. They were insensible to the great love of God displayed toward them. They were unaware of the enormity of their departure from the will and the way of the Lord. They lacked reverence for the Lord and actually despised Him. They were so lacking in spiritual perception that, when their deeds were pointed out to them (and this is not mere literary device), they saw no harm in them. Their attitude toward the Lord is revealed in the oft-repeated "Wherein?". The sins of Israel that provoked Nehemiah were the same that stirred up Malachi. The failures were: (1) the defilement of the priesthood; (2) foreign marriages with divorce of their Israelitish wives; and (3) neglect of the tithe and offerings. The prophet also indicates the place and outlook of the godly remnant in the nation.

The book is a continuous discourse. The prophet

ב‎ל‎ה‎מ‎ב‎

employs a direct, forceful, and pointed prose style.
There is the introduction of a dialectic form of instruction which became very popular in later Judaism. The eightfold controversy of the Lord with His
people is stated in 1:2, 6, 7; 2:14, 17; 3:7, 8, 13.
In each instance when they are accused of sin, they
contradict the Lord and ask for evidences of these
charges.

God's Love for Jacob

The designation of the prophecy as a burden indicates that the message is one of rebuke rather than
comfort or encouragement. The word is found here
and in Zechariah 9:1 and 12:1. The prophet directs his word to Israel, all the twelve tribes which
had returned. As indicated above, analogy with the
titles of other prophetic books would show that
Malachi is a proper name and not merely a designation of public office. The prophecy begins on the
glorious and heart-warming note of God's love for
Jacob. In the very last prophecy of the Old Testament and, as it were, on the last page of the sacred
Word, God reiterates the persistence of His love for
Israel. See Deuteronomy 10:15; 33:3; and Amos
3:2. The choice of Jacob was by undeserved love.
Romans 9:13. The doctrine of God's electing love
is neither capricious nor arbitrary, nor does it mini-
mize one whit man's responsibility before God. We
cannot restrict this love to the temporal advantages
of Palestine over Idumea, in that the former had
been restored from exile, while the latter had not.
For the whole prophecy of Malachi reveals God in
several relationships to His people: as Father, Lord,
God, and Judge. In response to this love Israel asks

with ungodly boldness, "Wherein hast thou loved us?" The root of all their sin was their unawareness of God's love and their own sin. Replying in infinite patience God repeats the fact of His love for Jacob rather than for Esau.

Over against the love of God for Jacob is set His hatred of Esau. Many interpreters of the book see the word "hate" in a comparative sense, and point for this usage to Genesis 29:30, 31; Deuteronomy 21:15, 16; Proverbs 13:24; Matthew 6:24; Luke 14:26 with Matthew 10:37, where the thought is love less or love more. This statement of God's hatred of Esau is quoted in Romans 9 from this prophecy, and not from Genesis. God does not exercise His sovereignty to reprobate any creature. The hatred of Esau had been well-deserved after the continued opposition to God through the centuries; it is mentioned at the end of Old Testament history and not in Genesis. There is no room here for the position of reprobation which is not taught in Scripture. The instance chosen to reveal the hatred of God for Esau is the desolation of his mountainous land, and the wasting of his heritage to make it a place for the jackals of the wilderness. Some understand the reference to be to the conquest of Edom by the Nabateans; others, the wars between the Persians and Egypt; and still others, the desolation by the Babylonians. The Chaldeans had invaded their country five years after the destruction of Jerusalem in 586 B. C. The word translated "jackals," the same as in Isaiah 13:22, cannot be rendered "abodes" (so the LXX) to preserve the parallelism with "desolation," because such a translation would

be meaningless in the Isaiah passage and the word
"abodes" is of uncertain origin. Though Esau in his
pride should attempt to rebuild his waste places, God
says He will throw down their building. Every attempt of theirs to rebuild their land will meet with
defeat. The threat here shows that God will never
allow Edom to regain its former position and power.
That which was properly and formerly known as the
border of Edom, the territory of Edom, will be called
the border of wickedness. Men will realize that the
desolate condition of Edom is because of their sins.
We do not need to assume that the prophet is speaking of a blotting out of the name of Edom entirely.
The degradation of Edom will be added proof to
Israel of the goodness and love of God extended to
them. Then they will bear witness that the Lord's
rule over their land is indeed a gracious one. The
goodness and greatness of the Lord will be manifest
upon His own people.

Polluted Sacrifices

How did Israel requite the Lord for His gracious
love? From the love of God the prophet now turns
to the ingratitude of His people. God has treated
Israel as a son; have they honored Him as Father?
They have sustained the relationship of servant to
Him as Master; have they rendered Him due reverence? The rightful respect due God has been withheld, due mainly to the ungodliness of the priests
against whom the charge is directed. The first sin
of the Levites was the neglect of their duties in the
temple. In this they were despising the name of the
Lord. The nature of the offense is stated in the next

verses. The priests were offering blemished sacrifices
on God's altar. Deuteronomy 15:21 forbad them
explicitly. That Malachi is referring to sacrifices,
that is, animal flesh, in the word "bread" is clear
from three considerations: (1) their connection
with the altar; (2) the mention of blind, lame, and
sick in verse 8; and (3) the use of "bread" for sacrifices in Leviticus 21:6, 8, 17. If the bread be the
sacrifices, then the table is the altar of sacrifice rather
than the table of showbread. Compare Ezekiel 41:
22. Contempt for God's appointed service implies
contempt of Him ("thee"). They were offering the
blind, the lame, and the sick which were forbidden
by Mosaic law. See Leviticus 22:20-25 and Deuteronomy 15:21. The repetition that such were no evil
is in rebuke and irony. It has been suggested that
the stronger rendering would be "is it not evil?"
They were always willing to modify God's requirements and laws by circumstances. They had the au-
dacity to offer to God what they would not have
dared to present to their governor, probably the Persian governor. The prophet is appealing to their
sense of propriety which is more sensitive on the
human plane than it is toward God. There are always those who love the praise of men better than
the praise of God.

The Displeasure of God

At first sight the charge to the people to entreat
the favor of God that He may be gracious to them,
appears to be a serious exhortation to repentance.
But it is best taken as ironical suggestion. The
prophet is saying, "Do you think that with such un-

acceptable offerings God will be pleased with you?" Their prayers could never avail as long as they were presenting such sacrifices. It was the doing of the priests and Malachi places the blame squarely upon them. As a result God could not regard them or respect their offerings. The wish is expressed that someone would shut the doors of the temple, so that fire might not be kindled upon the altar in vain. The word translated "in vain" can also mean "gratis." There are those who believe that the priests were so greedy and covetous that they demanded a price for the smallest exertion, even the closing of doors. Others think the priests were so lazy and careless that they did not close the temple doors at the right time. The best explanation is that, since the worship was outward and insincere, God would rather it ceased. See Isaiah 1: 11-15. It were better to have no sacrifices, than vain ones. The Lord had no pleasure in priests or sacrifices.

Acceptable Worship

But there is a well-defined worship which is acceptable to the Lord; it will be revealed and carried on throughout the whole earth. From the rising of the sun to its setting is an expression for the extremities of the earth. See Psalm 103: 12 and Zechariah 8: 7. This is not the accomplishment of this present age, but a prophecy relating to the millennial era. The last chapters of Ezekiel (40-48) show that in millennial worship in the rebuilt temple, incense and offerings will be present. There is no reference here that God regards the worship of the heathen as pure worship of Him, nor that the prophet is speaking of conditions in Malachi's own day (for which some writers contend), but of the future time we have outlined. Because the Lord will receive pure worship throughout the world, as His name is recognized and honored in every place, is given as the reason why He will not really be pleased with the polluted and heartless service of Israel. God will not accept the blemished offerings (verse 10) of His people, because He is the great God to be worshipped by incense and pure offering throughout the nations. Strangely enough, the Roman Church rests its practice of the mass on this passage among others. No more applicable to the prophecy is the view of the Church Fathers who understood the passage to be a prediction of the Eucharist (the Communion) in the Church.

Profaning Holy Things

Malachi returns to the theme of the sin of the priests and their contempt for the majesty of the Lord. The reproof of verse 7 is repeated. They were profaning the name of the Lord not in actual words, but their deeds testified so. The use of the participle in "profane" indicates they were habitually doing so. The altar and sacrifice of the Lord were considered contemptible. The whole service was burdensome and wearisome to them, because their hearts were not in it. Note Isaiah 43: 22-24 and Micah 6: 3 for similar thoughts. They disparaged and disdained the offering of the Lord; they snuffed at it, that is, they snorted and sniffed at it, treating it with utmost contempt. The priests cared little what they presented to God, so they offered that taken by violence, the lame, and the sick. How could God accept such a sham and insult as satisfactory to Him? And it was not because of poverty, but the difficulty was greed. The curse is pronounced upon the deceiver who thinks he can vow—in such cases the best was promised to God—a proper sacrifice, and then fulfill the vow with an unsuitable animal. Such offerings were an insult to the majesty of God, for He is a great King whose name despised (verse 6) and profaned (verse 12) by Israel, and yet to be exalted (verse 11) among the nations, is even now terrible and awful among the Gentiles. What an exalted God is our blessed portion, blessed be His name!

"I Loved Jacob"

This is a beautiful declaration of the supreme love of God for unworthy Jacob. Many speak of him as though he were the object of God's discipline and displeasure, and nothing more. No, God dearly loves him and that people that have sprung from him, the nation Israel. In this love God provided heaven's richest treasure, the Messiah and King of Israel, the Redeemer of men. We have the superlative privilege, which the angels cannot have, to declare to needy and distraught Israel in these our tragic days the love of God for them displayed in the finished redemption of Christ the Lord for them on Calvary. Do you count it a privilege? Do you avail yourself of the privilege?

QUESTIONS ON CHAPTER I

1. Discuss the authorship of this last prophetic book of the Old Testament.

2. What was the time of Malachi's ministry?

3. Describe the spiritual condition of Israel in his day.

4. Indicate briefly something of the style of the prophecy.

5. What is meant by the word "burden"?

6. What chord does Malachi strike first? Explain.

7. How do you understand God's hatred of Esau? Does it contradict John 3:16?

8. Is reprobation a doctrine of the Bible?

9. When was Esau's land made desolate?

10. In what way did God degrade Edom? (Verse 4.)

11. What was the first sin of the Levites in Israel? How did it manifest itself?

12. How do you interpret "it is no evil"? (Verse 8.)

13. Was the exhortation of verse 9 possible for them as long as they remained in their condition? Explain.

14. What is the meaning of the shutting of the doors? (Verse 10.)

15. Describe carefully the worship that is acceptable to God.

16. How did the priests profane the name of the Lord?

17. Indicate the highest expression of God's love for Jacob.

Chapter II

MARRIAGE AND DIVORCE

___

The Guilty Priest   *2:1-3*

THIS chapter continues God's rebuke of the priests begun in the first chapter, especially in 1:6. The prophet elaborates on the sinful condition of the priests who were supposed to know the will of God and teach it to the people. Malachi now sets forth the punishment awaiting them in case of impenitence. The commandment referred to is the decree, sentence, or threat of punishment stated in verses 2 and 3. For the priests refusing to give heed to God's warning and failing to glorify Him, there is pronounced the curse of Deuteronomy 27:15-26 and 28:15-68. The blessings spoken of are not to be restricted to the revenues of the priests only, but must include all the benefits of God's gracious hand, those promised the people by the priests by virtue of their office. See Numbers 6:24-26. Included here also are the blessings of life and peace noted in verse 5. These God had withheld because they had consistently denied Him their obedience. Moreover, He threatens to rebuke their seed. The word should not be translated "arm" as parallel to "faces" in the same verse. What is meant is the seed of their land, for since the priests were dependent on the increase of the harvest for their tithes, they would inevitably suffer if God cursed the seed. Furthermore, God warns them that He will spread the dung of their feasts upon their faces. This would be disgraceful treatment indeed. The maw was the assigned portion of the priests (Deuteronomy 18:3), but the dung in the maw of the sacrifices on feast days would be cast upon their faces. The priests would then have to be taken away with the refuse as an abhorrent thing. They would know by actual experience the nature of the admonition being sent to them. The implication is that there will be obedience or the Levitical covenant could scarcely remain in force. By their giving heed to the declaration of judgment, God could continue His covenant which He made with Levi in the beginning.

Godly Levi

Malachi here contrasts the culpable conduct of the ungodly priests of his day with the godly character and manner of life of their ancestor with whom the Lord had made the priestly covenant. The reference need not be limited to Phinehas (note the wording of Numbers 25:12, 13), for at Sinai Levi was faithful in spite of the sin of Israel at the golden calf. For this fidelity to God's honor the Lord made a covenant with Levi and his descendants. See Exodus 32:25-29 and Deuteronomy 33:8-11. The nature of the covenant was such that it guaranteed him life and peace (salvation). The Lord intended that His name should be feared, and Levi walked before Him in godly fear and reverence. The prophet continues his beautiful description of the true piety of Levi. His interpretation of the law, for the priest was the teacher of the people in the law of God, was not according to partiality or for selfish ends, but according to the strict norm of truth. His speech was in righteousness. He worshipped God and lived in the will of God. The expression "walked with" indicates a more intimate fellowship with the Lord than is implied in "walk after" as in 2 Kings 23:3. The result of such life and ministry was that many were led from sin to the fear of God. Compare Daniel 12:3. Verse 7 indicates the intended ministry of the priests in Israel: they were the regularly appointed teachers of the law of Moses to the nation. They are called messengers of the Lord. The word ordinarily refers to angelic beings, but is employed here of the priest as it was of the prophet in Haggai 1:13.

Ungodly Levites

But what a contrast there was between Levi of Israel's early history and the careless priests of Malachi's day. They departed radically from the way just outlined in verses 6 and 7. By false interpretation of the law and by their bad example they induced others to violate the law as well as they. They corrupted the covenant of Levi by making it inoperative through their inattention to its obligations. See Nehemiah 13:29. Because they treated the worship and service of the Lord as contemptible (1:7, 12), the Lord made them base before the people. Their degradation in the eyes of the nation was retribution in kind. They were partial in the performance of their duties, which included bribery as well as other methods of circumventing the just administration of the law.

Abominable Marriages

The offenses of the priests would have been sufficient if they had included only the ones already mentioned. But in addition to these the priests and the people had committed grievous sins against their fellow-countrymen, especially their wives. They were offenders in the matter of unholy and unsanctioned marriages. The prophet introduces the subject by asking whether they had not all one father, whether one God had not created them. The obvious answer is in the affirmative. The father spoken of must be God and not Abraham or Jacob. The force of the parallelism shows that a human ancestor could scarcely be meant here, when in the second part of the verse God is mentioned. The ultimate reference is to God as Father of all men by virtue of creation, but the primary reference here is to God as the Father of all Israel as the covenant people. If the verse is referred to God, it brings it into agreement with 1:6 ("a father"). Israel is being taught that men and women stand in the same relation before God as Father and Creator. Too, God had created them not only physically, but had made them His covenant people. Note Isaiah 43:1 and 60:21. Since God had made this unity, they dare not introduce divisive elements into the national life. The general term "brother" includes the injured wives. They were violating the covenant which the Lord made with their fathers to insure their remaining a people separated from all others. Compare carefully Exodus 19:5; Leviticus 20:24, 26; and Deuteronomy 7:1-4. The law of Moses thus forbad all marriages with the heathen as a safeguard against the importation of idolatry into Israel. Judah, Israel, and Jerusalem, the entire nation, had dealt treacherously with regard to the Jewish wives who were divorced to contract

marriages with heathen wives. These mixed marriages were mentioned in Ezra and Nehemiah. Ezra
9:1, 2; 10:1-4; and Nehemiah 13:25-27. Profaning the holiness of the Lord has reference to the
people of Israel themselves. See Jeremiah 2:3. This
they had done by wrong treatment of their wives
who were also set apart as holy to the Lord. What
a high regard we have here for women in contrast to
the usual status accorded them at that time in the
Orient. The daughter of a foreign god indicates an
idolatrous woman. A worshipper is regarded in
Scripture as a child to a father. Jeremiah 2:27. So
grievous and abominable is this sin in the sight of
the Lord that He threatens to destroy completely the
offender and all his family. The one who wakes and
answers has no connection with the Levites who kept
watch in the temple at night and called and answered
each other at certain times, nor with a teacher (Isaiah
50:4) and scholar, but is a proverbial expression
stating that no one would be left. The universality of
the judgment is meant. Anyone offering an offering
could not by this performance clear himself of his
guilt in mistreating his wife. How holy does God
regard the marriage ties!

The Evil of Divorce

The marriage of men of Israel with idolatrous
women had another aspect to it. There was a second
thing, a second sin. Such marriages involved divorcing their Jewish wives. These forsaken wives came
to the altar of the Lord and covered it with their
tears. Thus when the former husbands came with
their offerings, the Lord would not receive them with

good will. Because He had regard to the tears from their heart-broken wives, He had no regard for their offerings. Nowhere in the Old Testament do we have so much said concerning the evil of divorce. We need not press its applicability to our own day; it is a sin which cries out mightily unto God. But the contemporaries of the prophet ask why God should reject their sacrifices. The answer is because God was a witness to the legally contracted marriage where God was called to witness the covenant. Their Israelitish wives were the companions and wives of their youth, their choice in youth sharing both the joys and sorrows of life.

Verse 15 is a strong argument against divorce, but at the same time is considered the most difficult verse in the whole book of Malachi. It has always been a problem to interpreters, Jewish and Christian. Without dogmatizing we shall review the main views and indicate our preference. We can safely say at the outset that the first portion is as difficult as the latter portion of the verse is simple. The prophet is warning against continued treacherous dealing with their wives by divorcing them and marrying heathen wives. An alternate reading has been proposed for the first part of the verse: "And not one hath done so who had a residue of the spirit." This means that no one had contracted such marriages with foreign women and divorced their former wives, if he had anything of the Spirit of God. If this translation be adopted, it does not go smoothly with the remainder of the passage. The Targum and most Rabbis understood the "one" to mean Abraham who might be cited as a case where another wife was taken in addition to the first. The Jews would then in the prophet's day be defending their action by pointing to the example of Abraham who took Hagar after he had Sarah to wife. The view holds further that Abraham still had the Spirit of God, because his aim was not selfish pleasure but to obtain the godly promised seed. Thus the case of Abraham and the contemporaries of Malachi were not analogous. This appears to us to be too strained an exposition. It is most natural to see, since the prophet is speaking of divorce, a reference here to the original institution of marriage by God Himself. Compare Genesis 2:24: "one flesh" with "one" here. In the marriage relationship God made two into one. One wife was provided for one man, though God had the residue of the Spirit, He still had the creative power of the Spirit, to have made Adam a number of wives. But why did God make just one woman for the man? He was seeking a godly seed; He wanted to carry on a godly remnant. Polygamy and divorce are not conducive to nurturing children in the fear of God. And ultimately these practices were not helpful to obtain the godly seed in the stock of the promised Messiah. The purpose of God in a godly seed was being counteracted and set aside by their intermarriage and divorce. In view of all this, Malachi warns them to take heed diligently to themselves that they refrain from such godless deeds.

In short, God declares unequivocally that He hates divorce, the putting away of wives. This verse is not at variance with Deuteronomy 24:1 where divorce is allowed. This was countenanced because of the hardness of their hearts. See Matthew 19:3-8. The hatred of God is also expressed against the one who covers his garment with violence. The reference is to the old custom of putting a garment over a woman to claim her as wife. Note particularly Deuteronomy 22:30; Ruth 3:9; and Ezekiel 16:8. Instead of spreading their garment to protect their wives, they covered their garment with violence toward their wives. The garment symbolized wedded trust and protection. Again they are warned to take heed to themselves in this vital matter.

Wearying God

The third offense of the ungodly in Israel was an evil skepticism. By their ungodliness and unbelief they had wearied God; they had exhausted His patience. They brought forward the old argument against the providence of God from the prosperity of the wicked and the suffering of the righteous. They had endured so many trials in exilic and postexilic times, that they were ready to believe that God delighted in and favored the cause of the wicked, the heathen who enjoyed prosperity, over against the godly. They complained that God did not judge wickedness severely enough. And if such were not the case, where indeed is the God of justice of whom they heard continually. Many connect this verse with the next chapter (and it is related in thought), because the answer to 2:17 is found in 3:1. God never fails to answer such a question put forth in such skeptical spirit. It rounded out the tale of their misdeeds and revealed them to be ripe for judgment.

Cursing the Blessings

How the heart of man delights in the blessings and benefits he receives from the hand of God, even when he does not thank God for them. Israel, too, took these blessings for granted. They did not realize their continuance was conditioned upon faith and obedience. As a result their blessings were replaced by curses. And is it not so all too often in the lives of believers also? They forget that the blessings of God are dependent upon our walking in obedience and upon our making Christ known to Jew and Gentile alike. God will withhold these blessings if we walk in self-will. The blessing of the provision of a Savior for Israel can turn out for them to be an ultimate curse if they avail not themselves of this blessed opportunity. They will hear the curse of doom pronounced upon their unbelief, if we bestir not ourselves for their salvation. That which was appointed unto blessing can eventuate in a curse if we be found unfaithful. What is our answer to the prompting of the blessed Spirit in this matter?

QUESTIONS ON CHAPTER II

1. What punishment is foretold for the guilty priests? Be specific.

2. Indicate the godly life and conduct of Levi.

3. Why is he introduced here?

4. What were the definite duties of the priest in Israel?

5. In what way had the priests and people sinned in the matter of marriage?

6. Discuss fully the Scriptural position on marriage presented here.

7. What punishment is declared for the offenders?

8. Who were covering the altar of God with their tears? Why?

9. Explain clearly and fully the meaning of verse 15.

10. Does this passage on divorce contradict Deuteronomy 24:1? Explain.

11. How did the ungodly in Israel show an evil skepticism?

12. How do blessings become curses?

Chapter III

MESSIAH AND HIS FORERUNNER

CHAPTERS 3 and 4 of this prophecy are undoubtedly better known than the first two chapters of the book. These last chapters are full of prophetic disclosure concerning the first coming of the Messiah and His second coming. As in so many other Old Testament passages, we have both appearances joined together. The chapter begins with the alerting word, "Behold." The Lord promises that He will send His messenger. This is God's answer to their brazen and skeptical question of 2:17. In the words "my messenger" we have a play on the name of the prophet Malachi. But who is this messenger? It has been suggested that in the light of 4:5 this may be Elijah the prophet, but the whole matter is too uncertain in this view. The possibility has been advanced that the prophet may not have had any specific person in mind. This is scarcely tenable. Most students of the prophecy have rightly seen here the prediction of the coming of the forerunner of the Messiah from the nature of his ministry indicated in the verse under consideration. The messenger is undoubtedly John the Baptist. Note carefully Matthew 3:3; 11:10; Mark 1:2, 3; Luke 1:76; 3:4; 7:26, 27; John 1:23. These passages show unequivocally that the one prophesied of is John the Baptist. His work is described as preparing the way before the Lord. This prediction rests on the prophecy in Isaiah 40:3-5. Reference is to the custom of Eastern kings to send men before them to remove every barrier and obstacle in their path. In this instance it meant removal of opposition to the Lord by the preaching of repentance and the conversion of sinners to Him. Such was the objective in the ministry of John.

The ungodly in the nation had asked, "Where is the God of justice?" The answer is that the God whom they sought will suddenly come to His temple and the messenger of the covenant whom they professed to desire. When the passage states that the Lord would suddenly come to His temple, it is not implied that this was to occur in Malachi's day, but rather unexpectedly in the appointed time of His coming. This was partially fulfilled in the first coming of Christ, and will be completely accomplished in His second advent to the earth. Who is meant by "the messenger (or angel) of the covenant?" Is it the same person as the messenger already mentioned in the first clause of the verse? The expression occurs only here, and some think the meaning cannot be determined. But the case is not so hopeless. A comparative study of the Old Testament Scriptures bearing on the subject will reveal that this person is the Angel of the Covenant of Exodus 23:20-23; 33:15; and Isaiah 63:9. The Angel is God's self-revelation. He is the Lord Himself, the Angel of the Lord of Old Testament history, the preincarnate Christ of the many theophanies (appearances of God in human form) in the books of the Old Testament. Jewish commentators like Abenezra and Kimchi make this person the Lord, and the latter commentator even refers both "the Lord" and "the Messenger of the covenant" to the Messiah. We dare not miss the three undeniable proofs of the deity of the Messiah given here: (1) he is identified with the Lord: "he shall prepare the way before me . . . saith the Lord of hosts"; (2) he is indicated as the owner of the temple: "to his temple"; and (3) he is called "the Lord" whom they sought.

What covenant is meant in the phrase "messenger of the covenant?" Some interpreters understand this designation of the new covenant of Hebrews 9:15. It is rather the one already in force in the Old Testament, as seen in the many manifestations of God throughout the old economy. It is the one already made with Israel. See Exodus 25:8; Leviticus 26: 9-12; and Deuteronomy 4:23. The mass in Israel in the time of Malachi and in the days of Christ were seeking and desiring a temporal Deliverer. To them this promise would be ironical; but the desire of the godly was sincere. Mark well that the gospel began with Israel in the first coming, and so it will be in the second advent. Israel is central in the purpose of God in both comings of the Lord Jesus Christ to the earth.

Messiah the Refiner

Just as the first verse blends the first and second coming of Christ—a feature known in Old Testament prophecy as in Isaiah 61:1-3—so the second verse combines elements of both appearances of the Messiah to His people Israel. The prophet had indicated they were desiring the presence of the Lord, but he asks now who among them could abide the day of

His coming? The expected answer, in view of the ungodly in the nation, is no one will abide that day. It was certainly true in Malachi's day; it was eminently applicable in the day of Christ's first coming when He scrutinized all and then decreed the destruction of Jerusalem and the scattering of Israel; and it will be true when He comes again. Compare Joel 2:11; Malachi 4:1; Matthew 3:10-12; and Revelation 6:15. The coming will be in judgment to purge out the dross, that is, the iniquity, from Israel. The refiner's fire is a vivid figure from the field of metallurgy to show that the Messenger of the covenant would not come merely as an earthly monarch and liberator to bestow temporal benefits, but as the Searcher of hearts and lives. For the same figure of refining see Zechariah 13:8, 9. The thought of cleansing is further brought out by the figure of the fullers' soap.

The Lord is seen sitting as Judge. The refiner sits with the crucible before him watching both the intensity of the fire and the metal being purified of its dross. When judgment comes, it truly begins at the house of God. 1 Peter 4:17. The entire nation will be purged, beginning with the sons of Levi (Ezekiel 48:11). These are specified because their offerings had been unacceptable on account of their godlessness. They will be cleansed of the sins described in chapters 1 and 2. Then they will offer to the Lord offerings in righteousness, as in 2:6 and not as in 1:7-14. They will be righteous offerings, because they will be given from hearts in the right condition before the Lord. Most Roman Catholic commentators think this is a prophecy of the offering of the Eucharist, but it actually refers to millennial conditions when He shall have returned and have set up His righteous kingdom on the earth. In the days of cleansed and restored Israel their offering will indeed be acceptable to God as an offering in righteousness. The offerings of millennial days (Ezekiel 40-46) will commemorate the sacrifice at Calvary, as the Lord's Supper does now. Many believers forget that, although the Church has remembered the death of the Lord Jesus Christ on Calvary for sinners in the Lord's Supper, Israel has thus far had no such memorial of His work in the centuries of their unbelief. The millennial sacrifices will perform the function of such a memorial for the redeemed nation. It cannot be argued against them that they would not be efficacious sacrifices in the millennial kingdom, for even in Old Testament times the sacrifices had no real efficacy. See Hebrews 10:4. In the Old Testament economy sacrifices were sign-posts; in the millennial day they will be memorials looking back to the central event of Calvary. The days of old mentioned by Malachi are the times of Moses or perhaps also the times of David and the early part of the reign of Solomon. At that time the offerings were indicated as pleasing to the Lord.

Judgment Foretold

The prophet now speaks to his contemporaries, threatening them with the judgment of God. Evildoers must still be judged. This is still the answer of God to their insolent challenge of 2:17. The first to come under the chastisement of God will be the sorcerers. Note Exodus 22:18. Magic prevailed in Israel in post-captivity days, a sin into which they were probably led because of their foreign idolatrous wives, and which continued even down to New Testament times. Acts 8:9. Adulterers will also experience the rod of God's displeasure. This term probably applies to those who were living with foreign wives, after divorcing their Hebrew wives, those of 2:16. The judgment will also be directed against the false swearers, those who practiced false witnessing. Perjury is condemned in Exodus 20:16; Leviticus 19:12; Deuteronomy 19:16-20; Jeremiah 29:23; and Proverbs 19:5. Those who deal falsely in the wages of a hired servant are classed with the foregoing. Finally, those under sentence are the oppressors of the widow, the fatherless, and the sojourners, classes which are the special objects of God's care and love. And all their defections are traced to their source; they all stemmed from their lack of fear of God. But because God is the unchanging and steadfast Lord, who has purposes of mercy toward them which He must accomplish, He will carry out to fruition His purposes of grace in spite of their wayward ways. The Lord is declaring that, though He must punish them, yet He will not utterly destroy them, because He is unchanging in His covenant promises. The nation is called "sons of Jacob" in relation to the Lord's covenant with the patriarch. In short, Israel owes its existence in spite of its sins to the unchanging purpose of the Lord to grant her abundant grace and mercy. All the nations' hope, as ours as well, is grounded in the never-failing, unchangeable character of our covenant-keeping God.

Robbing God

But just as God is unchangeable in His goodness, so they have not changed from their evil ways. For a long while now, even from the time of their fathers, they have gone astray from the commandments of the Lord. This is no novel action with them; it is one in which they have had much evil experience. The call of God to them is to return to Him in penitence and He would return to them in blessing. See Zechariah 1:3. In spite of the length of time involved in their departure from the Lord, He is willing to receive them if they turn to Him in true penitence. In their self-righteousness the ungodly majority in the nation, satisfied in their careless ways, do not see the need for real turning back to the Lord, and ask wherein they need to mend their ways. The answer is clear enough. Could it be possible that puny man would rob the infinite God? Yet they robbed God. They had robbed Him in tithes and offerings. In all probability they had decreased their tithes and offerings because of adverse conditions, which is labelled here as robbery of God. Compare Deuteronomy 14: 22-29 and 26:12-15. It is interesting that tithes are never mentioned in the New Testament. The offerings in Israel were the first-fruits, not less than one-sixtieth of the corn, wine, and oil. Deuteronomy 18: 4. There were several kinds of tithes: (1) the tenth of the remainder after the first-fruits were taken, this amount going to Levites for their livelihood (Leviticus 27:30-33); (2) the tenth paid by Levites to the priests (Numbers 18:26-28); (3) the second tenth paid by the congregation for the needs of the Levites and their own families at the tabernacle (Deuter-

onomy 12:18); and (4) another tithe every third
year for the poor (Deuteronomy 14:28, 29). These
tithes were not being properly given by the people in
the days of Nehemiah and Malachi (Nehemiah 13:
10), so the people are rightly accused of robbing God.
In seeking to rob God they robbed themselves, for
they had failure of the harvest and famine, judgments
corresponding to their sin. Thus were they cursed
with the curse, for they were still defrauding (the
participle is used) God. And the evil was being perpetrated by the whole nation.

The Pathway of Blessing

However, all is not hopeless. The prophet sets
forth the pathway of God's favor. There is an important spiritual principle enunciated here which is
applicable in every age: God meets with blessing the
heart wholly devoted to Him. If we want God to
open His storehouse, we must first open ours. The
nation is counselled to bring the whole tithe into the
storehouse, that there may be food in the Lord's
house. The storehouse was the chambers in the temple where the tithes were brought. See Nehemiah
10:38 and 13:12. In obedience to this exhortation
they would find by practical test that the Lord would
open the windows of heaven and pour them out such
a blessing, that there would not be room enough to
contain it. God loves to be put to the practical test
as in 2 Chronicles 31:10. God would send them
abundant rains; abundant blessing is compared to
rain. Nothing would be withheld in the way of
blessing. The land had evidently been suffering from
drought as indicated in verse 11. Now there would

be a superabundance and not room enough to receive it. God promises that every injurious thing, the locust or any similar scourge from God, would be withheld for their sakes. When the rain watered the fields, the scourge would not destroy the crop. The locust especially is called the devourer because of its insatiable greed. In the way of obedience and as a result of the blessing of God upon them, all nations would call them blessed. Both God and man would find delight in her. Then would be fulfilled the words of Deuteronomy 33:29; Isaiah 62:4; and Zechariah 8:13.

"Return Unto Me"

This is the pathetic cry of the Lord to Israel throughout the Old Testament. To realize the blessing of God in their national life they need only to return to God through the Savior, the Lord Jesus Christ. Let us sound forth continually the call to Israel to return unto God!

Stout Words Against God

The same type of skepticism displayed by the godless priests in 2:17 is now seen to have infected the remainder of the nation. Their words had been obstinate, unbearable against the Lord. But the insensibility of their conceited and wilfully ignorant hearts made them ask what they had spoken amiss against their God. Actually, they had said it was useless to try to serve God. They claim to have kept His charge and walked mournfully before Him, all to no profit or avail. They were wholly in error with regard to God's service for they regarded it in a mercenary

spirit, as though to be profited thereby were the chief
and sole goal. God looks at the motive, however, and
not at self-interest. They thought the outward appearance would suffice instead of genuine humili-
ation, so they walked in sackcloth and ashes pretend-
ing to be grieved for their sins. See Isaiah 58:3-8
for the meaning of true worship. Not satisfied with
complaining over their lean lot, they called the proud
happy. Since they have not prospered in their half-
hearted worship of the Lord, they pronounce the
proud the favored of the Lord. Some think the proud
are the godless heathen outside of Israel, while others feel they are the godless in Israel. Neither view
excludes the other, and there is no reason why both
positions could not be true. They esteemed the proud
anywhere as the favorites of the Lord. They made
much of the prosperity and flourishing of the wicked,
who tempted God by presumptuous words and deeds
and yet escaped all judgment.

God's Book of Remembrance

When the wicked are blatantly mouthing their un-
speakable blasphemies against God, then the godly
must be forewarned how to meet these cavils against
the Lord. In the midst of spiritual failure and corruption on every hand, the godly remnant are drawn
together by their mutual spiritual needs and desire,
in the fear of the Lord. This is an important truth
for us to bear in mind today in the midst of fearful
spiritual declension. When gathered together, the
godly held mutual converse with reference to truth
and godliness, strengthening themselves in their trust
in the Lord. The word "often" found in the Author-

ized Version is not in the original Hebrew text.
While the remnant spoke together of Him, the Lord
inclined His ear and heard. Then these acts of communion were written in a book of remembrance before Him. This is the language of appearance, for
nothing is past to God to be remembered and He
needs no keeping of books. But it is for the encouragement and assurance of the godly. That books
are kept in heaven is attested already in Psalm 56: 8.
It is thought that the figure of the book is taken from
the custom of Persian kings to keep a record of the
names of those who did service for the king with a
statement of that service. Compare Esther 6: 1, 2.
But this is not necessarily so, for we read of a book
in Daniel 12: 1 and the passage already cited from the
Psalms. God tenderly keeps before Him those that
truly reverence Him and think on His name.

He calls them His in a peculiar and special sense,
even His own possession. This designates that which
is especially valuable. It is applied to Israel in Exodus 19: 5; Deuteronomy 7: 6; 14: 2; and 26: 18.
They will be particularly remembered in the day God
has appointed for the carrying out of His purposes,
the day of His judgment when He comes again. God
will spare them the doom of the wicked as a loving
father does his devoted and dutiful son. See Psalm
103: 13. Then the great chasm between the righteous
and the wicked, between those who serve Him and
those who do not, will be manifest. There are those
who think the "ye" refers to the wicked murmurers
in Israel, but it is better to see here a reference to
the righteous. The godly have had ample opportuni-
ties to see that God does not treat all alike whether

righteous or ungodly; it will be all the more evident when the Lord gloriously delivers the godly and sovereignly destroys the wicked.

QUESTIONS ON CHAPTER III

1. Indicate the importance of chapters 3 and 4 for the future of Israel.

2. How does the promise of 3:1 answer the insolent question of 2:17?

3. Who is the messenger of 3:1? Present proof from Scripture.

4. Of whom is Malachi speaking in the designation "the angel of the covenant"? Defend your view.

5. What three clear proofs of the deity of the Messiah are given here? (Verse 1.)

6. What covenant is alluded to in verse 1? How do you know?

7. What coming of the Lord is in view when He is seen as Refiner? Give the reason for your answer.

8. Do the offerings of verse 3 speak of the Eucharist? Of what do they speak?

9. Explain clearly the reason for offerings in the millennium. Give Scripture proof.

10. What groups come under the judgment of God? Why?

11. What is the meaning of verse 6?

12. How were the people robbing God?

13. What is the remedy?

14. What kinds of tithes were given in Israel?

15. What will be the result of obedience?

16. What insolent words were uttered against God?

17. Was real penitence present?

18. How are the ungodly to meet the cavils against the Lord?

19. Where did Malachi get the figure of the book?

20. Does God ever treat the ungodly and godly exactly alike? Explain.

Chapter IV

"THE SUN OF RIGHTEOUSNESS"

The Day of Burning Wrath   4:1

MOST editions of the Hebrew Old Testament and most manuscripts of the original text include the six verses of chapter 4 as a continuation of chapter 3. All the versions have the division as it is found in our English translations. There are those who think the chapter break is unfortunate, but we fail to see that it does violence to the thought of the passage. We should view these final words with solemnity of heart, for this chapter gives us the last message of the Old Testament prophets. After this prophetic word the heavens were silent for four centuries until the voice of John the Baptist was heard calling Israel to repentance in view of the coming of the Messiah. The day spoken of is the important Day of the Lord so prominent throughout the Old Testament; it is the time of the wrath of the Lamb revealed in the New Testament. The language is short and abrupt, which brings out the dread reality of the prediction. Because God's judgment is often likened to fire, the day is said to burn as a furnace. Among many passages note carefully Isaiah 10:16; 30:27; Jeremiah 21:14; Ezekiel 20:45-48; Amos 1:4; and Zephaniah 1:18; and 3:8. Before the fire of God's judgment the wicked will be as stubble to be burned up root and branch. The intensity of the heat sets forth the greatness of the wrath of God.

Notice the end of the proud; it is quite different from their thought expressed in 3:15. Root and branch, as the two extremities of the tree representing the whole, is a proverbial expression for totality. All will be utterly destroyed. All that offends will be purged from the kingdom. Matthew 13:41, 42. Annihilationists make much of this verse for their erroneous teaching that the wicked will be blotted out of conscious existence completely. But the passage speaks of judgment on the body of the wicked; the soul and spirit will be judged at the Great White Throne. Scripture knows nothing of souls that go out of existence through the judgment of God. The godly are in conscious bliss eternally, while the wicked are in conscious woe throughout eternity. Revelation 20:11-15.

The results of the coming day of judgment for the wicked are indicated in verse 1; in verses 2 and 3 we have the consequences of that day for the righteous. Nothing in Scripture outlines with greater demarcation the vastly different lots of the believing and unbelieving when the Lord cometh to judge the earth.

The Sun of Righteousness

Those who fear the name of the Lord (the same as in 3:16) have a blessed portion assigned them. For them there will not be the blasting heat of the furnace, but the genial heat and warmth of the Sun of righteousness with healing in its wings. He who is an oven to the wicked, is like the sun to the righteous. Some interpreters see no more in the phrase "sun of righteousness" than a period of blessing for the godly. We believe the sun is used here figura-

tively of God Himself, and specifically of the Lord
Jesus Christ, Israel's Messiah. Note Psalm 84: 11;
see also 2 Samuel 23: 4 with Isaiah 9: 2 and 49: 6.
He is called the Sun of righteousness, because He is
the Lord our Righteousness. Jeremiah 23: 5, 6 and
1 Corinthians 1: 30. There is spiritual healing in this
Sun, for just as the rays of the physical sun give light
and heat for the growth of plant and animal life, so
the Sun of righteousness will heal the wounds in-
flicted upon and borne by the righteous. The beams
of the sun are here spoken of as wings because of
the speed with which they spread over the earth.
Israel's hope is the Sun of righteousness; the hope
of the Church is the Morning Star. 2 Peter 1: 19 and
Revelation 22: 16. Mark the distinction between the
Morning Star, which ushers in the dawn, and the
Sun of righteousness, which brings in the bright day.
Through the redeeming activity of the Deliverer the
godly will go forth, escaping the judgment to come
upon the evil-doers. Such will be their freedom from
outward constraint, their vitality, and their joy, that
they will gambol as calves of the stall. And they will
tread down the wicked; God will reverse what is
usually the condition between the righteous and the
wicked. The ungodly are compared to ashes, the result of the fire of God's judgment. All this will
transpire in the day that God has appointed.

Moses and Elijah

Since no prophet was to appear from Malachi's
time until the coming of Messiah's forerunner, it was
all the more needful that they give closest heed to
the Mosaic law. Moses gave the law, but it was not

from himself, for in this as in all his ministry, he was a servant of the Lord. Mark it well that the law was given for all Israel and not for any others, the vaporizings of the Seventh Dayists to the contrary notwithstanding. Moses is connected here with Elijah (verse 5), as they were at the Mount of Transfiguration and, as many believe, they will be in the Great Tribulation, Revelation 11:3-12. In verse 5 we have the third great "Behold" in the latter part of the prophecy of Malachi. See 3:1 and 4:1. Compare the wording at the beginning of this verse with 3:1. Commentators are divided into two distinct camps on the subject of whether Elijah is meant personally or ideally (representatively) through John the Baptist. Those who take the reference ideally of John the Baptist point to passages like Matthew 11:14 and Luke 1:17 where John is said to have come in the spirit and power of Elijah, and where he is spoken of as representing Elijah to them, if they would receive him. This view explains the denial of John 1:21 as referring only to the personal sense of the term, that is, he was denying that he was Elijah literally. Matthew 17:10-13 is also explained in such a way as to give the force that Elijah had come in John the Baptist. The great and terrible Day of the Lord is explained as the dreadful time of judgment which resulted in the destruction of Jerusalem by the Romans. Actually, there is no such usage of the phrase "day of the Lord" in Old Testament prophecy, as that just noted. Jewish commentators and Christian interpreters generally have taken it to refer literally to Elijah the Tishbite. With this view we are in agreement. John the Baptist himself testi-

fied that he was not Elijah (John 1:21). He knew
by the Spirit that he was referred to in a sense in
Malachi 4:5 (Luke 1:17), yet he knew also by divine illumination that he did not completely fulfill
all the conditions and requirements of this prophecy.
There is a future fulfilment. Even after the transfiguration experience, the Lord in Matthew 17:11
speaks of Elijah's coming as still future, although in
the person and ministry of John the Baptist he had
come in a certain sense. The mention of the Day of
the Lord shows that John cannot be meant exclusively here, for his ministry preceded the day of
Christ's grace and not the day of His judgment. As
John the Baptist came in the spirit and power of Elijah before the first coming, so Elijah will come in
person before the second coming. In short, John the
Baptist's coming was a testimony to faith, not the
fulfilment of this prophecy. The ministry of Elijah
to Israel had been one of calling apostate Israel back
to the Lord whom they had forsaken. He will come
again in order to avert the curse of God from Israel.
This work John did not accomplish in his ministry.
Some believe the two witnesses of Revelation 11 are
Moses and Elijah, thus fulfilling this prophecy. Note
there the nature of the miracles performed. The aim
of the ministry of Elijah when he comes before the
great and terrible Day of the Lord, is to turn the
hearts of the fathers to the children and those of the
children to their fathers (the very opposite of what
took place in the first coming, Matthew 10:34-36),
lest the Lord come and smite the earth with a curse.
The reconciliation worked for is (on the basis of
Luke 1:16, 17) to be between the unbelieving chil-

dren and the believing ancestors and forefathers
(like Jacob, Levi, Moses, and Elijah, mentioned in
1:2; 2:4-6; 3:3; and 4:4). If the restoration is
not brought about, the coming of the Messiah will be
a curse upon the earth and not with a blessing. The
curse or ban meant destruction and extermination.
See Leviticus 27:28, 29 and Deuteronomy 13:16,
17. It is both interesting and instructive that the
final word of the last prophet of the Old Testament
should be "curse," while the first word of the Messiah on the Mount was "Blessed" (Matthew 5:3),
and the last word of the New Testament is one of
"grace" (Revelation 22:21). The Jews repeat verse
5 after verse 6, because Malachi ends with the pronouncement of a curse. In four Old Testament books
the Jewish scholars indicated that the last verse but
one was to be repeated in the reading. These are
Isaiah, the Twelve (the minor prophets concluding
with Malachi), Lamentations, and Ecclesiastes. Compare their last verses.

The Remedy for the Curse

The Book of Genesis shows how the curse entered
the human race, and Malachi indicates the curse still
threatens. The Book of Matthew begins with the Son
of David, the Son of Abraham who came to be made
a curse for us by hanging upon a tree, declared a
curse in the Word of God, that we might have blessing, joy, and eternal life through faith in His name.
Only through Messiah Jesus the Lord can Israel escape the awful curse. The hour is tragically late.
When, when will we tell them simply and clearly the
remedy and escape from the curse?

QUESTIONS ON CHAPTER IV

1. Does the Hebrew Old Testament have four chapters in the Book of Malachi? Why?

2. Why are these last words of great importance?

3. What day is spoken of in the passage?

4. What is meant by leaving neither root nor branch?

5. Is there ground here for annihilation doctrine? Explain clearly.

6. What passage or passages can you give to show the eternal nature of the punishment of the wicked?

7. What is the contrast between verses 1 and 2, 3?

8. How do some interpret "sun of righteousness"?

9. What is meant by the figure? Present your proof.

10. Compare the hope of Israel with the hope of the Church.

11. Why does Malachi emphasize the law of Moses here?

12. In what instances are Moses and Elijah joined in Scripture?

13. Will Elijah return to earth personally or ideally before the coming of Christ? Defend your position in detail by Scripture.

14. How would you characterize the ministry of John the Baptist?

15. Do you see any connection between this passage and Revelation 11? Explain.

16. Why is Elijah promised? What is he to accomplish?

17. Compare the conclusion of the Old Testament with the end of the New.

18. What custom do the Jews follow when reading this book? Why?

19. Is the entire human race under the curse?

20. If a believer are you under the curse?

21. How can Israel be rescued from this curse?

22. Do you care to do anything about it?

INDEX OF SUBJECTS

INDEX OF SCRIPTURE REFERENCES

On University Studies

Ohio University Press

Athens, Ohio

F. W. J. SCHELLING

On University Studies

Translated by E. S. Morgan

Edited and with an introduction by

Norbert Guterman

Contents

Chronology

1775   (January 27) Friedrich Wilhelm Joseph (later *von*) Schelling born at Leonberg, Württemberg.

1790   Admitted as student to the theological seminary at Tübingen (though three years below the admission age). Makes friends with Hegel and Hölderlin, both born in 1770.

1793   Publishes essay *On Myths.*

1794   Writes his first philosophical essay, *On the Possibility of Form in Philosophy* (published in 1795).

1795   *On the Ego as Principle of Philosophy* and *Philosophical Letters on Dogmatism and Criticism.* Is graduated from Tübingen. For next three years tutors two sons of Baron Riedesel.

1796   (March) Accompanies his pupils to Leipzig. Meets Schiller at Jena. Studies mathematics, physics, medicine.

1797   *Ideas toward a Philosophy of Nature.*

1798   *On the World Soul.* (May) Visits Jena and meets Goethe. (July) Appointed professor of philosophy at Jena. Resigns his post as tutor. Spends six weeks (July/August) in Dresden where he frequents romantic avant-garde and studies art at the Gallery. Friendship with August and Friedrich Schlegel. Meets August's wife, Caroline, as well as Novalis, Tieck, and Henrik Steffens.

1799 *First Outline of a System of Philosophy of Nature* and *Introduction to the Outline, or On the Concept of Speculative Physics.*

1800 *System of Transcendental Idealism.*

1801 *Exposition of My System of Philosophy.*

1802 *Bruno, or On the Divine and Natural Principle of Things.* Honorary Doctor of Medicine, University of Landshut.

1802/3 Edits with Hegel the *Critical Journal of Philosophy.* Gives course of lectures on the philosophy of art.

1803 *Lectures on the Method of University Studies.* Marries Caroline Schlegel (recently divorced) on June 28. From October of this year to April 1806, professor at the University of Würzburg.

1804 *Philosophy and Religion.*

1806 Moves to Munich at invitation of Bavarian government.

1807 Member of the Academy of Science and Secretary of the Academy of Fine Arts in Munich. Gives lecture "On the Relation of the Plastic Arts to Nature."

1809 (September 7) Caroline dies. *Philosophical Inquiries into the Nature of Human Freedom.*

1810 Gives course of lectures at Stuttgart.

1811 Writes *The Ages of the World.*

1812 Marries Pauline Gotter.

1815 *On the Divinities of Samothrace.*

1820 Moves to Erlangen.

1820/23 Lectures on the history of modern philosophy and on the philosophy of mythology.

1827 Recalled to Munich. Appointed: Chief Curator of Bavarian scientific collections, Director of Bavarian Academy of Science, and professor at university of Munich.

1833 Corresponding member of the French Academy. Member of the Légion d'Honneur.

1841 Begins Berlin lectures.

1843 Attacks on Schelling by Engels, Feuerbach, Paulus, and others.

1854 (August 20) Dies at Bad Ragaz, Switzerland.

Introduction

In 1802, when Schelling delivered these lectures, he was
only twenty-seven years old but already had a brilliant
philosophic career behind him. He began to philos-
ophize at nineteen when he was studying with the theological faculty of Tübingen. His first essay, written in
1794 and published in 1795, established him as the most
articulate champion of Fichte's subjective idealism
(which Fichte believed to be an improved version of
Kantianism), and until 1801 he was regarded as a disci-
ple of Fichte. Adversaries of the new system called him
"a street peddler of the Ego"; its defenders, "the second
founder of the Theory of Knowledge." There were more
adversaries than defenders: they included anti-Kantians
who clung to the old "dogmatic" philosophy, orthodox
Kantians, theologians who saw in Kant's radical separation between the theoretical and practical reason a se-
curing of the dogmas of religious faith against the
inroads of rationalism, and finally philosophers who had
their own "improved versions" of Kantianism. As
Fichte's companion-in-arms, Schelling distinguished
himself by vigorous polemics. In the heat of the struggle

the two allies bent on their immediate goals overlooked or underestimated their differences: strange as it may seem, neither took the trouble to read the other's writings carefully.

Eventually the two philosophers became conscious of their divergence. However, from the beginning Schelling's conception of the nature of philosophy and of the philosopher's task was clearly his own. As early as 1795 Schelling felt the need of going beyond the subjective principle of cognition. "The purpose of critical idealism," he says, "namely, to set mankind free, could not be attained if its system were based solely upon our cognitive faculty" (*Werke,* I, 290).[1] It is not true, he goes on to say, that critical idealism is the only possible system; dogmatism is just as possible, and its most coherent expression, Spinozism, is irrefutable by Kantian arguments. The choice between the two systems is the result of a free act, which Schelling calls "aesthetic," and which today might be called "existential." The true philosopher rebels against being the prisoner of any system. The moment he thinks he has completed his own system, he ceases to be creator, is degraded to the role of an instrument of his own creation. "How much more intolerable the idea that a system could be forced upon him by someone else!" (*Werke,* I, 306).

The highest dignity of philosophy, Schelling declares, consists in staking everything on human freedom. Hence nothing could be more pernicious than attempts to hold philosophy within the straitjacket of a theoretically universally valid system (*Werke,* I, 307).

"A universally valid philosophy is an inglorious fig-

---

[1] *Werke,* followed by indication of volume and page, refers to the complete edition (Stuttgart and Augsburg, 1856–1861) published by Schelling's son, K. F. A. Schelling.

ment of the imagination," he wrote in 1797 (*Werke*, II, 7)—a statement that directly contradicts the possibility of ever founding a philosophy "as self-evident as geometry," which was Fichte's goal (*Fichte's Leben*, II, 2, xviii). Similarly incompatible with Fichte's conception of philosophy was Schelling's interest in natural science. In 1796, before he began to develop his philosophy of nature, he wrote: "While the Kantians, ignorant of what is going on outside themselves, are grappling with figments of their imagination, their 'things-in-themselves,' men of truly philosophical spirit are quietly making discoveries in natural science, which healthy philosophy will soon put to use" (*Werke*, I, 348n.).

Also in 1796 Schelling drafted what is known as the earliest program of German idealism. The original of this draft has been lost, but a copy in Hegel's handwriting (discovered by Franz Rosenzweig in 1914) survives; only the beginning is missing. I have translated the entire document.[2] Although it is written in a casual style, as one would expect of a letter addressed to a close friend, it offers revealing insights into the young Schelling's mind:

> . . . an ethics. Since the whole of philosophy will eventually become a part of morals—Kant with his two practical postulates gave us merely one example: he did not exhaust the subject—ethics becomes a complete system of all Ideas, or, what amounts to the same thing, a system of all practical postulates. The first Idea is naturally that of my own self as an absolutely free being. As I become aware of myself as free, a whole world emerges —out of nothing—the only true and conceivable creation out of nothing.— At this point I shall descend to the field

2 *Das älteste Systemprogramm des deutschen Idealismus*, Heidelberg, 1917. Reprinted in Franz Rosenzweig, *Kleinere Schriften*, Berlin, 1937.

of physics. The question is this: How must a world be constituted for a moral being? Our physics is advancing slowly and laboriously through experiment—I should like some day to give it new wings.

And so—once philosophy has provided the Ideas, the experience, the data—we can at last have a physics in the grand manner, such as I expect later ages to create. It does not seem that present-day physics can satisfy a creative spirit such as ours is or ought to be.

From nature I pass to the works of man. The Idea of humanity first—I want to show that there is no Idea of the state, for the state is something purely mechanical —no more than there is an Idea of a machine. Only an object of freedom can be called Idea. Thus we must go beyond the state!— For every state treats free men as cogs in a machine, and this is not to be tolerated, hence the state must be abolished. You see yourself how all ideas about perpetual peace, etc. are subordinate to a higher Idea. At the same time I want to set down the principles for a history of mankind and lay bare the whole wretched business of state, constitution, government, legislation. Lastly come the ideas of a moral world, godhead, immortality, the collapse of all belief in a hereafter, Reason turning on the priests [3] who at the moment are hypocritically invoking it.— Absolute freedom of all minds that carry the intelligible world within themselves and seek no God or immortality outside themselves.

Finally the Idea that unifies all Ideas, the Idea of Beauty, the term taken in the higher Platonic sense. I am now convinced that the highest act of Reason, the one in which she encompasses all Ideas, is an aesthetic act, and that the True and the Good are united only in the Beautiful. The philosopher must possess just as much aesthetic power as the poet. Your literal-minded

[3] Schelling probably refers to the theologians who were exploiting Kant to their own purpose.

philosophers are men without any aesthetic sense. The philosophy of the spirit is an aesthetic philosophy. It is impossible to be intelligent, it is impossible to reason intelligently even about history without an aesthetic sense. Here it should become apparent just what is lacking in people who do not understand Ideas—who are frank enough to admit that everything becomes obscure to them the moment knowledge goes beyond lists and tabulations.

In this way poetry takes on a higher dignity. It becomes in the end what it was at the beginning: the teacher of mankind—for there is no philosophy any more, no history; the poetic art alone will outlive all the arts and sciences.

At the same time we hear so often that the mass of the people needs a sensuous religion. Not only the masses, the philosopher too needs one. Monotheism of Reason and the heart, polytheism of the imagination and art— this is what we need.

First of all I shall speak here of an idea which, so far as I know, has not yet come to any man's mind—we must have a mythology of the Ideas—an eventual mythology of Reason.

Until we have made the Ideas aesthetic, i.e., mythological, they are of no interest to the people; and conversely, until mythology has been made rational, the philosopher can only be ashamed of it. And so enlightened man and unenlightened man must at last hold out a hand to each other; mythology must become philosophical in order to make the people rational, and philosophy must become mythological in order to make the philosopher sensuous. Then only will eternal unity prevail among us. No more contemptuous glances, no more blind trembling of the people before their wise men and priests. Only then can we have an equal development of all energies, those of the individual, and those of all individuals alike. No more repressing of energies. Only then shall we have the reign of universal freedom and intellectual equality!— A higher mind sent by Heaven must found this new religion among us, which will be humanity's last great achievement.

Schelling, as promised above, "descended to the field of physics" in 1797, when he published *Ideas for a Philosophy of Nature*. In 1798 he published *Of the World Soul,* a work which Schiller sent to Goethe. Upon reading it, Goethe expressed a desire to meet the author, and in July 1798, thanks largely to Goethe's influence, Schelling was appointed professor at Jena: he was then twenty-three. Other works on the philosophy of nature followed in rapid succession.

Schelling's goal in this first phase of his philosophical career was to formulate a theory which could account for both nature and our knowledge of nature. The effort is to overcome the Cartesian dualism which had led to the mechanistic conception of nature (i.e., everything external to the human mind viewed as dead matter subject to the law of inertia) and to formulate a "dynamic" theory. Schelling is not trying to replace empirical science, but to supplement it: what he has in mind is another kind of knowledge, more poetic and less detached from the creative imagination.[4]

[4] It was this ambitious aim that instantly attracted many scientists and such men of letters as Goethe and Coleridge. Coleridge contrasts Schelling with Fichte whose theory "degenerated into a crude egoismus, a boastful and hyperstoic hostility to Nature, as lifeless, godless, and altogether unholy" and admires him "not only as a great and original genius, but as the founder of the Philosophy of Nature, and as the most successful improver of the Dynamic System which, begun by Bruno, was reintroduced (in a more philosophical form, and freed from all its impurities and visionary accompaniments) by Kant. . . . With the exception of one or two fundamental ideas, which cannot be withheld from Fichte, to Schelling we owe the completion, and the most important victories of this revolution in philosophy." (*Biographia Literaria,* ix)

Schelling's point of departure is a critical analysis of the assumptions of his age's science. Following Kant, he shows that the concept of matter presupposes the existence of dynamic forces; but he rejects teleological hypotheses of an extra-natural purpose governing organic life, and identifies creative nature with the unconcious activity of mind. To Fichte, nature was merely the object, the non-self; to Schelling, it is an enlarged self which is both object and subject. Nature is visible mind, just as mind is invisible nature.

In 1800, having by this time shown how the unconscious mind becomes conscious throughout the world process, Schelling published his *System of Transcendental Idealism*. Here his point of departure is the mind, and he shows how the progressive stages of its development are correlated with corresponding stages in nature. "What we call nature is a poem encoded in secret and mysterious signs, but if the riddle could be solved, we would recognize in nature the Odyssey of the mind" (*Werke*, III, 628). The work concludes with an exaltation of art as "the organon of philosophy."

In 1801, in his *Exposition of My System*, Schelling for the first time explicitly rejects Fichte's subjective idealism. Refusing to subordinate matter to spirit or vice versa, he considers them, in the manner of Spinoza, as correlatives, both having their common root in the absolute. At this point Schelling's main philosophical position had been outlined, and only much later, sometime between 1820 and 1830, did he look back at it as merely the first, "negative," phase of philosophy, which would now have to be supplemented with a "positive" philosophy, dealing not with mere ideas but with concrete being.

So, in 1802, when Schelling delivered the present lectures, he had just discovered the absolute. He was only beginning to grasp the far-reaching implications of his new system, and the need to bring his earlier formulations into harmony with it. Shortly after the appearance of these lectures in book form, Friedrich Schleiermacher in a lengthy review [5] noted that the title refers only to their "exoteric" content, and that the book has a more important "esoteric" content, namely, the system of absolute idealism. Schleiermacher particularly recommends Schelling's discussion of absolute knowledge in the first lecture to those who "have misunderstood" the earlier *Exposition of My System*. Schleiermacher's distinction between the two aspects of the book is well taken. Indeed, perhaps the most important single characteristic of these lectures is the way Schelling succeeds in blending a "practical" discussion of education with his own metaphysical aims.

The exoteric or ostensible theme—the conception of the university as a living community of scholars dedicated to the extension of knowledge—remains topical to this day. Schelling's observations on the bewilderment of freshmen making their first contact with the campus, on the inadequacy of their preparatory training, on the shortcomings of a teaching system which emphasizes memorized learning rather than the spirit of each discipline—all this is at least as relevant today as it was nearly two centuries ago. The ideal of the teacher whose major purpose is to stimulate the creative capacities of his pupils in most cases still remains an ideal. Nor is some of the esoteric (i.e., metaphysical) content irrelevant to

[5] *Jenaische Allgemeine Literatur-Zeitung*, No. 96 and 97, April 1804. Reprinted in *Aus Schleiermachers Leben*, Berlin, 1863; v. IV, pp. 579–593.

present-day preoccupations. To be sure, Schelling's view that all science should take its cue from philosophy—and, needless to say, he means *his* philosophy—can scarcely be accepted today. Since 1802 science has developed efficient methods of its own for assessing its hypotheses and results. But the very advance of science has served to underline the need for an over-all view of the relation of science to our life as a whole. The moral dilemma faced by latter-day nuclear physicists is but one glaring example. There is also the deepening gulf between "the two cultures," and, within science itself, realization that the irresistible trend to specialization narrows the intellectual horizon of the scientist. Schelling in his own fashion anticipates this state of affairs and attempts to remedy it by formulating a principle that includes the physical sciences, history, and art in a single harmonious universe of knowledge.

This little book has often been described as the best available introduction to Schelling's thinking as a whole. His contemporaries, who were more or less familiar with his earlier work, saw in it a popular exposition of his philosophy. Readers today may find it difficult or obscure at certain points; my notes (indicated by asterisks and placed after lecture fourteen) are meant to clarify the author's intention at what I take to be such passages. It is not surprising that this youthful work, composed when his career was at its most brilliant pitch, should radiate optimism and self-confidence. Schelling had not yet discovered the reality of evil. His obsession with the darker sides of existence was to come later. As a mature man Schelling's great question was, "Why is there something rather than nothing?"

Until about 1804, Schelling continued to publish a great deal; as Hegel tartly noted, he was "carrying on his education in public." After 1804, he published much more infrequently. The latter part of his writings in fact did not appear until after his death; of those works posthumously issued in fourteen volumes, more than half of the pages are devoted to previously unpublished material. The reason Schelling gave for publishing so little in his later years was dissatisfaction with his work. No doubt this had a great deal to do with his gradual loss of influence. By 1812, as Hegel's star was rising, Schelling's had begun to set.

Hegel died in 1831. In 1833 his *Lectures on the History of Philosophy* appeared, which contains a lengthy chapter on Schelling. Hegel credits Schelling with first formulating the main features of Hegel's own system— the idea of the absolute, the idea that the absolute can be conceived of only as process, etc., but criticizes him for making philosophy a matter of talent or genius, of brilliant intuition rather than hard thinking, "as though only Sunday's children were capable of philosophy." [6] He also chides Schelling for resorting to vague analogies in lieu of rigorous logical proofs, and above all for his failure to carry through the development of his own thought. Hegel's analysis deals mainly with Schelling's early works. The *Inquiry into the Nature of Human Freedom* (1809) is only briefly mentioned. It is "profound and speculative," Hegel says, but it is an "isolated" treatise, and "in philosophy nothing can be developed in isolation." [7] The over-all impression Hegel gives is that Schelling's philosophy is but a crude, primitive version of Hegel's own; Schelling is in effect relegated to the role of historical precursor.

[6] G. W. F. Hegel, *Vorlesungen über die Geschichte der Philosophie.* Ed. by H. Glockner. Stuttgart, 1928; v. III, p. 654.
[7] *Ibid.,* p. 682.

Most later writers have reflected this judgment. Heinrich Heine may have been acquainted with Hegel's *Lectures on the History of Philosophy* when, in 1835, he spoke of Schelling as a ghostly image of failure, embittered by Hegel's success. Heine no doubt exaggerated. When, in 1841, Schelling inaugurated a lecture series at Berlin, the event attracted international attention. His opening address was attended by a distinguished audience that included Kierkegaard, Burckhardt, and Engels. Translations appeared in France, Poland, Russia, and the United States. It is interesting to note that the American periodical which published the first of the Berlin lectures was none other than *The Dial* (issue of January 1843)—Emerson was one of Schelling's admirers. Shortly before the Berlin lectures, Emerson wrote to a friend: "To hear Schelling might well tempt the firmest rooted philosopher from his home, and I confess to more curiosity in respect to his opinions than to those of any living psychologist." In another letter (Aug. 4, 1842) Emerson wrote: "There is a grandeur in the attempt to unite natural and moral philosophy which makes him a sort of hero."

However, though Emerson may at this date still have been enthusiastic about Schelling, others had already spoken against him. Following the Berlin lectures Schelling was attacked by both left- and right-wing Hegelians, by both orthodox and liberal theologians. Kierkegaard, at first admiring, was quickly disillusioned: he recognized that Schelling, despite his assurances to the contrary, sacrificed, as Hegel did, the concrete individual to the world spirit. (This did not prevent him from borrowing Schelling's biting critique of Hegel in those same Berlin lectures.) Feuerbach indignantly denounced Schelling as "the philosophical Cagliostro of the nineteenth century." [8] Friedrich Engels, who had not as yet met Karl Marx, wrote three pamphlets against Schelling [9] condemning the Berlin lectures as the latest reactionary attack on free philosophy. He too relegates Schelling to the dustbin of history, and says that he deserves respect only as "Hegel's precursor" and "the discoverer of the absolute."

In 1856, two years after Schelling's death, when the complete works began to appear, not only Schelling but metaphysics generally had gone out of fashion. Schelling's later philosophy as expounded in the Berlin lectures, his speculations on the nature of freedom and God, and his theories of mythology and revelation, were dismissed as incomprehensible or preposterous. His philosophy of nature was again and again—over the generations—held up as a prime example of the aberrations into which reliance on pure thought can lead. The dominant belief was that science would provide future generations with answers to all traditional metaphysical questions—that total truth would be attained (if ever) by careful observation of "the facts." The era of positivism had begun.

Not until the early years of this century did philosophers begin to rediscover Schelling. His philosophy of nature, it began to be allowed, contained valuable ideas. As Josiah Royce put it in 1906, "His . . . leading ideas in regard to nature are of decidedly more importance than the first glance indicates." [10] It has taken somewhat longer for Schelling's so-called "positive" philosophy to be appreciated, but Whitehead, Tillich, and Ernst Cas-

---

[8] In the preface to the second edition of *Essence of Christianity,* 1843.
[9] Reprinted in *Marx-Engels Gesamtausgabe,* I, 2, pp. 173–249. Berlin, 1930.
[10] *Lectures on Modern Idealism* (Yale University Press, 1964), p. 77.

sirer (among others) have variously paid tribute to aspects of his later thought.

These Jena Lectures of 1802 show Schelling at his best: a restless, far-ranging mind, with all the virtues of the traditional metaphysician. Constantly striving to create a "system," yet always putting freedom above the confines of all systems including his own, his conception of philosophy which aims at an all-encompassing vision of reality is no mere systematizing of known facts. He refuses to be overwhelmed by the crushing weight of facts, insisting on the philosopher's right to interpret them. He has unbounded faith in man's destiny and in the power of reason. Nowhere better than in these lectures does he make clear that philosophy consists not in accepting another man's vision, in memorizing the works of other philosophers, but in re-creating the world and one's self. At the same time he is convinced that however rich and varied the expressions of philosophy may be, they reflect the one true perennial philosophy, just as in his vision of the absolute, nature in all its multiformity reflects the world of the eternal archetypes.

Schelling of course has also all of the metaphysician's vices. His speculative boldness often leads him astray. Inconsistencies abound. His occasionally oracular tone is often ill-fitted to his matter. He does not always practice what he preaches. His very faults are perhaps the best antidote to the misconception that any philosophy can provide us with ready-made solutions and spare us the labor of thinking for ourselves. Coleridge sums up the virtues and the vices very well in a letter of 1817 to J. H. Green (*Letters*, 683): "Schelling . . . is a man of great genius: and, however unsatisfied with his conclusions, one cannot read him without being *whetted* and improved."

In English, only the following works by Schelling have appeared in book form:

1. *The Philosophy of Art: An Oration on the Relation Between the Plastic Arts and Nature.* Trans. A. Johnson. London, 1845. v+34 pp.
2. *Of Human Freedom.* Trans. James Guttmann. Chicago, 1930. lii+128 pp.
3. *The Ages of the World.* Trans. F. Bolman. New York, 1942. 253 pp.
4. *Excerpts from the System of Transcendental Idealism.* Trans. Albert Hofstadter. In *Philosophies of Art and Beauty.* The Modern Library, New York, 1964 (pp. 347–377).

The Method of University Study was translated by Ella Morgan and published in the *Journal of Speculative Philosophy* (St. Louis, Mo.) over the years 1877–1881. The present version began as a revision of that translation but has ended as a virtually new text.

This book arose out of a continuing study of Schelling which has been made possible by a grant from the Bollingen Foundation. My ultimate interest is in the philosopher's views on art, mythology, and symbolism.

Norbert Guterman

On University Studies

Lectures on the Method of University Studies

Author's Preface to First Edition (1803)

These lectures were given at the university of Jena in the summer of 1802. Since they attracted a considerable number of listeners, some of the ideas expressed may eventually influence the development of our universities. Although these lectures cannot, by their very nature, be expected to cast new light on basic principles, their generally accessible style, as well as the view they offer of the sciences as a whole, may be of some interest to a wider public. These reasons, the author felt, justified publication.

1 The Concept of Absolute Knowledge

A brief statement of the particular reasons why I have decided to give these lectures may not be superfluous. Surely, it would be pointless for me to prove at great length that lectures on the method of university study are not only useful but indeed indispensable to the student, and may even serve to further the revival of science itself and a better understanding of its goal.

It is at the very beginning of his university career that the young man first comes into contact with the world of science. The more taste and inclination he has for science, the more likely it is that this world will strike him as a chaos, a confused mass, a vast ocean upon which he is launched without star or compass. Students who really enjoy a clear sight of their goal are unfortunately rare exceptions to this rule. What usually happens is that the better-organized minds throw themselves haphazardly into every conceivable study. Striking out in every direction at once, they never get to the heart of any one subject, which is the only way to attain a many-sided, well-rounded culture. At best, by the end of their academic career they are rewarded with insight into how fruitless their labors have been—they see how much they have learned to no purpose and how many essentials they have neglected. Lesser minds, meanwhile, practice resignation from the outset, keep to the beaten track, and at most try to assimilate—applying themselves mechanically, merely memorizing—only as much knowledge as they suppose will be profitable in their future trade or profession.

The dilemma in which the superior student finds himself with regard to choice of subject and method of study often leads him to heed unworthy counselors, to adopt their low opinion of—or even contempt for—the sciences.

For this reason it is imperative that universities give general instruction in the aims and methods of academic study, both as a whole and in respect to its particular subjects.

There is another consideration. In science and in art the particular has value only insofar as it implies the universal and absolute. But it happens too often that concern for universal culture is neglected in the individual's concern for his profession: the student trying to make himself a good lawyer or physician loses sight of the far higher purpose of learning, which is to ennoble one's mind through knowledge. Some people might here point out that study of one of the broader sciences should provide a sufficient antidote to cultural narrowness. Generally speaking, I would be the last person to deny this. Mathematics, and especially geometry, clears the mind for purely rational cognition, independent of practical application. Philosophy, which comprehends the whole man, is even better suited for freeing the mind from the limitations of a one-sided culture and for elevating it to the realm of the universal and absolute. However, it must be observed that the broader sciences have no necessary bearing upon a given student's field of specialization—at least, science at its most universal does not trouble to make such a relation clear. As a result, most students when they concentrate on mastering a special science, are left without guidance. Rather than expend their powers struggling for insight into the living whole of knowledge, they confine themselves narrowly to some one specialty.

Consequently, knowledge of the organic whole of the sciences must precede special training for a particular profession. The student who devotes himself to a special field must learn where it stands in the whole—the particular spirit that animates it as well as how it is related to the harmonious structure of the whole. He must also grasp the particular science in such a way that he is not a slave to it, but a free man within it. And this means that he must view it in the spirit of the whole.

You can see from the foregoing that a methodology of university study must be rooted in actual and true knowledge of the living unity of all the sciences, and that without such knowledge any guidance can only be lifeless, spiritless, one-sided, limited. Perhaps this requirement was never more pressing than at the present time, when everything in science and art seems to be tending toward unity,* when matters that long seemed remote from each other are now recognized to be quite close, when every tremor at or near the center is communicated quickly and immediately to the parts, and a new more universal vision, encompassing almost all disciplines, is taking shape.

An epoch such as our own is surely bound to give birth to a new world.* Those who do not actively contribute to its emergence will inevitably be forgotten. The noble task of shaping the future devolves upon the fresh, unspoiled energies of youth. Every young man has an opportunity to take part in this process of universal renewal: no field of activity falls outside it. To assist the advance, we must be inspired by the spirit of the whole; each of us must conceive of his special field of study as an organic part of the total body of knowledge. Whether by our own efforts or with the aid of others, we must recognize our particular function in the emergent new world before our minds have hardened in outdated molds, before the spark of our higher aspirations has been stifled by prolonged spiritless drudgery—that is to say, in early youth, at the beginning of academic training.

Who is to set the young student upon the right road? Whom is he to trust in this connection? First of all himself, his own good genius, always a reliable guide; [1] next, those who because of the nature of their own special fields are unmistakably committed to a universal view of human knowledge. Surely, no one who lacks such a view is capable of imparting it to others; a man who confines himself to studying a subordinate discipline, however praiseworthy his industry may be, cannot be expected to rise to the vision of knowledge as an organic whole. This vision can be found only in the science of all sciences, in philosophy, and it is only the philosopher who can communicate it to us, for his own special field is the absolutely universal science.

Such considerations as these have led me to prepare these lectures, the purpose of which is perhaps already clear to you. To what extent I shall cover the topics

[1] Every man has a friend within himself whose promptings are purest in youth; he is frightened away by frivolity, and eventually silenced as vulgar purposes come to the fore. [This and the following footnotes are comments added by Schelling in the margins of a printed copy of these Lectures. *Ed.*]

satisfactorily is something else again. All I can say is that I shall try to deserve the confidence you have shown in me in the past.

So much, then, for preliminaries. Let us proceed at once to the pivotal issue upon which everything else turns. What is that issue? It is the idea of an intrinsically unconditioned knowledge, one and entire—the primordial knowledge, which in the phenomenal world exists only in separate branches, no longer as one single great tree of knowledge. As the knowledge of all knowledge, it must be based on the same assumption as every individual science. However we express this assumption— whether as adequacy of knowledge to its object or as the resolution of the particular in the universal or in some other formula—it is not conceivable without a higher assumption: true ideality is ipso facto true reality; there is no other ideality.

This essential identity of the real with the ideal cannot, strictly speaking, be proven even in philosophy: it is the assumption upon which all true science is founded. All that can be proved is that without it there can be no science, that the merest claim to knowledge implies search for this identity, for resolution of the real in the ideal.[2]

All universal laws of nature—such as the various sciences boast they have discovered—imply this identity; indeed, every effort to discover them unconsciously presupposes it. Their aim is to resolve the concreteness and opacity of particular phenomena in a universal rational knowledge which should be self-evident and transparent. The validity of this presupposition is recognized in special fields with respect to particular cases, even though

2 And vice versa, the possibility of fully translating the ideal into the real.

it is not understood and, consequently, not acknowledged in an absolute and universal sense, as it is in philosophy.

The geometrician more or less consciously bases his science on the absolute reality of the purely ideal when he proves that in any possible triangle the sum of the angles equals two right angles. To do this he does not refer to actually existing triangles but to the archetype. His insight is rooted in the nature of knowledge itself, which is purely ideal and thereby purely real. Even if we restricted the possibility of knowledge to merely finite knowledge, the empirical truth of the latter could never be accounted for by reference to any so-called object—for knowledge is already presupposed when we speak of an object. In fact, knowledge would be altogether inconceivable unless the intrinsically ideal, which in temporal knowledge appears in finite form, were not itself the reality and substance of things.*

But this first assumption of all the sciences, this essential identity between the absolutely ideal and the absolutely real, is possible only because that which is the one is also the other. Now, this is nothing less than the Idea of the absolute—that is, in relation to the absolute, Idea is also Being. In other words, the absolute is the supreme presupposition of all knowledge, the first knowledge.

In virtue of this first knowledge, all other knowledge is in the absolute and is itself absolute. For, although primordial knowledge is originally present only in the absolute itself, it is also present in ourselves in the idea of the essence of all things and in the eternal idea of ourselves; and our total system of knowledge can be only a copy of that eternal knowledge. Needless to say, I am not referring to individual sciences insofar as they have separated from this total knowledge and moved away from their true archetype. Only knowledge in its totality can be a perfect reflection of the archetypal knowledge, but each single insight and every individual science are organic parts of this whole, and hence all knowledge that is not directly or indirectly related to primordial knowledge is without reality or meaning.

Our ability to engage in a given discipline with intelligence and the higher inspiration called scientific genius depends upon our ability to relate our particular insights to the original whole. Every thought not conceived in this spirit of unity and totality is intrinsically empty, of no account. Whatever cannot be incorporated into this active, living whole is dead matter to be eliminated sooner or later—such is the law of all living organisms. The fact is, there are too many sexless bees in the hive of sciences, and since they cannot be productive, they merely keep reproducing their own spiritual barrenness in the form of inorganic excretions.

Now that I have formulated the idea of the purpose of knowledge, I need not add anything concerning the dignity of science as such. Whatever norm for the development or study of science I may formulate in the following lectures originates in this one idea.

Historians of philosophy relate that Pythagoras changed into *philosophia* (the love of wisdom) the name of the discipline that until his time had been called *sophia* (wisdom), and that he justified the change on the grounds that God alone is wise. Whatever the historical accuracy of this story, the change and the alleged reason for it imply recognition that all knowledge is a striving for communion with the divine essence, for participation in the primordial knowledge of which the visible universe is the image and whose source is the fountainhead of eternal power. Accordingly, since all knowledge is one, and every branch of knowledge is a part of the whole, all sciences and kinds of knowledge are parts of philosophy, which is itself the striving to participate in primordial knowledge.

Everything, then, which springs directly from the absolute is itself absolute; it has no purpose outside itself, is an end in itself. Knowledge in its totality is one of the two aspects of the universe, and it is as absolute as the other aspect, Being or nature. In the domain of the real, finitude rules; in the domain of the ideal, infinitude; the former is what it is through necessity, the latter is to be achieved through freedom. Man—and the same is true of all rational beings—is intended in a sense to supplement the phenomenal world. The purpose of his activity is to develop that without which God's revelation is not total —for nature contains the whole of the divine essence in its real aspect. Man as a rational being is meant to express the image of the same divine nature as it is in itself, i.e., in its ideal aspect.

The unconditional character of philosophical knowledge is often challenged. Formulated in the most general terms, the argument against it runs as follows: knowledge is only part of the task of elucidating the absolute, merely one means to an end, and that end is action.

Action! action! * is a call that resounds on many sides, but is uttered most loudly by those who cannot get ahead with knowledge.

Much can be said in favor of such calls for action. It is supposed that anyone can act, for this depends only on freedom of will. On the other hand, knowledge, particularly philosophical knowledge, is not within the reach of all even with the best will in the world.

We ask: What kind of action is it in relation to which

knowledge is a means, and what kind of knowledge is it in relation to which action is an end? What grounds can be advanced for so much as the possibility of such an antithesis?

Even though the propositions which I must refer to here can be fully illumined only by philosophy, there is no reason why they should not be clear enough for our present purpose. Anyone who has even a general notion of the absolute will see that there can be but one conceivable basis for any antithesis. The nature of the absolute is this, that as the absolutely ideal it is also the absolutely real. This implies that (1) as ideal, the absolute fashions its essence into form as the real, and (2) because this essence can only be absolute, it in turn dissolves form into essence eternally in the same way, so that essence and form are perfectly fused. These two aspects of the absolute constitute the single act of primordial knowledge; but since this knowledge is indivisible, i.e., both real and ideal at every point, these two inseparable aspects must be present in every act of absolute knowledge. The two aspects must be one in both what is manifested as the real and in what is manifested as the ideal. Thus, just as nature is the image of the divine transformation of ideality into reality, reality is re-transformed into ideality by light and ultimately by reason, so that in the whole conceived of as ideal we find again a real (objective) and an ideal (subjective) aspect. In knowledge, subjectivity manifests itself as objectivity; in action, the particular is conceived of as absorbed in the universal.

The foregoing summary statement is sufficient to show that knowledge and action are opposed only at the finite level. Clearly, if knowledge is the ideal embodiment of the infinite in the finite, and action of the finite in the infinite, at the level of the Idea or being-in-itself each expresses the same absolute unity or primordial knowledge.

Temporal knowledge, like temporal action, posits conditionally and successively what in the Idea exists unconditionally and simultaneously. This is why knowledge and action are just as necessarily separate at the temporal level as they are inseparable—because both are equally absolute—in the Idea. Similarly, in God as the Idea of all Ideas, absolute wisdom is absolute power—directly, in virtue of its absoluteness. In other words, in God action is not determined by a prior intention, and for this reason, His wisdom is also absolute necessity.

The same applies to all other antitheses, which are antitheses only to the extent that each of the opposing terms is not conceived absolutely for itself, that is to say, conceived only from the point of view of the finite discursive reason. Consequently our antithesis is rooted in a notion of knowledge as imperfect as the notion of action which is supposed to be ennobled when it is viewed as an end in relation to knowledge. But knowledge as such cannot be a means to truly absolute action, for such action, precisely because it is absolute, cannot be determined by a cognition. The world of action, like that of knowledge, is a self-contained absolute world. This is of course not the case at the phenomenal level, where knowledge and action have reality only in their opposition.

Those who regard knowledge as the means and action as the end derive their idea of knowledge from everyday activities, in which knowledge indeed serves as a means to action. They expect philosophy to teach them what their duties in life are; in other words, they do not act out of a freely accepted necessity, but in obedience to notions supplied by theoretical knowledge. More generally, theory is supposed to tell them how to raise crops, how to develop the arts and crafts, and how to rebuild their dissipated powers. They think that geometry is fine, not because it is the most self-evident science, the most objective expression of reason itself, but because it teaches how to measure fields and build houses or is useful in plotting the courses of merchant ships; the fact that it is also useful in warfare, according to them, diminishes its value—after all, war is quite incompatible with universal philanthropy. As for philosophy, it is valueless even in war; the one war in which it might serve as a weapon would be a war against the shallow apostles of practicality in science—and this makes it all the more objectionable to them.

Those who fail to grasp the unity of knowledge and action bring forward such trivial objections as this: that if knowledge and action were one, the latter would always follow from the former, whereas it is quite possible to know what is right without doing right. They are quite correct in saying that action does not result from knowledge, thus implying that knowledge is not a means to action. They are wrong only in expecting such a result. They do not understand relations between absolutes, how each can be unconditioned in itself, and by making one a means and the other an end, they make each dependent on the other.

Knowledge and action can never be truly in harmony except envisaged as equally absolute. Just as there can be no true knowledge which is not directly or indirectly the expression of primordial knowledge, so there can be no true action which does not express—through no matter how many interposing links—the primordial action, and through it the divine essence. The freedom sought for and believed to exist in empirical action is as little true freedom and as much an illusion as the truth allegedly found in empirical knowledge. There is no true freedom save by virtue of absolute necessity,[3] and there is the same relation between freedom and necessity as between absolute knowledge and absolute action.[4]

[3] (It must be integrated with necessity.)
[4] In freedom, i.e., in action itself, necessity is restored, just as on the other hand truly absolute knowledge is knowledge at once absolutely necessary and absolutely free.

2 The Scientific and Moral Functions of Universities

The concept of university studies led us to the higher concept of an existing body of scientific knowledge and thence to the highest Idea, namely, primordial knowledge. We shall now discuss the actual conditions under which the various sciences are taught in our universities.

It might seem that a philosopher should confine himself to drawing a picture of the body of scientific knowledge and formulating general methodological principles, without going into organizational matters or the temporal forms of our institution. However, I hope to show that these forms are not arbitrary, that they reflect the spirit of the modern world, and that they make it possible for the disparate elements of modern culture to interpenetrate. This process of interpenetration will eventually do away with the present confusion and give rise to superior institutions.

The reason why knowledge has a temporal aspect will be clear from the previous lecture. Just as the unity of the ideal and the real in its finite reflection expresses itself in space as a self-contained whole, as nature, so this unity, viewed in the infinite, expresses itself in the universal form of endless time. However, time does not exclude eternity, and science, though it manifests itself at the phenomenal level as a product of time, introduces an element of eternity. The true, like the good and the beautiful, is by nature eternal, and in the midst of time is independent of time. Science is temporal only insofar as it is expressed by individuals; in itself, knowledge is no more a matter of individuality than action is. Just as a true action is one that might take place in the name of the whole race, so in true knowledge it is not the individual but reason that knows. Science is essentially independent of time; it belongs to mankind, which is itself eternal. Therefore, like life itself, science must be passed on from individual to individual, from generation to generation—this process is an expression of its eternal character. This is not the place to prove in detail that all sciences and arts of the present generation of man have been bequeathed to us. It is inconceivable that man as he is today raised himself by his own efforts from instinct to consciousness, from animality to rationality: we must assume there existed before us a race which ancient legend celebrated as gods and the first benefactors of mankind. The hypothesis of a primordial people [i.e., the modern version of this ancient legend] can do no more than account for the already deformed traces of a high prehistoric culture which preceded the first separation of peoples and—if we refuse to assume the existence of an inborn earth spirit common to all men—it might also account for the similarities in the myths of the oldest peoples; but it does not account for the beginnings of culture, and, like any empirical hypothesis, merely pushes the explanation further back in time.

However that may be, it is well known that the earliest vehicles for transmitting higher ideas were actions, ways of life, and symbols; even dogmas of the earliest religions were not stated explicitly but merely implied in prescriptions for religious practices. The states, laws, and institutions which were created to secure the preponderance of the divine principle in mankind were essentially expressions of speculative ideas. The invention of writing at first served only to stabilize tradition; the idea of using the spiritual medium of language to record artistic expression and thus give it enduring form could not arise until later. Even morality in the finest period of mankind was not an individual characteristic but reflected the spirit of the collectivity which was its source and its goal; similarly, science thrived in the light and air of public life as part of the collective organism. Subsequent ages were marked by a retreat from external reality and an internalization of life, which also affected science. The modern world is in every way, especially in science, a divided world which lives both in the past and in the present. The history of our sciences shows that the modern era took the past as its point of departure. The modern world had behind it a vanished world of the most magnificent scientific and artistic achievements. Separated from this ancient world by an unbridgeable gulf, it was linked to it only by the external bond of historical tradition, not by internal bonds of continuous organic growth. When the sciences revived in our part of the world, the reawakened urge to knowledge could not first aim at original productions, but at understanding, admiring, and explaining the glories of the past. Rediscovery of forgotten ancient knowledge became the object of an additional new science. For this reason, and because good minds are needed even to gain insight into knowledge achieved by others, the terms scholar, artist, and philosopher came to be regarded as equal in dignity, and men who had not enriched previously existing knowledge by a single original insight were honored as men of science. Whereas the Greeks, as an Egyptian priest told Solon, were eternally young, the modern world was already old and experienced in its youth.

To study the history of the arts and sciences has become a kind of religion. In it philosophers discern more clearly the intentions, so to speak, of the world spirit. The profoundest minds, the greatest talents, have devoted themselves exclusively to this branch of knowledge.[5]

It is one thing to make the past an object of scientific investigation, another to put acquaintance with the past in the place of knowledge itself. Historical erudition in this sense becomes an obstacle to true knowledge; what it asks is no longer whether a thing is true, but whether it is in conformity with some derivative of the original insight, some imperfect copy of it. Aristotle in his writings on natural science interrogated Nature directly; in later times this direct approach was so completely forgotten that Aristotle took the place of Nature, and his

[5] Changes in the external world correspond to quieter but no less profound changes in the minds of men, in accordance with a necessary law. To believe that intellectual changes—scientific revolutions and the ideas they produce, as well as works expressing a specific scientific or artistic spirit—reflect no necessity and are produced not in accordance with law but by chance, is utter barbarism. Classical antiquity must forever remain sacred to us; it is no less piety to make pilgrimages to surviving ancient remains than religion to search for a saint's alleged relics in devout simple-mindedness. As Goethe said:

> Eagerly the pilgrim trudges: will he find his saint?
> Will he hear and see the man who worked the miracles?
> No, Time has carried him off; only bits are left;
> A skull, a few bones have been preserved.
> We are all pilgrims, who go in search of the past;
> What we honor with such joy and piety is but scattered bones.
> (Venetian Epigrams, No. 21)

authority was invoked against Descartes, Kepler, and others who clearly spoke in the name of Nature herself. Even today the majority of so-called scholars hold no idea important until it has passed through other brains and become historical, a thing of the past.

Our universities were organized more or less in the spirit of this historical knowledge, not so much perhaps in the early Renaissance as in later times. The whole of their organization could be inferred from the divorce which historical learning brought about between knowledge and its original object. Knowledge was divided into as many different branches as possible and the living whole was fragmented primarily because there was a great mass of already existing material still to be assimilated. Since all isolated parts of knowledge, i.e., the special sciences, can serve only as means to the attainment of absolute knowledge once the universal spirit has left them, this fragmentation eventually brought about a situation in which knowledge itself was almost lost sight of in an ever narrower concern for means and institutions. While a host of busywork scholars were mistaking the means for the end and trying to impose this view, knowledge, which is one and entire—and absolute in its oneness—withdrew to the higher disciplines and even there rarely exhibited much independence.

In the face of this situation, we have first of all to answer the question: What should be done within the accepted limitations, the actual structure of our universities today, in order that the unity of the whole may re-emerge amid the widespread specialization? I shall not be able to answer this question without mentioning a requirement that has to be met by the university teachers themselves. I shall not hesitate to speak frankly of such things to you. The young student, as he starts his

academic career, is getting his first experience of eman-
cipation from blind faith; for the first time he is acquir-
ing and exercising his own judgment. No teacher worthy
of his vocation will demand respect on any other
grounds than the superiority of his intelligence, the
breadth of his learning, and the zeal with which he seeks
to communicate them. It would be an ignorant, incapable teacher who could wish to be respected on any
other grounds. The reason I am speaking out on this
matter is the following. How far a student's expectations
of the university faculties will be rewarded depends in
part on the character of those expectations. The scientific spirit once awakened among students reacts favor-
ably on the whole body of the university, because the
higher their expectations, the more the unfit teachers
will be frightened away and the fit encouraged to greater
efforts.

Since our demand—namely, that all sciences should be
treated in the spirit of universal absolute knowledge—is
inherently right, the question, Where are capable teachers to be found? is easily answered. The teachers themselves have had the experience of a university education;
were they but given intellectual freedom, not shackled
by scientifically irrelevant considerations, they would be
able to rise to the occasion and be in a position to form
other capable teachers.

It may be asked whether it is proper to make philosophical demands on the universities when everyone
knows that they are instruments of the state and must be
what the state intended them to be. If the intention
were to impose on science a certain caution and modera-
tion, to limit it to ordinary practical matters, we could
hardly ask teachers to be progressive and to cultivate
their disciplines in a philosophical spirit.

Surely, all of us assume—as we must—that the state intends the universities to be real scientific institutions and that whatever we say about them is valid only on this condition. Incontestably, the state has the authority to suppress the universities or to transform them into industrial training schools; however, it cannot intend the universities to be real scientific institutions without desiring to further the life of ideas and the freest scientific development. If the latter objective were abandoned for petty reasons, the incapable teachers would certainly be protected, but genius would be blocked and talent crippled.[6]

6 The usual view of the universities is that they should produce servants of the state, perfect instruments for its purposes. But surely, such instruments should be formed by *science*. Thus, to achieve such an aim through education, science is required. But science ceases to be science the moment it is degraded to a *mere* means, rather than furthered for its own sake. It is certainly not furthered for its own sake when, for instance, Ideas are rejected on the grounds that they are of no use in ordinary life, have no practical application, are unrelated to experience. Such may very well be the case, as far as experience at a given moment is concerned, experience that has become what it is precisely because the Ideas have been neglected and for this reason cannot be in harmony with them. What is true, real experience, must be determined by the Ideas in the first place. Experience is doubtless a good thing if it is *genuine* experience, but whether and to what extent it is genuine, and what is really experienced in experience, that is the great question. For instance, Newtonian optics is allegedly based on experience, and yet its fundamental conception, as well as its consequences are recognizably false to anyone who has conceived the Idea of light. Similarly the alleged experience of physicians may often contradict true theory derived from the Ideas; but if, for instance, the physician himself produces morbid symptoms and then attributes them to spontaneous effects of nature, we are not dealing with genuine experience; rather, had the physician treated the disease on the basis of a correct conception derived from Ideas, the symptoms in question would not have been produced, and he would not attribute them to his "experience," or at least would not see in them a contradiction to true theory. What Kant says of practical ideas is applicable to theoretical ideas: namely, that nothing is more harmful or unworthy than appeal to experience, which after all would not exist in the first place, had it not been guided by crude notions.—But I digress.

The fact that all the sciences are represented is not sufficient in itself to assure the true organic life of knowledge, which is supposedly the goal of universities (as their very name indicates). For this is required a spirit of co-operation which can come only from absolute science, the special sciences its willing instruments in supplying the objective, real aspect to complement it. I cannot dwell longer upon this view; however, it is clear that we are not here dealing with some "application" of philosophy such as has been attempted from time to time in every profession, even in connection with the most trivial subjects (trivial with respect to philosophy) —even agriculture, obstetrics, and the theory of first aid have not escaped this kind of "philosophical" treatment. Nothing is sillier than efforts by lawyers and physicians to give a "philosophical" cast to their professions, when they are ignorant of the first principles of philosophy. It is as though someone who did not know Euclid's first proposition were to try to measure a globe, cylinder, or other solid.

What I am referring to is the formlessness prevalent in most practical disciplines today, the total absence of art or logic, the kind of obtuseness which is incapable of rising above the particular, the inability even to imagine that every branch of knowledge, even one dealing with practical, empirical matters, must aim at the universal.

Only the universal as such is the source of Ideas, and Ideas are the life of science. He who knows his particular profession only as a specialty, who is unable to see what is universal in it or to express it in terms of universal scientific culture, is unworthy to be a teacher and custodian of science. He may be useful in various ways—as a physicist in the erection of lightning rods, as an astronomer in composing almanacs, as a physician in utilizing

galvanism for therapeutic purposes, etc.—but the vocation of teacher requires more than mechanical skills. As
Lichtenberg* observed, "Drawing boundary lines to
fence off scientific fields may be very useful for farmers,
but Reason, looking for unity, warns the philosopher at
every step to take no notice of the fences, which are often
matters of convenience or a sign of narrow-mindedness."
Undoubtedly it was not just special skill in his profession but ability to inform it with a universally cultivated
mind that made Lichtenberg the most intelligent physicist of his time and the best teacher in his field.

The demand that a particular profession be treated
in the spirit of the whole is often interpreted in the
sense that it should be only a means. Actually, the very
opposite is the case: a scientist is faithful to the spirit
of the whole only to the extent that he considers his
field an end in itself, an absolute. Nothing can be
conceived of as part of a true totality if it functions
merely as a means. A state is perfect if every citizen,
while a means in relation to the whole, is also an end in
himself. Precisely because the particular is absolute in
itself, it is within the absolute and an integral part of
it, and vice versa.

The more a scholar conceives of his particular domain
as an end in itself, even making it, as far as he is concerned, the central point of all knowledge—hoping to
expand it into an all-embracing totality [7]—the more he
is striving to express universal and absolute ideas in it.
Conversely, the less able he is to conceive of it as universal, the more will he—consciously or unconsciously
—comprehend it only as a means, for that which is not
an end in itself can only be a means. This would be intolerable to a man who respects himself; hence, such

[7] So that it might reflect the whole universe.

narrowness is usually associated with pettiness and want of genuine interest in science—science is looked upon merely as a means to very tangible ends.

I am fully aware that in the eyes of very many, particularly those who appreciate science only for its practical uses, universities are no more than institutions for the transmitting of knowledge, places where a young man learns all that has been accomplished in science down to his own day; in this view, it might seem sheer accident if the teachers, besides communicating knowledge, were also to enrich science with discoveries of their own. But even granting that this alone is or ought to be the purpose of a university, we still demand that the transmitting of knowledge be intelligently effected. Otherwise, why should lectures by living men be at all necessary in a university? The student could as well be referred to popular textbooks expressly written for him or to voluminous compilations which exist in every branch of knowledge. But there can be no doubt that to transmit knowledge intelligently one must be able to understand the discoveries made by others, to understand them correctly, clearly, in all their implications. Many of them are of a kind whose inner essence can be grasped only by a kindred genius through a rediscovery in the literal sense of the word. A teacher who merely transmits will often give a radically false version of what he learned. Do we possess an exposition of ancient philosophy, even of a single philosopher of the ancient or modern world, which we can point to confidently as a successful exposition, at once true and adequate? A man who lives within his science as though on another's property, who is not himself in possession, who has never acquired a sure and living feeling for it, who is incapable of sitting down and reconstructing it for himself, is an unworthy teacher even when he attempts no more than to expound ideas of others. He is out of his depth, struggling at a task beyond his powers. Intelligent transmitting of knowledge certainly involves good judgment. But if a correct and comprehensive understanding of the discoveries of others is impossible without capacity for original thought, how much more impossible, then, is accurate judgment of them. To be sure, in Germany many self-styled "critics" from whom no original thought would drop if they were held upside down, pass judgment on everything. But such judgments are of no use whatever to knowledge.

A man incapable of reconstructing the totality of his science for himself, of reformulating it from his own inner, living vision, will never go beyond mere historical exposition of the science. This is the sort of thing we get in a well-known introduction to philosophy: "When we direct our attention to ourselves, we become aware of various manifestations of a something we call the soul. These various activities we refer to as different faculties; we call them faculties according to the different ways in which they manifest themselves—as sensation, understanding, imagination, etc."

What could be more stultifying, more senseless, more mind-killing than such a statement? Furthermore, we must remember that the university lecturer is supposed to explain his subject genetically. This is the real advantage of live instruction: the lecturer does not merely give results, as the writer does, but shows—in the higher sciences at least—how these results were reached, and at every point builds up the whole science, as it were, before the student's eyes.* How can a man who has not reconstructed his science for himself teach it in such a way that it appears not as something ready-made, but as something the student must rediscover for himself?

Mere transmitting of knowledge without personal creative understanding is not enough if the teacher is to obtain the results he should. At the same time, no one can teach a science unless he has previously mastered it as completely as possible. In every craft, even the lowliest, proofs of completed apprenticeship are demanded before one is allowed to practice it as a master. But considering how easy it is to attain a professorship in many universities, it would seem as though no vocation makes fewer demands than that of teaching. Under the circumstances, creative minds that expect to obtain a professorship speedily on the grounds that capacity for original work goes hand in hand with learning are likely to be disappointed.

We have so far examined how much universities could do to achieve—were it only the original purpose for which they were founded—the furthering of knowledge. But it would seem that they could do more than that, and that their original purpose was too narrow. We do not grant the validity of the antithesis between knowledge and action; we have seen that the antithesis vanishes as each of the opposing terms approaches its perfection, its absoluteness. If our universities have not yet begun to further culture in the universal sense, in addition to serving as nurseries of knowledge, it is because, even with respect to knowledge, they remain at a low level.

Here we must also consider the constitution of our universities in so far as it influences their ethical function in the community.

Civil society for the most part shows a decided want of harmony between the ideal and the actual. This is because for the time being its aims cannot be ideal and because the means have taken on so much importance that they defeat the ends. As universities are simply associations for the cultivation of the sciences, they need, apart from voluntary support from the state in it own interest, no further regulations than those rooted in the Idea itself. Wisdom and prudence here agree: it is necessary only to do what the Idea of a scientific institution prescribes in order to make the constitution of a university perfect.

Civil society, so long as it is obliged to pursue empirical ends to the detriment of absolute ends, can have only an apparent and forced identity, not a true inner identity. Universities can have only an absolute purpose —beyond that they have none.

To accomplish its aims the state must impose divisions—not such as arise out of inequalities of rank, but far more essential—by isolating and setting in opposition individual talents, by repressing many individualities and directing energies into various channels where they will serve more effectively.

All the members of a scientific association share a single purpose, namely, to give no weight to any other consideration but science and to permit no other distinctions save those of talent and culture. Men who are there only to assert themselves in other ways—by extravagance, by wasting their time in frivolous amusements, in short, the same sort of privileged idlers as are found in civil society (and they are chiefly responsible for rowdiness at universities)—ought not to be tolerated. Whoever cannot prove his diligence and readiness to work should be expelled.

If science were the paramount concern of all minds, there could be no misdirection of the noble impulses of youth. After all, the young are primarily interested in ideas. In this view, whenever misconduct did occur (or should it occur again), the fault lies with the teacher or the supervising personnel whose duty it is to foster the proper spirit.

Were teachers communicating nothing but the genuine scientific spirit to those around them, giving consideration to nothing but the advancement of science, and were not outbreaks of vulgarity which disgrace the vocation of teaching tolerated by the low standard of the community itself, those who are capable of distinguishing themselves only by their savagery would soon quit the student ranks of their own accord.

The realm of the sciences is not a democracy, still less an ochlocracy, but an aristocracy in the best sense of the word. The incapables whom nothing but some convenience or other recommends, the ambitious chatterboxes who dishonor the scientific estate with their petty pursuits, should be kept down. Left to their own devices and in no way encouraged, they would receive the contempt that ignorance and intellectual incapacity deserve; indeed, since these are usually associated with ridiculousness and meanness, they would serve as the sport of youth, whose natural aversion to such as they too often is blunted by the conditions prevailing today.

Talent needs no special protection so long as its opposite is not fostered; intellectual capacity naturally creates for itself the highest and most decided influence.

This is the only policy we need in order to make institutions of knowledge flourish, to give them all possible dignity within their walls and earn them respect outside. To make the university a model of organization, nothing is necessary beyond realizing what is in any case desirable and doing so consistently. Inasmuch as I do not concede the existence of a gulf between knowledge and action, I cannot allow it in reference to the university.

Training for rational thinking, by which I understand no superficial habit but a cultivation that goes deep into the innermost essence of man—the only really scientific culture—is also the only training for rational action. Ends that lie beyond this absolute sphere of scientific culture automatically fall outside the concern of universities by the very nature of their function.

A man who has mastered his particular science has thereby come close to absolute knowledge, has entered the realm of clarity and rationality. The most dangerous thing that can happen to a man is to be under the sway of muddy thinking. It is a great gain when such sway has been cut down to a minimum, and the process is complete when he has pressed on to the attainment of absolute consciousness and walks wholly in the light.

Science guides the mind directly to the vision which in a continuous self-creating process leads us to identity with ourselves and thereby to a truly blessed life. The experience of life educates slowly, not without loss of time and strength. To him who dedicates himself to knowledge it is granted to anticipate experience, to recognize directly and in himself that which after all is the only fruit of the most cultivated, most richly experienced life.

3 Prerequisites to University Studies

The high goal we pursue in dedicating ourselves to knowledge has been, I believe, sufficiently clarified in the foregoing lecture. And so I can be brief in formulating the requirements that must be met by those who choose a scientific vocation.

The idea of study as such, especially in modern culture, has two aspects. First, the historical, which involves no more than learning. That the student of any science must surrender his will in obedience to the thing to be learned needs no further proof. What misleads even the better class of minds in meeting this condition is the result of a very common illusion.

The fact is, they feel that learning requires effort rather than real activity; and because activity is the more natural condition, they consider every kind of activity a higher expression of their innate faculties even though the reason they find it easy to have original ideas lies in their ignorance of the true objects and real problems of scientific knowledge rather than in a genuinely over-flowing productiveness. When we learn, even guided by a teacher, we have no choice: we must take it all in our stride, the difficult and the easy, the attractive and the less attractive. We do not pick our tasks arbitrarily according to some association of ideas or inclination, but according to an inherent necessity. When we merely play with ideas, a moderately active imagination, especially if we are unaware of scientific requirements, is sufficient to enable us to pick out what we like and to omit what we don't like or cannot discover by ourselves without effort.

Even a student who is by nature fitted to take up subjects in a new branch of knowledge not previously treated will not be successful unless he has trained his mind by the process of learning. Without this training his progress will be desultory even in original endeavors. Only those who have learned all there is to be learned in a given field, who can grasp it with a sure instinct as an organic whole, will be able to work in it creatively.

A certain popular tone in the higher sciences, which is supposed to make them everybody's affair and suited to everybody's comprehension, has greatly encouraged intellectual laziness to such an extent that pleasant superficiality has become the mark of a so-called finer education. In the end, the purpose of university culture has become to taste only so much of the wine of the higher sciences as might properly be offered to a lady.

The universities deserve some credit for having checked the rising tide of superficiality which recent reformers of education have been encouraging. In all fairness, however, it must be allowed that these same dubious methods of instruction represented a reaction to the stodginess, the listlessness, and the boring pedantry into which the university faculties had lapsed.

Besides its own peculiar aspect of inquiry, every science has another which it shares with the arts. This is the aspect of form, which in some sciences is quite inseparable from content. All excellence in art, all shaping of a precious material into adequate form is rooted in the limitations the artist imposes upon himself. Perfect form is attained only by dint of practice, and all true instruction should emphasize technique rather than content.[8]

Some forms are transient and perishable, and the forms in which the spirit of science is clothed are but eternally different modes of the manifestation of genius forever renewing itself. In particular forms, however, there dwells a universal and absolute form of which the particular forms are but symbols, and a work of art is the greater the more it succeeds in revealing this single universal form. But the arts, too, have an aspect which can be acquired only through learning. To dislike forms and alleged limitations is to dislike the "art" involved, i.e., the creative aspect in science.

Ready-made knowledge can only be memorized; knowledge is not truly our own until we are capable of reproducing the given content in a form of our own making. Memorizing is but a negative condition; true intussusception or organic assimilation is impossible without inner transformation of what we learn. All rules for study are summed up in this one: learn only in order to create. Only by his divine capacity for production is man truly man; without it, no more than a tolerably well-devised machine. He who has not—with the same high impulse as the artist who out of the raw material calls forth the image of his soul—his own invention, who has not fashioned the image of his science in all its parts

[8] It should exercise the organ rather than transmit subject matter. But the organ of science, too, is art, and art must be learned and developed by practice.

and features in perfect harmony with the archetype, has not truly grasped it.

All creation is the result of a meeting between the universal and the particular, an interpenetration of the one and the other. The secret of creation is to seize sharply the opposition between the particular and the absolute, and in the same indivisible act, simultaneously to grasp the former in the latter and the latter in the former. In this way are produced the higher points of confluence between the separate parts and the Idea—the higher formulas in which the concrete is resolved, "the laws born of the heavenly ether, not generated by man's mortal nature."

In the ordinary division of knowledge into rational and historical, the former includes investigation of causes, the latter is defined as a mere science of facts. It might be argued that causes, too, can only be known historically, but the point is that then they are not conceived of as causes. The sciences that are most obviously susceptible of utilitarian application are disparagingly called "bread-and-butter" sciences. But no science in itself deserves such a name. To a student who treats philosophy or mathematics as a means, they are as much bread-and-butter sciences as law or medicine to the student who has no higher interest in them than their usefulness to his career. The purpose of "bread-and-butter" study is merely to learn the results of a science. The causes or principles are either entirely omitted or learned solely for some extraneous purpose, such as exhibiting a minimal knowledge at the regular examinations.

Students of this kind pursue knowledge exclusively for utilitarian purposes; in other words, they look upon themselves as a mere means. Surely, no one with a spark of self-respect holds so low an opinion of himself as to value science purely as an apparatus for achieving material ends.

The consequences that follow necessarily from such an attitude to science are these: First, it is impossible properly to assimilate knowledge acquired in this way, and as a result it is falsely applied since the possessor of it does not rely on a living vision but merely on his memory. All too often universities turn out just such bread-and-butter scholars who have memorized all there is to be learned in their profession, but are completely wanting in judgment, utterly incapable of subsuming the particular under the universal. Living interest in scientific knowledge develops the creative imagination, the intuitive vision in which the universal and particular are always one. The merely bread-and-butter scholar, on the other hand, lacks vision and imagination when faced with particular problems. And inasmuch as his school could scarcely prepare him for every problem he might conceivably encounter, his learning turns out to have been of no avail to him much of the time.

Another inevitable consequence is that such a scholar is quite incapable of keeping up with the advancement of knowledge, incapable of going beyond what he has learned. He thus lacks the chief characteristic which distinguishes a man, especially the true scholar. The reason is that genuine advances in knowledge cannot be judged by the standards of an earlier teaching; they must be judged on their own merits in the light of absolute principles. At best the bread-and-butter scholar will be receptive to some new-fangled remedy, to one or another new theory that arouses curiosity, a new formula, a learned novelty, etc. He can grasp only the particular for only the particular can be learned—and once it is learned everything becomes a particular. Hence such a man becomes the sworn enemy of every genuine discovery in the realm of the universal, of every idea he cannot grasp, of every real tuth that disturbs his peace of mind. If he forgets himself so far as to declare that he is against it, he puts himself in the awkward position of judging the new according to the very principles and theories it challenges, invoking principles and authorities which were valid in an earlier stage of knowledge. Or, conscious of his own emptiness, he stoops to slander and abuse, smugly convinced that every new discovery is really a personal attack on him.

How much any student accomplishes at the beginning of his study depends to some extent on what type and degree of knowledge he brings with him to the university. Of the intellectual and moral culture required at this early stage I shall not speak; all that could be said about it is self-evident.

As for so-called preparatory training, the kind acquired before entering the university, it surely cannot be described otherwise than as practical familiarity with the elements of knowledge. As far as this knowledge is concerned, no doubt we should recognize an upper and a lower limit within which the student should have been prepared.

The higher sciences cannot be mastered in the same way as the mechanical rudiments used in their study. It would be inadvisable to try to impart to children, incapable of attaining absolute insights, the kind of knowledge that is inherently absolute and communicates this quality to all other knowledge. Indeed, even in the case of the lower sciences, when they contain elements that can be truly appreciated only in the context of the whole, the elements should not be taught to the student before familiarity with the higher sciences has made him capable of understanding this whole. Otherwise, he would forget what he had been taught without deriving any benefit from it. In recent years some zealous reformers have tried to turn the lower schools into something little short of universities, but they have only given fresh encouragement to superficiality.

It is necessary that the student spend enough time at every stage of learning to acquire a firm footing. It *seems* that a few can skip one or another stage, though this is never really so. Newton as a child read the *Elements* of Euclid with as great ease as if he had himself written it for his own amusement. He was thus able to pass directly from elementary geometry to higher investigations.

As a rule, what happens is the exact opposite: the training offered in preparatory schools is woefully inadequate. What the student should have acquired before entering the university is the rudiments or elementary mechanics of the sciences. Every science has a mechanical aspect. Thus, in mathematics there are elementary and general operations to be performed. The university professor can develop the scientific principles underlying these operations, but it is not for him to teach arithmetic. In some disciplines, mechanical aids are indispensable—for example, knowledge of ancient or modern languages—since they alone give access to the highest sources of culture and science. More generally, preparatory training should include just about everything that can be memorized; memory is at its sharpest and needs most to be exercised in the young.

In this connection, I shall speak chiefly of language study, which is not only an indispensable preliminary in all scientific education but also has an independent value.

The wretched arguments advanced by modern educators against study of the ancient languages need no longer be refuted. Such arguments merely confirm the intellectual poverty upon which modern education is based and are primarily prompted by mistaken zeal against what an empirical psychology regards as excessive cultivation of the memory. We are supposed to be convinced by the fact that certain scholars who memorized a rich store of information of all kinds were nonetheless unable to acquire in this way what nature had denied them. The fact that no man can be a great general, mathematician, philosopher or poet without possessing a strong, capacious memory seemed to these reformers of no moment—after all their purpose was not to form great generals, mathematicians, philosophers or poets, but rather useful and industrial burghers.

I know of no occupation better calculated to exercise at an early age the dawning wit, acumen, and powers of invention than study of the ancient languages. What I have in mind here is not linguistics in the abstract sense, not language as a direct expression of reason and, as such, an object of scientific construction. Nor do I refer to philology in relation to which knowledge of languages is but a means to a much higher end. To call the mere linguist a philologist is to misuse the term; the philologist stands with the artist and the philosopher at the highest peak—or rather, he is both artist and philosopher. His task is the historical construction of works of art and science; he must understand their history and expound it vividly. At the university, philology in this sense only should be taught; the university professor should not be a mere teacher of languages. But I digress.

Language in itself, even considered from the grammatical point of view, is a continuously applied logic.

True scientific culture consists in the ability to recognize possibilities, whereas ordinary knowledge grasps only realities. When a physicist has recognized that under certain conditions a phenomenon is actually possible, he has also recognized it as real. Study of language as an art of interpretation, encouraging conjectural improvements on the reading of a text, cultivates this ability to recognize possibilities, at first in ways appropriate to childhood and youth, in later life as a pleasant diversion for the adult who has retained something of his youth.

Nothing forms the intellect so effectively as learning to recognize the living spirit of a language dead to us. To be able to do this is no whit different from what the natural philosopher does when he addresses himself to nature. Nature is like some very ancient author whose message is written in hieroglyphics on colossal pages, as the Artist says in Goethe's poem.* Even those who investigate nature only empirically need to know her language in order to understand utterances which have become unintelligible to us. The same is true of philology in the higher sense of the term. The earth is a book made up of miscellaneous fragments dating from very different ages. Each mineral is a real philological problem. In geology we still await the genius who will analyze the earth and show its composition as Wolf * analyzed Homer.

It is not possible here to go into each division of the university curriculum to explain the whole edifice from the ground up without at the same time discussing the various branches of knowledge and showing that they form an organic whole. I shall accordingly begin by showing how all the sciences are interlinked and how their internal organic unity is expressed objectively in the external organization of universities.

In a sense, this outline might take the place of a general encyclopaedia of the sciences. However, I shall never consider these purely in themselves, but always in special relation to my course of lectures, and hence you cannot expect me to present a system of the sciences rigorously deduced from the highest principles. In these lectures I cannot aim at an exhaustive treatment of the subject. That could be done only by actually developing and demonstrating the whole system. I shall leave unsaid much which perhaps deserves to be said, but, on the other hand, I shall avoid saying anything which is better left unsaid either because of its own nature or because silence is dictated by present conditions, especially those obtaining in the sciences.

4 The Purely Rational Sciences: Mathematics and Philosophy

The absolute unity of primordial knowledge is both the source of all the sciences and their final destination. By being embodied in concrete forms, primordial knowledge, flowing from a single center, shapes the whole of cognition. Those sciences which reflect primordial knowledge most directly, which come closest to it, are, so to speak, the sensorium of the organic body of knowledge. We must start from the central organs and trace the life that flows from them through various channels to the outermost parts.

Those not already in possession of this primordial knowledge can be led to it in only one way—by being shown how it is opposed to other kinds of knowledge.

This is not the place to explain how we arrive at the cognition of particular things; all we can show here is that cognition of this kind cannot be absolute and, hence, cannot be unconditionally true.

This is not to be understood in the sense of a certain empirical skepticism, which doubts the truth of sensory knowledge—that is, representations of particular things —on the ground that the senses can deceive us, implying

that if there were no optical or other illusions, we might
be fairly certain of the knowledge derived from the
senses. Nor do we have in mind the crude kind of empiricism which doubts the truth of sensory knowledge on
the ground that the original impressions from which it
derives are distorted by being communicated from one
mind to another. The idea of any causal relation between knowledge and being is itself the result of a
sensory illusion, and if the knowledge in question is
finite, it is so in virtue of an inherent, not an extraneous,
determination.

The very fact that this knowledge is determinate
makes it dependent, relative, and subject to constant
change; its determinateness is its form, which accounts
for its multifariousness and variability. The *essence* of
knowledge is one, the same in all things, and for that
reason cannot be determinate. Hence, that which distinguishes one insight from another is the form, which in
the case of particular knowledge is not identical with the
essence (in this sense, we can call the essence the universal). But form apart from essence is not real, is mere
appearance; consequently, particular knowledge as such
is not true knowledge.

The particular is opposed to the pure universal; separated from the particular, it is called the abstract. It is
impossible here to explain the origin of this knowledge;
all we can show is that whereas in particular knowledge
the form is not adequate to the essence, the pure universal must appear to the understanding as essence without form. Where the form is not recognized in and
through the essence, we are dealing with an actual thing
which is not conceived on the basis of its potential
being. Thus, the particular sensible determinations of
the eternal substance cannot be deduced from the uni-

versal concept of substance. This is why those who do not go beyond this opposition admit the existence of, besides the universal, the particular under the name of "matter," as the sum total or quintessence of sensible diversities. At the other extreme, pure, abstract potentiality is conceived, from which no way leads to actuality. The two, as Lessing put it, are separated by the big ditch which the common herd of philosophers have never been able to cross.

It is sufficiently clear that the ultimate ground, the condition of the possibility of all truly absolute knowledge must consist in this, that the universal is also the particular, that the very thing that for the discursive reason is mere potentiality without actuality, essence without form—this very thing is also actuality and form. This is the Idea of all Ideas, and hence the Idea of the absolute itself. It is no less evident that the absolute considered in itself, precisely because it is *only* this identity, is neither the one nor the other of the opposites but— being the essence of both and, hence, their identity —can manifest itself *either* in the real *or* in the ideal, not in both.

The two aspects of knowledge, the one in which actuality precedes potentiality, and the other in which potentiality precedes actuality, can thus be opposed as the real and the ideal. If the pure identity of actuality and potentiality could conceivably come into view in the real or in the ideal, absolute knowledge would doubtless be possible even at the phenomenal level.

Consequently, if the identity of actuality and potentiality could be reflected as such in the real, it would be neither an abstract concept (because it would be a potential being opposed to an actual being) nor a concrete thing (because it would be an actual being opposed to a potential being).

Furthermore, because it would be reflected in the domain of the real, it would appear as pure being and, since activity or change is the opposite of being, as the negation of all activity. The same can be inferred from the principle stated earlier, namely: everything which has its opposite in some other thing is again the identity of itself and its opposite only insofar as it is absolute in itself. For according to this principle, the real can appear as identity of potentiality and actuality only insofar as it is itself absolute being and, hence, does not admit of opposite predicates.

Such a pure being with negation of all activity is, beyond any doubt, space. Space is not an abstraction—otherwise there would be many spaces, and space is only one in all spaces; nor is it concrete—otherwise there would be an abstract concept of space of which concrete space would be an imperfect expression. But space is fully what it is; its being is entirely congruent with its concept, and precisely because it is absolutely real, it is also absolutely ideal.

The same identity in the domain of the ideal can be defined as the counterpart of space. Space represents pure being, which is the negation of all activity; its counterpart represents pure activity (or change), which is the negation of all being. Because it is *pure* activity, it is also, according to the principle stated, the identity of itself and its opposite, that is, of potentiality and actuality. Such an identity is time. No being as such is in time, but only changes of being—expressions of activity or of negations of being. In empirical time, potentiality as cause precedes actuality, whereas in pure time they are one and the same. As identity of the universal and the particular, time is neither an abstract idea nor a concrete thing, and in this respect it has the same characteristics as space.

We can see now that in the pure intuition of space and time we have a truly objective intuition of the identity of potentiality and actuality. We also see that both are only relatively absolute, since neither space nor time is the Idea of all Ideas, but each is only a separate reflection of it. For the same reason, neither of them is an attribute of being in itself, and if the unity expressed in both is the basis of an insight or a science, such an insight or science pertains merely to the reflected world, though they must be absolute in respect of form.

If then—I cannot prove this here, but will presuppose it as proven in philosophy—mathematics, in both the analytical and geometrical branches, is based wholly upon these two modes of intuition, it follows that the dominant mode of knowledge in the mathematical sciences must be absolute in form.

Reality in general, and the reality of knowledge in particular, is not defined exclusively in terms of the universal, nor exclusively in terms of the particular. Mathematical knowledge is neither of mere abstractions nor of concrete things, but of the intuitively apprehended Idea. The representation of the universal and the particular in their unity is called construction, which does not differ from demonstration. The unity is expressed in two ways. First, underlying all geometrical constructions, such as the triangle, the square, the circle, etc., is the same absolute form, and to grasp them in their particularity nothing is required beyond the one universal and absolute unity. Second, in respect to every figure the universal is identical with the particular. For instance, what is true of the triangle in general is also true of any particular triangle, and conversely. The particular triangle stands for all triangles and is both unity and totality. The same unity is expressed as form and essence, since the construction, which—in the sense of a cognition —would seem to be mere form, is also the essence of the construct itself.

It is easy to apply the foregoing remark to the analytical branch of mathematics. The position of mathematics in the system of knowledge leaves no doubt as to the spirit in which it should be studied. Mathematics transcends the law of causality which dominates ordinary knowledge (many so-called "sciences"); it rises into the realm of pure rational identity and, hence, is an end in itself. Although great results have incontestably been achieved by applying mathematics to the general laws of motion in astronomy and physics, those who esteem it for these results alone do not grasp its absolute character, because some of these results are based on a misuse of purely rational evidence. Modern theoretical astronomy aims solely at replacing absolute laws derived from the Idea with empirical laws, and it has achieved this aim to its complete satisfaction; in fact, mathematics as it is understood today cannot be concerned in the least with grasping the essence or being-in-itself of nature or its other objects. For this, mathematics would first have to go back to its source and arrive at a more universal conception of the type of reason expressed in it. Insofar as mathematics is the most perfect objective expression of reason itself in both its abstract and its concrete (i.e., natural) aspects, all the laws of nature, as they are resolved into pure laws of reason, must find their corresponding forms in mathematics: this, however, not in the sense that mathematics determines these laws and that nature plays the part of a mere mechanism, but in the sense that mathematics and the science of nature are two aspects of one and the same science.

The forms of mathematics, as understood today, are symbols the key to which has been lost—certain statements of ancient writers suggest that Euclid still possessed it. We can rediscover it only if we conceive of mathematical forms as forms of pure reason and expressions of Ideas. Present instruction in mathematics is not likely to lead back to the original meaning of these forms; it is to be hoped that philosophy, by proceeding in the direction it has now taken, will supply the means for decoding the symbols of mathematics and restoring that ancient science.

The student should above all—indeed exclusively—keep this objective in mind. He must also pay attention to the important opposition between geometric and analytic mathematics, which corresponds strikingly to the opposition between realism and idealism in philosophy.

We have shown that mathematics is absolute knowledge only in the formal sense, and it will retain this formal character so long as its symbolism is not completely understood. The world of mathematics is merely a copy; the absolute identity of primordial knowledge is present in it only in a reflected form and, hence, separated from the rest. Only the science which deals directly with primordial knowledge as such can be absolute in every respect. The science which has no archetype except primordial knowledge itself is necessarily the science of all knowledge, that is, philosophy.

It cannot be our purpose here to convince everyone that philosophy is the science of primordial knowledge. All we can prove is that such a science is necessary and that any other definition of philosophy is not a definition of philosophy or even of any possible science.

Philosophy and mathematics are alike in that both are founded upon the absolute identity of the universal and the particular.[9] Hence, both are purely intuitive, since every relationship of this type is perceived through intuition. But whereas mathematical intuition is a reflected one, philosophical intuition is rational or intellectual intuition and identical with its object—with primordial knowledge itself. Philosophical construction interprets what is grasped in intellectual intuition. The particular identities, which like the universal identity, express absolute primordial knowledge can be grasped only in intellectual intuition, and in this sense are Ideas. Philosophy is therefore the science of Ideas or the eternal archetypes of things.

Without intellectual intuition no philosophy! Even pure space and time are not perceived in the ordinary consciousness; they, too, are grasped through intellectual intuition. However, because space and time are reflected in the sensible, the mathematician has the advantage of being able to visualize his objects; the philosopher lacks this advantage—intellectual intuition is his only guide. Those who do not have intellectual intuition cannot understand what is said of it, and for this reason it cannot be communicated to them. The minimum requirement is clear and genuine insight into the nothingness of all merely finite knowledge. Intellectual intuition can be developed; in the philosopher it must become his

9 Does the geometrician see what is concrete in the actual circle? By no means; nor does he see in it only the universal concept. And yet he does see the universal in the particular. Thus he intuits only the absolute, the circle in itself, not the concrete circle. However, he does not eliminate the concrete, does not *negate* it, is merely indifferent to it —it has no bearing on his *cognition*.

character, as it were—a regularly employed tool, a faculty for seeing things solely as they are in the Idea.*

I have not spoken of philosophy as such; my purpose was only to discuss it to the extent that it has a bearing on basic education in the sciences.

To speak of the uses of philosophy I consider beneath its dignity. Anyone who can ask what its usefulness might be is assuredly not capable of any conception of it. By its very nature it is exempt from consideration of utility. It exists for its own sake alone; its very essence would be destroyed if it existed for the sake of anything else.

However, I consider it necessary to speak of the criticisms which are leveled against it. Philosophy does not recommend itself by its usefulness, but neither should it be hampered in its development by false accusations that it is harmful.

5 The Usual Objections to Philosophical Study

I do not pass silently over the frequent charge that philosophy is a danger to religion and the state, because I believe that most of those who defended philosophy against this attack were not able to do so adequately.

The obvious reply to such a criticism must surely be: What kind of state and what kind of religion can be endangered by philosophy? If there really were a danger, the fault would be in the so-called religion and the so-called state. Philosophy follows its own inherent principles and can give little concern to whether everything devised by mankind agrees with it. Here I shall not speak of religion. I shall try to show later that religion and philosophy are closely related and how the one begets the other.

As for the state, I put the question generally: On what scientific grounds can anyone claim that philosophy is, or might be, a danger to the state? Surely the answer to this question will tell us whether philosophy is dangerous and whether any danger to the state can be caused by it.

In my opinion there is one philosophical tendency

that is pernicious to the state and another that under-
mines its foundations.

We have the first tendency when ordinary knowledge
claims that it is absolute knowledge or that it can act as
judge of the latter. Let the state permit the common
understanding to be arbiter in the realm of Ideas, and it
will soon set itself above the state whose constitution is
founded on Reason—something it comprehends as little
as it comprehends Ideas. It can use the same popular
arguments advanced against philosophy more convinc-
ingly to attack the principal forms of the state. I must
explain what I mean by the common understanding. I
do not mean solely—or even primarily—the understanding which is crude and entirely uncultivated, but the
understanding nurtured by false and superficial education, taught to be content with hollow, empty ratiocina-
tion and to think of itself as highly cultured—the sort of
understanding that has expressed itself in modern times
chiefly by deprecating everything that rests upon Ideas.

It is to this lack of Ideas, which boldly calls itself
"enlightenment," that philosophy is most strongly opposed. It must be granted that no nation has succeeded
better than the French in this elevation of the ratiocina-
tive understanding above reason.[10] Consequently, it is
the greatest historical absurdity to say that philosophy
is some sort of threat to the preservation of the principles of justice. (I use this expression because there might
be constitutions or conditions to which philosophy,
though not dangerous to them, cannot give its approval.)
France, the very nation which, save for a few individuals
in former times (who will surely not be accused of influ-
encing the political events of a later time), had no phi-

---

[10] And we, Germans, after all, are but poor dull preachers compared
with the French writers.

losophers at any epoch, least of all in the years preceding the Revolution—this was the nation that set the example of a revolution characterized by atrocities as criminal as those perpetrated afterward when it reintroduced slavery in new forms.* I do not deny that France is full of *raisonneurs* in all the sciences and on every topic, who have usurped the name of philosophers, but there is scarcely a single one of them to whom we would concede it. It is not surprising that a strong government in such a nation should proscribe those empty abstractions of which the scientific ideas of the French wholly or chiefly consisted, and we would even be inclined to applaud such a measure if we were not enlightened about its real purpose. With the empty notions of the understanding it is, indeed, as impossible to build up a state as to develop a philosophy, and a nation which has no access to the Ideas is justified in picking over the ruins for forms that once existed.

The elevation of the common understanding to the role of arbiter in matters of reason leads inevitably to ochlocracy in the realm of the sciences and sooner or later to mob rule in every other domain. Dull or canting speakers who would like to put a certain sickly-sweet mixture of so-called moral principles in place of intellectual authority merely betray how little they know of morality. There is no morality without Ideas, and all moral action is moral only as an expression of Ideas.*

The advocates of the other tendency, which absorbs the first and which must result in the destruction of everything founded on Ideas, aim only at the useful. Once this becomes the highest norm, it must also apply to state constitutions. But surely nothing is more variable and less reliable than such a norm; what is useful today will be harmful tomorrow. More than that: should this tendency become widespread, no matter how, it must stifle all sense of greatness and energy in a nation. According to its standards, the invention of the spinning wheel would be more important than that of a world system, and the introduction of Spanish sheep raising would be regarded as a greater achievement than the transformation of a world by the almost godlike powers of a conqueror.[11] If a philosophy could make a nation great, it would be one wholly founded on Ideas—not a philosophy that ruminates about pleasure or sets love of life above all else, but one teaching contempt of death. Such a philosophy would not be concerned with psychologically dissecting the virtues of great men. In Germany, only a spiritual bond, a ruling religion or philosophy, could restore the old national character which has disintegrated and is disintegrating to an ever greater extent and which no material union can restore. It is certain that a small peaceful nation, which is not destined to achieve greatness, needs no great motives; such a nation seems satisfied so long as it can eat and drink tolerably well and devote itself to industry. Even in larger states poverty of the soil forces governments to promote the utilitarian spirit and to guide all arts and sciences in that direction; doubtless philosophy can be of no use in such states. And when rulers begin to make common cause with the people and kings are ashamed of being kings, wishing only to be "First Citizens," * philosophy too has no choice but to turn into a middle-class

---

[11] When supreme value is assigned to usefulness, the state's ignominious self-seeking must eventually produce a similar attitude in the individual, and self-seeking must become the sole remaining bond between the state and the individual. But there is no bond more fortuitous than this one. The only true bond, whether linking people or things, must be a divine one, i.e., one in which every member is free, because each wills only the unconditioned.

morality and climb down from its exalted heights to the level of workaday life.

The constitution of the state is modeled on the constitution of the realm of the Ideas. In the latter, the absolute is the power from which all things flow, the monarch; the Ideas represent not the nobility or the people —for these two notions have no reality except as opposites of each other—but the entire body of the free citizens; the individual material things are the slaves and bondsmen. There is a similar hierarchy in the sciences. Philosophy lives only in the Ideas; it leaves dealing with particular real things to physicists, astronomers, etc. However, these are, of course, merely "eccentric views"; in these times of humanitarianism and enlightenment, who still believes that the state has an exalted mission?

If anything could arrest the rising tide that ever more visibly is wiping out all barriers between the superior and the inferior—even the rabble has now begun to write, and every plebeian aspires to be a critic—then it is philosophy, whose natural motto is *Odi profanum vulgus et arceo*. [I hate the unhallowed crowd and bid it to keep out (Horace, Odes, III, 1).]

After philosophy had been decried (not without effect) as dangerous to the state and to religion, officeholders in various scientific fields began to join the chorus, as if it were also somehow harmful to them. They argue that philosophy diverts energies from serious sciences, represents these as superfluous, etc.

It would doubtless be an excellent thing if scholars in certain disciplines could be promoted to the rank of the privileged classes and if the state could forbid all progress, even all change, in any branch of knowledge. This has not yet gone so far, at least not on any wide scale, and probably never will. No science is inherently opposed to philosophy; rather, all the sciences are one in and through philosophy. Only a science as it exists in some human brain can be opposed to philosophy, and if it is at odds with the science of all sciences, so much the worse for it! Otherwise, how could geometry have been left so long in undisturbed possession of its theorems and allowed to progress peacefully?

I know of nothing so calculated to inspire respect for science as a thorough study of philosophy although this respect may not always be respect for the sciences as they are today. And when those who, thanks to philosophy, have acquired some idea of the true turn their backs on the groundless, bottomlessly inconsistent thing offered them under the name of science in other disciplines— when they try to go deeper, to find something more solid and more consistent—then it is pure gain for science itself.

That men who approach the sciences still fresh, without preconceived opinions, with their original desire for truth still unperverted, should be carefully insulated from doubting any alleged truth or even demonstrable untruth—that they should be embalmed like intellectual mummies—this is something I, at least, am utterly opposed to.

Even to be able to study other sciences, one must first have received the idea of truth from philosophy—and surely anyone will be the more interested in a science the more ideas he brings with him. I myself, during the time I have taught here, have seen how interest in all branches of natural science has been awakened through the influence of philosophy.[12] Those who have so much

12 Philosophy, by its nature, strives for the encompassing, the universal. In the individual or in a whole race, once the universal spirit of higher science and enlightenment by Ideas is associated with the

to say about philosophy's injurious influence upon the young can be divided into two groups: those who have really acquired the science of philosophy and those who have not. Most often the latter is the case. How, then, can they judge? As for the former, they owe to the study of philosophy itself the benefit of seeing that it is of no benefit. Thus we say of Socrates that he knew enough at least to know that he knew nothing. But they should pass on the benefit to others and not expect to be believed on their word; after all, a man's own experience is always more convincing than another's assurance. Not to mention the fact that their ingenious arguments against philosophy could not be understood by the young, and their innuendoes, however obvious, were lost on readers who have no knowledge of philosophy.

Such detractors of philosophy console themselves and each other for the ineffectiveness of their warnings and admonitions by saying, "After all, philosophy will not last much longer; it is a fashion that will pass like so many others; and anyway, there is a new philosophy every week." And so on.

The first part of this statement reminds me of the peasant who, seeing a stream for the first time, supposes it is just rain water and sits down to wait for it to drain off:

---

most living and diverse cognition of the particular, then we have the condition for cultural harmony such as gives rise to healthy, straightforward, productive knowledge and action. However, when striving for the encompassing and the universal, such as philosophy stimulates, is balanced neither by the richness of classical culture nor by genuine experience based on the observation of nature, the lopsided structure must sooner or later topple. Philosophy is not to blame for such a misfortune, but rather the shortcomings of its counterpart, which together with philosophy represents the complete cultural organism.

Rusticus expectat, dum defluat amnis; at ille labitur et labetur in omne volubilis aevum.

[The peasant waits till the river flows past, but it glides on and will glide on rolling for ever and ever (Horace, Epist. I, 2).]

As for the second part—about the speed with which philosophies succeed one another—such critics are in no position to judge to what extent really different *philosophies* are involved. The seeming changes in philosophy exist only in the eyes of the ignorant. These changes do not concern philosophy at all, although many writings are published in our day which call themselves philosophical and yet have nothing to do with philosophy. But even to distinguish a work that calls itself philosophical from a work that is actually philosophical, the matter must be investigated, and as the young today are the investigators of tomorrow, the study of philosophy is still necessary. Or, if these alleged changes really have some bearing on philosophy, then they pertain to its forms.* For the essence of philosophy is immutable and has not changed since it was first expressed; but it is a living science, and an artistic instinct is involved in philosophy no less than in poetry.

The fact that changes are still taking place in philosophy proves that it has not attained its final and absolute form. There are higher and lower, more or less complete forms, but every so-called new philosophy must mark an advance in form. Each philosophy sharpens the mind and kindles the impulse to create a new one. But even were philosophy presented in its absolute form—and has it not always been, to the degree it could have been?—no one is forbidden to remold it and give it his personal stamp. Philosophers have this peculiar advantage that, like mathematicians, they are in perfect agreement as to what constitutes their science (this applies to all philosophers who truly deserve the name), and yet that, unlike mathematicians, they can still be original. The other sciences could congratulate themselves if they too began to change their forms in earnest. To arrive at the absolute form, the mind must experiment with all forms; this is the universal law of all free creation.

The slanderous remark that philosophy is a mere thing of fashion cannot be taken seriously. People who say this ought to be all the more willing to make their peace with philosophy. Even if it is true that they don't care to take up every new fashion, still they don't care to be thought old-fashioned either, and so, whenever they manage to pick up a little something, be it only one term, from the newer or newest philosophy, they do not scorn to boast of it. Were it really but a thing of fashion, as they pretend, and were it as easy to construct a philosophical system as it is to replace one style of dress or headgear with another, or to formulate a system of medicine or theology on the latest principles, then such people would not fail to do so! It would seem, after all, that philosophy is not so simple a matter as that.

6 On the Study of Philosophy

If all knowledge is an end in itself, this must be even truer—in the preëminent sense—of the knowledge that unifies and is the soul and life of all else.

Can philosophy be learned, can it be acquired with practice and industry? Or is it an endowment, something one must be born with? I have already shown that philosophy as such cannot be learned. What can be acquired in this way is only familiarity with its various forms. The student of philosophy should acquire this knowledge in addition to cultivating his faculty for grasping the absolute, which is something that cannot be acquired. When we say that philosophy cannot be acquired, we do not mean that no practice is needed in mastering it, that philosophizing just comes down to ordinary reflecting, the mere combining of thoughts. Most of our contemporaries who pass judgments on philosophical matters and even go so far as to launch new systems might cure themselves of their conceit by learning more of all that has existed before them. Then, many things that have become commonplace would turn up less frequently, such as the notion that people can be converted to errors they have renounced by shallower arguments than had convinced them to begin with, or that people should not doubt their ability to conjure up the spirit of philosophy and to grasp its great subjects with the aid of a few clichés.

What can be, if not learned, at least practiced at school is the technical aspect of philosophy, what is generally called dialectics. Without the art of dialectics there is no scientific philosophy. Its very goal—which is to represent the all as unity and to do this in forms which are originally reflective but which nonetheless express primordial knowledge—proves this. This relation between speculation and reflection is the basis of all dialectics.

It is the very antinomy between the absolute and its finite forms, as well as the fact that art [i.e., technique] and subject matter are as inseparable in philosophy as form and content are in poetry, that proves that dialectics, too, has an aspect which cannot be learned, and that it, no less than what in the original sense of the term might be called "the poetry of philosophy," also rests upon the creative faculty.[13]

An emanation coming from the inner essence of the absolute, which is the eternal unity of the universal and the particular, manifests itself at the phenomenal level as reason and imagination, which are one and the same, save that the former is in the domain of the ideal, the latter in that of the real. Those equipped with nothing more than a dry and barren understanding might be pleasantly surprised to hear that imagination is required in philosophy. Actually, they have no idea of what true imagination is; all they are famliar with is a certain

13 Intellectual productivity is thus the first condition of all genuine science, but above all the science of all knowledge [i.e., philosophy].

capacity for verbal associations which only obstruct thinking, or else with the false imagination, i.e., the disorderly reproduction of sensory images. Every genuine work of art, created by the imagination, is a unity of the same opposites as those unified in the Ideas. The merely reflective understanding grasps only simple successions and conceives of the Idea as a synthesis of opposites, i.e., a contradiction.

The creative faculty, if it is present, can be developed, enhanced, and its resources multiplied ad infinitum. It can also be nipped in the bud or at least retarded in its development. Consequently, if there can be any guidance in the study of philosophy, it must be of a rather negative kind. Feeling for Ideas cannot be created where it does not exist, but it is possible to prevent its being crushed or misled.

The impulse and the desire to investigate the essence of things is so deeply implanted in men that they eagerly snatch at the partial and the false if it but has the appearance of truth and offers any hope of leading to knowledge. Otherwise it would be incomprehensible that the most superficial attempts in philosophy should arouse the interest of the most earnest minds, once such attempts hold out the promise of certainty in any sphere.

The understanding which nonphilosophy calls sound common sense wants the truth in hard cash, as it were, and tries to get it regardless of the inadequacy of its resources. When the understanding oversteps its limits, it produces the monstrosity of a crude dogmatic philosophy, which seeks to measure the unconditioned by the conditioned and to extend the finite into the infinite. The kind of logic by means of which the understanding can infer one finite thing from another is supposed to help it cross the gulf separating the relative from the absolute. As a rule, however, it does not soar so high, does not go beyond what it calls "the facts." The most modest philosophy of this type proclaims that experience is the only or primary source of knowledge. It concedes that Ideas may have reality, but if so, this reality is wholly inaccessible to human knowledge. We may well say that to study such a philosophy is worse than to study none at all. The original purpose of all philosophy is precisely to go beyond the facts of consciousness and to arrive at something absolute in itself. Had true philosophy never existed, it would never have occurred to anyone to maintain that a description of the facts of consciousness is philosophy.

Nor can mere doubt concerning the common, finite aspect of things be called philosophy. This doubt must yield to the categorical knowledge of their nothingness, and this negative knowledge must become equivalent to positive intuition of the absolute before it can rise even as high as genuine skepticism.

What is commonly called logic, too, falls entirely within empirical philosophy. If logic is defined as a science of forms, dealing only with the technical aspects of philosophy, it can only be what we have referred to above as dialectics. But such a science does not yet exist. If logic were to treat of the forms of finitude in their relation to the absolute, it would necessarily be scientific skepticism, and even Kant's transcendental logic cannot be called this. But if we understand by logic a purely formal science, divorced from the content or matter of knowledge, then it would be a science directly opposed to philosophy, for the latter rests upon the absolute unity of form and content; in setting aside matter in the empirical sense, as the concrete, it deals with absolute reality which is also absolute ideality. Consequently, the discipline that formulates the laws of the common understanding as absolute is entirely empirical. For example, the law that of two contradictory terms one only may be predicated of any entity is perfectly true in the finite sphere, but not in speculation which begins by positing opposites as identical. In the same way logic formulates laws governing the various functions of the understanding—judging, classifying, and inferring. But it proceeds empirically without proving their necessity. Therefore it appeals to experience, as when it proves that a syllogism with four terms or a division which does not proceed according to a single principle at every stage produces absurdities.

If logic undertook to prove these laws on speculative grounds, as necessary for this reflective cognition, it would not be an absolute science, but only a stage in the development of the general system of reason. Kant's *Critique of Pure Reason* is founded wholly on the assumed absoluteness of logic; in this work reason is subordinated to the understanding. According to Kant, reason is the faculty of inference, whereas it is rather a mode of absolute knowledge, and knowledge arrived at by syllogisms is entirely conditional. If there were no other cognition of the absolute except by means of syllogisms and no other reason than that in the form of the understanding, then, as Kant teaches, we should indeed have to renounce all direct categorical knowledge of the unconditioned and supersensory.

According to Kant, it was a mistake to soften the natural aridity of logic and give the students, by way of introduction to this subject, a brief survey of anthropology and psychology. In fact, teachers who did this only showed they had the right idea of the value of logic; and it is not surprising that thinkers to whom logic is the whole of philosophy have a kind of inborn taste for psychology.

As for psychology, the foregoing remarks make it clear what I think of this so-called science. It rests upon the assumption that soul and body are opposites, and it is easy to see what can result from explorations of something that does not exist, namely, a soul without a body. The true science of man must be based on the essential and absolute unity of soul and body, i.e., the Idea of man; empirical man is but a relative manifestation of the Idea.

Psychology should actually be a part of physics. The latter, as it is today, deals only with the body and assumes that matter and nature are dead. The true science of nature cannot be based on such premises but only on the identity of soul and body in all things.[14] No real antithesis exists between physics and psychology. But even if such an antithesis existed, neither of the two could be put in the place of philosophy.

Because psychology deals with the soul not as it is in the Idea, but as a phenomenal reality, it tends inevitably to see everything in terms of cause and effect, to ignore all elements derived from the absolute or essence, and thus to degrade everything that is uncommon and sublime.[15] The great deeds of the past, once they have been dissected with psychological knives, appear as the natural result of a few quite understandable motives. The Ideas of philosophy are accounted for by a number of crude psychological illusions. The great accomplish-

14 For the living element in things, just as in the soul, is solely the Idea.
15 Particularly with the effect of promoting the notion that nothing in the human being is divinely produced. All arguments against philosophy viewed as cognition and science of the absolute originate in this psychology, and can be extended with similar results to religion, art, and virtue.

ment and the great men of antiquity are seen as the natural products of certain natural faculties. Shakespeare, we are told, is a great poet because of his superior knowledge of the human heart, his exceedingly refined psychology. One of the main results of this theory is the general leveling of talents.[16] Why should there be any such thing as imagination, genius, etc.? At bottom all men are alike, and what such terms designate is but the preponderance of one mental faculty over another, i.e., a morbid condition, an abnormality;[17] whereas in reasonable, orderly, sober men all things are nicely balanced and perfectly healthy.

Neither empirical philosophy resting on facts nor formal, merely analytical philosophy can lead to any knowledge whatever; a one-sided philosophy cannot lead to absolute knowledge because it treats its object from a limited point of view.

A genuine speculative philosophy can be one-sided, too, when it takes as its absolute principle a particular form of the fundamental identity, conceived at a subordinate stage of reflection (for this identity recurs at all possible stages, changing in form only). Such a philosophy is speculative because it can rise to the universal pure and simple merely by going beyond the limits of its conception and by ceasing to regard the particular form of identity as the absolute. It is one-sided insofar as the picture it draws of the whole remains distorted.

The modern world is in general a world of antitheses, whereas in antiquity, except for individual stirrings, the finite and the infinite were united under a common veil. The spirit of the modern era tore this veil and showed the one in absolute opposition to the other. We can see

16 *Sans-culottisme.*
17 A kind of madness, really, but yet with some method in it.

only a small part of the far longer course which fate has prescribed for the modern world; and so the antithesis may easily seem to be essential, while the unity into which it is destined to resolve itself may seem purely accidental. Nevertheless, it is certain that this unity will be restored on a higher plane and will be to the old identity between the finite and infinite (which was in a sense unconscious) as the work of art is to the organic work of nature. However that may be, in the modern world the antithesis inevitably manifests itself in one form or another, and it will manifest itself time and again in science and in art until it is transcended in truly absolute identity.

Dualism, an inherently necessary and necessarily recurrent expression of the modern era, was bound to be its dominant philosophy. The philosophies of identity, which were developed by a few individual thinkers, can be counted for almost nothing; rejected by their contemporaries, these philosophies were looked upon by posterity only as remarkable examples of error.

As the old political institutions and even the idea of a universal church lost their hold on men's minds, the divine principle withdrew from the world; and visible nature came to be conceived of as the soulless body of the finite. The light turned inward, and the antithesis between subjectivity and objectivity reached its highest pitch. Since Descartes, who formulated dualism with scientific precision, down to our own day there has been no philosophy to oppose it (apart from Spinoza's). Even Leibnitz expressed his theory in a form which dualism was able to make its own. Once the Idea had been split in two, the infinite lost its significance and became just as subjective as the antithesis itself. To assert this subjectivity completely to the point of negating the reality of the absolute was a first step toward the restoration of philosophy. This step was the so-called critical philosophy. The idealism of [Fichte's] *Wissenschaftslehre* [Theory of Science] drew the ultimate conclusions from this philosophy without transcending its dualism. But it eliminated the infinite or the absolute (in the sense of the dogmatic philosophy) more resolutely [than Kant had done], denying it any kind of reality. As the thing-in-itself, the absolute must be objective, i.e., altogether outside the self; but this is unthinkable; for, by being posited outside the self, it is posited for the self and, hence, in the self. This eternal, insoluble circle of reflective thinking is expounded fully in the *Wissenschaftslehre*. The idea of the absolute had tended irresistibly toward subjectivity since Descartes; the objectivity it had been endowed with in a mistaken dogmatism was illusory. It was restored entirely to subjectivity when it was recognized as real only with respect to action. This form of idealism marks the point where modern philosophy becomes fully conscious of its own implications and achieves its most complete expression.

It was Descartes who first steered the course toward subjectivity with his *cogito ergo sum*. The arguments given in his *Meditations* are in effect repeated in later formulations of idealism. In Descartes, however, subjectivity and objectivity did not yet seem entirely sundered from each other. But his actual intentions and his ideas of God, the world, and the soul were more clearly formulated in his physics than in his metaphysics; they could still be misunderstood at all only because they were based on the ontological proof of the reality of God, a last remnant of genuine philosophy. It is noteworthy that mechanical physics was first given systematic form in modern times by the thinker who clearly formulated philosophical dualism. Descartes, with his comprehensive mind, succeeded in annihilating nature in his physics just as effectively as did the form of idealism just mentioned. For it makes not the slightest difference, from a speculative point of view, whether nature in its empirical form exists in a real or in an ideal sense. Whether individual things are conceived of in a crude empirical manner or defined as affections and determinations "of every I"—the latter regarded as the absolute substance in which they exist—comes to the same in the end.

Nature is truly destroyed when it is conceived of as consisting entirely of absolute qualities, limitations, and affections—something like ideal atoms. However, no proof is needed to show that a philosophy which turns its back on all oppositions and has not truly arrived at absolute harmony has not attained to absolute knowledge, let alone provided us with a guide to it.

The task every student should set himself as soon as he takes up philosophy is to strive for the one truly absolute knowledge, which by its nature includes knowledge of the absolute, to strive for it until he has perfectly grasped the whole as unity. In the absolute, free from all oppositions which limit it subjectively or objectively, philosophy discloses not only the realm of the Ideas but also the true fountainhead of all knowledge of nature, which is itself only the organ of the Ideas. I have shown earlier that the modern world is ultimately destined to formulate a higher, truly comprehensive unity. Both science and art are moving in that direction, and it is precisely in order that this unity may exist that all oppositions must be made manifest.

So far we have discussed oppositions within philosophy itself. In the course of the next lecture I shall mention a few antiphilosophical attitudes rooted in the prejudice and in the misguided and superficial thinking of our age.

7 Philosophy vs. the Positive Sciences

One of these antiphilosophical attitudes derives from the previously mentioned opposition between knowledge and action. This attitude is not grounded in the spirit of modern culture as such; it is a recent product, a direct offspring of the pseudo-enlightenment. According to this school, there is, strictly speaking, only a practical philosophy, not a theoretical philosophy. Kant, after reducing in his theoretical philosophy the Idea of God, of the immortality of the soul, etc., to mere "ideas," tried to give the latter a kind of foundation in the moral disposition. In a like manner, rejection of theoretical philosophy expresses the belief that we have at last achieved the happy state of complete freedom from Ideas; an alleged morality is now supposed to serve as their equivalent.

Morality is a godlike disposition whereby we rise above all concrete limitations into the realm of the pure universal. Philosophy, too, rises above ordinary life and, therefore, is closely connected with morality—not subordinated to it, but essentially, inherently identical with it. There is but one world, which both philosophy and morality seek to reflect as it is in the absolute, each in its own way—knowledge as knowledge, action as action. The world of action is inherently no less absolute than the world of knowledge, and ethics is no less a speculative science than theoretical philosophy. Each particular duty corresponds to a particular Idea and is a world in itself, just as each species in nature has an archetype which it strives to resemble as nearly as possible. Morality, no more than philosophy, cannot be conceived with an a priori construction. I am aware that a system of ethics in this sense does not yet exist, but the principles and elements of such a system are implied in the absolute character, now restored, of philosophy.

What, on the subjective plane, is the individual's moral disposition, is, on the objective plane, universal freedom—what might be called public morality. The system of ethics, like the system of nature, rests upon the Ideas, and theoretically speaking the decline of individual and public morality should be reflected in the decline of philosophy. But the shallow rationalism which, no longer able to appear in its natural form, parades under the borrowed name of morality merely reveals its impotence—its feeble voice is like the chorus in classical drama, no more than a weak accompaniment to the vigorous action that marks our epoch.

One of the tasks of philosophy will be to disclose the positive forms of morality; it has long been formulated only in negative terms [i.e., in the form of prohibitions]. The fear of speculation, the hasty abandonment of pure theory for the sake of practice, leads to the same shallowness in action as in knowledge. The study of strictly theoretical philosophy introduces us directly into the realm of Ideas, and only Ideas can lend point and ethical significance to action.

Another source of opposition to philosophy is religion. The two are not diametrically opposed to each other as reason and faith were in former times; the more recent view is that religion and philosophy are simply incompatible because religion is pure intuition of the infinite, while philosophy, being a rational system, cannot remain on the plane of pure identity. We shall first try to clarify the meaning of this antithesis in order to discover the purpose it is designed to serve.

It has often been asserted that philosophy, by its nature, is entirely within the domain of the absolute and never goes outside it. It knows no transition from the infinite to the finite and rests entirely upon the possibility of grasping the particular in the universal and the universal in the particular, which is the foundation of the theory of the Ideas. "But the very fact that philosophers deduce the particular from the absolute," it is argued, "instead of having direct intuition of each in the other (naturally, as it were) presupposes an antecedent differentiation, a stepping outside the absolute identity." According to this view, then, the mind comes closest to the absolute when it is in a state of unconsciousness or total stupor, a state of perfect innocence in which the "intuition" of the infinite could not even be conceived of as religion, since any such conceiving would imply reflection and stepping outside the "identity."

Thus, now that philosophy has restored the idea of the absolute, freeing it from the limitation of subjectivity, and has endeavored to present it in objective forms as far as possible, religion is used as the last remaining weapon of subjectivity to disparage science. What science is in effect criticized for is its universal validity, its opposition to vagueness; in short, it is criticized for being scientific. In an age when a certain dilettantism leaves its mark in nearly every other field, it is not surprising that even the most sacred is not spared and that this kind of incapacity or unwillingness to know takes refuge in religion to escape the more difficult task of grasping the absolute intellectually.

Praise be to those who are proclaiming anew the essence of religion, who expound it with life and energy and assert its independence of morality and philosophy! Yet if it is true that the road to religion does not lead through philosophy, it must also be granted that philosophy does not need religion and cannot be replaced by it. No special objective talent is needed to achieve inner harmony and spiritual beauty, but to formulate this beauty objectively, be it in science or in art, requires something very different from merely subjective endowment. Those who mistake aspirations to this harmony (in itself praiseworthy) or simply their need of it for the ability to express it in objective terms merely express their longing for poetry and philosophy—they do not thereby *practice* poetry or philosophy. They go in search of the formless, disparaging systematic philosophy, which is out of their depth and whose symbolism they are incapable of understanding.*

Poetry and philosophy, which another variety of dilettantism imagines to be opposites, are alike in that both require a self-produced, original view of the world. Most people believe that with a merely social view of the world they are adequately equipped to produce works of art and express its eternal Ideas. And it is true that such as they are relatively superior to scribblers who, without the least experience of life, in the simplicity of childhood, write melancholy poetry. Empiricism is today dominant in poetry to an even greater extent than in philosophy. Some people, having heard that all art begins and ends in contemplation of nature and the universe, and assuming nature to consist merely of particular phenomena or even the peculiarities of things, imagine that they have perfectly grasped the poetry inherent in nature when they treat the phenomena as allegories of feelings and states of mind. It is easy to see that in this way both empiricism and subjectivity are unduly exalted.

In philosophy, nature and God, science and art, religion and poetry are linked with one another from the beginning. When philosophy has overcome its internal oppositions, it meets no external oppositions save those that may be produced by empiricism or a shallow dilettantism, as formless as it is frivolous.

The subject of philosophy is primordial knowledge itself, but it is the science of this knowledge only ideally. An intelligence that could in a single cognitive act apprehend the absolute whole as a system complete in every part, including both the ideal and real aspects, would thereby cease to be finite, would apprehend all things as actually one and, for this very reason, would not apprehend anything as determinate.

The real (as opposed to ideal) aspect of primordial knowledge is represented by the other sciences, but in them all things are isolated and separated; they can never actually be unified in the individual, only in the species, and then only in an intellectual intuition that perceives the infinite progress as a simultaneous presence.

Now, it is clear that the process by which an Idea is progressively realized—such that the whole (though never the particulars) is adequate to it—must express itself as history. History is neither a purely rational process subject to the concept, nor is it purely irrational;

rather it combines necessity in the whole with the appearance of freedom in the individual. Actual knowledge, since it is the gradual revelation of primordial knowledge, has necessarily a historical aspect, and insofar as all history aims at realization of an external organism as the expression of the Ideas, science, too, strives to have an objective, external existence. The latter can only be a copy of the internal organism of primordial knowledge itself and, hence, of philosophy, with the difference that objective science represents as separated what in primordial knowledge and in philosophy is one.

Accordingly, we must first of all deduce the internal type of philosophy from the common source of form and content in order to determine the corresponding form of an external organism in which knowledge becomes truly objective.

Pure absoluteness as such is necessarily also pure identity, but the absolute form of this identity is to be eternally its own subject and object—this we may presuppose as already proved. Neither subject nor object in this eternal act of cognition is the absolute, but that which is the identical essence of both and which, therefore, cannot be differentiated. One and the same essence is in that which may be called the objective aspect of the absolute—which embodies ideality in reality—and in the subjective aspect, which embodies reality in ideality. Thus the same subject-object is posited in each, while in the absolute form the whole essence of the absolute is posited.

Each of these two aspects may be termed a unity complete in itself, but the absolute as such is neither the one nor the other, for it is precisely the identity, the essence of each and, thereby, of both. Accordingly both are in the absolute, although not distinguishable within it, for in both form is identical with essence.

Once we have conceived the absolute as that which is pure identity in itself and, as such, the necessary essence of the two unities, we have thereby conceived the absolute point of indifference between form and essence—the point from which all cognition and science flow.

Within the absolute each of the two unities is what the other is. But just as the essential unity of both is necessarily the character of the absolute itself, so both necessarily manifest themselves in the nonabsolute as separate and different. For if only one of them were distinguished at the phenomenal level, it would also be *qua* one within the absolute, thereby excluding its opposite; thus, it would not be absolute itself, which contradicts our assumption.

Therefore, the two are necessarily differentiated at the phenomenal level, somewhat as the absolute life of cosmic bodies is expressed by the fact that they have two relative centers. Form, which in the absolute was identical with essence—and was essence itself—now becomes differentiated into the form of the natural world and the form of the spiritual world. As the embodiment of eternal unity in multiplicity, of the infinite in the finite, it is the form of nature, which, as it manifests itself, is at each given moment only a stage or transitional point in the eternal act by which identity becomes embodied in difference. Considered in itself it is the process through which things or Ideas move away from their center and are in themselves. Hence nature in itself is only one of the two aspects of all things. As the embodiment of multiplicity in unity, of the finite in the infinite, it is the form of the ideal or spiritual world. Considered in itself it is the unity in virtue of which things return to their center and are in the infinite identity instead of in themselves.

Philosophy views the two unities only in the absolute and, accordingly, as opposed only ideally, not really. Its fundamental task, therefore, is to show that the absolute center is equally present in the two relative centers—the real and the ideal—and that both are in the absolute. This defines the basic pattern of philosophy as a whole, which also recurs necessarily in every part.*

This organic pattern inherent in primordial knowledge and in philosophy is expressed externally in the various sciences, which are thus constituted as a single body of knowledge.

Knowledge becomes objective only in action, which in turn expresses itself externally in ideal creations. The most universal of these is the state, which is formed (as was said earlier) on the model of the world of Ideas. But since the state itself is objectified knowledge, it, too, necessarily comprehends within itself a material organization of knowledge, something that might be called the ideal, intellectual state. The sciences that attain to objectivity within the state and in function of it are called "the positive sciences." The transition to objectivity necessarily divides the sciences from one another—in primordial knowledge they are one. But the separate sciences fall into a pattern which necessarily reflects the internal structure of philosophy. The three cornerstones of this structure are: first, the absolute point of indifference, in which the ideal and the real worlds are apprehended as one; second, the real aspect of the absolute, which is the center of the real world; third, the ideal aspect of the absolute, i.e., the center of the ideal world. The external body of knowledge will be similarly structured. It comprises three primary sciences, distinct from each other and yet linked externally.

The first of these sciences is the objective counterpart of the absolute point of indifference: the science of the absolute and divine being, i.e., theology.

The second science is the objective counterpart of the real aspect of the absolute. This is the science of nature, and because this science not only concerns itself primarily with the organism, but also, as will be shown later, can be a positive science only in respect of the organism, it is the science of organism, i.e., medicine.

The third science is the objective counterpart of the ideal aspect of the absolute. This is history in the broadest sense of the term; since its supreme goal is a world order based on law, it comprises the science of right, or jurisprudence.

Insofar as the sciences attain actual objective existence in and through the state and become a power, they are organized into so-called faculties. A few remarks are necessary concerning their relative rank—especially since Kant in his *Contest of the Faculties* seems to have treated the question from a very one-sided point of view. Clearly, theology, as the science in which the innermost core of philosophy is objectified, must have the first and highest place. Since the ideal is a higher potency or level of the real, it follows that the law faculty has precedence over the medical. As for philosophy, I maintain that there is no such faculty, nor can there be, for that which is all things cannot for that very reason be anything in particular.

It is philosophy itself which becomes objective in the three positive sciences, but it does not become objective in its totality in any single one of them. Philosophy in its totality becomes truly objective only in art; for this reason there can be no faculty of philosophy, but only a faculty of the arts. But the arts can never be an external power, nor can they be privileged or subject to restrictions by the state. Consequently, organizations of art can only be free ones, i.e., not dependent on the state. The *collegium artium* in the old universities, whose members were called artists and which has today become the so-called Faculty of Philosophy, was never intended to serve the state. This difference between the faculty of philosophy and the others has survived down to the present day, for it does not, as they do, create masters (*doctores*) who for their privileged status have duties to the state; it merely creates teachers (*magistri*) of the free arts.

The above assertion is confirmed by the fact that where philosophical faculties have so far lost their original character of free colleges for the furthering of the arts and their special corporate spirit, as to become caricatures of their former selves, they are objects of general scorn, whereas in view of their purpose they are supposed to enjoy universal esteem.

It is generally acknowledged that theology and jurisprudence have a positive, i.e., a historical, aspect. It is more difficult to show that the science of nature, too, has a positive aspect. Nature is the self-contained, distinct process by which primordial knowledge becomes objective; whereas history stands under the sign of the infinite, nature stands under the sign of the finite. The historicity of knowledge here is not immanent in the object but in the subject. Nature as a whole always acts with evident necessity; particular actions or events in nature require the intervention of a subject. Such a determining of nature to act, under certain conditions and to the exclusion of others, is what is called "experiment." It is the experiment that gives the science of nature a historical aspect, since it is a deliberately contrived event, the witness of which is the one who contrived it. Even in this sense, however, the science of nature is not "positive" to the same extent as, e.g., jurisprudence. For this reason, it is included among the positive sciences only insofar as the knowledge it contains involves public duties, and this is the case only with medicine.*

We have now surveyed the positive sciences as a whole, distinguishing them from philosophy; we have made fully clear the opposition between absolute and historical knowledge. What we said about the study of special disciplines in the spirit of unity and totality must now be justified by the test of practicability.

8 The Historical Construction of Christianity

The real sciences can be distinguished from the absolute or ideal science only because they contain a historical element. Theology, however, apart from this element, stands in a special relation to history.

It is primarily in theology, which deals with speculative Ideas, that philosophy becomes objective. For this reason, theology is the highest synthesis of philosophical and historical knowledge. To demonstrate this is the chief purpose of the following remarks.

My assertion that theology stands in a special relation to history is not based solely on the fact that religion, like every other type of knowledge, like civilization itself, could only have originated in the teachings of superior beings—in other words, that from the very outset religion was tradition. The current explanations—according to which the idea of God or gods was produced by fear, gratitude, or some other feeling or was a crafty invention on the part of early lawgivers—are unsatisfactory; in the former hypothesis the idea of God is reduced to a purely psychological phenomenon, while the latter fails to explain how it ever occurred to anyone to make himself a lawgiver in the first place, or how anyone could have used religion as a threat to enforce obedience unless religion had already existed. Among the falsest and shallowest writings in recent times are the so-called histories of mankind. Their views of the primitive conditions of our species are inspired by travelers' accounts stressing the rudeness of savage peoples. Actually there is no condition of barbarism that is not a degenerated form of vanished civilization. The history of the earth will eventually prove that the savage tribes of today are the remnants of nations which were separated from the rest of the world as a result of revolutions. Unable to communicate with each other, robbed of their earlier cultural possessions, they have regressed to their present state. I firmly believe that the earliest condition of the human race was a civilized one and that the first states, sciences, arts, and religions were founded simultaneously - or, more accurately, that they were not separated but were perfectly fused, as they will again be one day in their final form.

Nor does my assertion that theology has a special relation to history refer merely to the fact that the particular forms of Christianity in which religion exists among us can be known only historically. What makes this relation special is that in Christianity the universe is viewed as history, as a moral kingdom, and that this view constitutes its fundamental character. We can fully understand this only by comparing Christianity with the religion of ancient Greece. If I do not mention still older religions, notably that of India, it is because in this respect they provide no contrast (this is not to imply, however, that they are closer to Christianity). The limits of the present lecture do not permit a complete exposition of this view; hence, I shall only outline it briefly. The mythology of the Greeks was a self-contained world of symbols for the Ideas, which could be visualized as real only in the form of gods. Each particular divinity and the world of the gods as a whole were conceived of as clearly delimited on the one hand and as absolute on the other. The infinite was perceived only in the finite and, in this way, even subordinated to the finite. The gods were beings of a higher nature, abiding, immutable figures. Very different is a religion which is concerned directly with the infinite, in which the finite is not conceived of as a symbol of the infinite —nor as existing at the same time for its own sake—but only as an allegory of the infinite, wholly subordinated to it. The system in which the ideas of such a religion become objective is necessarily infinite itself, not a world completed and bounded on all sides; the figures which represent the godhead are not abiding but transitory— not eternal beings of nature but historical figures in which the divine is revealed transitorily, its fleeting appearance held fast by faith, yet never transformed into an absolute presence.

Where the infinite itself can become one finite thing, there it can also become many, there polytheism is possible. Where the infinite is only *represented* by the finite, it remains necessarily one, and no polytheism is possible except as a coexistence of divine figures. Polytheism arises from a synthesis between absoluteness and limitation, a synthesis in which neither formal absoluteness nor limitation is abolished. In this respect, a religion like Christianity cannot be rooted in nature, for it does not conceive the finite as symbol of the infinite, nor as existing for its own sake. Consequently, Christianity can be rooted only in what falls within time—that is, in history; and hence Christianity is, in the highest sense and in its innermost spirit, historical. Every moment of time is a revelation of a particular aspect of God, in each of which He is absolute. That which the Greek religion had as simultaneity, Christianity has as succession in time, although it has not yet achieved its definitive form.

It has already been pointed out that nature is to history what the real is to the ideal; the same is true of the relation between the Greek religion and the Christian religion. In Christianity the divine principle no longer reveals itself in nature and is recognizable only in history. Nature as such is the sphere in which things are in themselves, i.e., in which things have a life independent of the Ideas (though they symbolize the Ideas in virtue of the fact that their finitude embodies the infinite). This is why God becomes, so to speak, exoteric in nature; the ideal manifests itself in something different from the ideal—in an existent. Yet the divine is truly exoteric only insofar as this existent is taken for the essence, and the symbol is viewed as independent of the Idea; in terms of the Idea it is esoteric. The divine unveils itself in the ideal world—above all, in history; here the mystery of the divine kingdom is disclosed.

In nature the intelligible world is present only symbolically. In Greek poetry it was as though wrapped in a cocoon, still veiled objectively and unexpressed subjectively. By contrast, Christianity is the revealed mystery, and whereas paganism is inherently exoteric, Christianity is inherently esoteric.

With the advent of Christianity the relation between nature and the ideal world was thus inevitably reversed. In paganism nature was made manifest while the ideal world was veiled in mystery. In Christianity the ideal world was progressively revealed while nature inevitably receded into the background as mystery. To the Greeks,

nature as such was divine; their gods were not supernatural or extra-natural. To the modern world nature
was a closed book, for she was not conceived of in herself, but only as a metaphor of the invisible spiritual
world. The most active phenomena of nature, such as
electricity and chemical change, were scarcely known to
the ancients—at least they failed to arouse the widespread enthusiasm they arouse in the modern world.
The highest religious feeling, as expressed in Christian
mysticism, holds the mystery of nature and the mystery
of the Incarnation to be one and the same.

Elsewhere (in the *System of Transcendental Idealism*)
I have shown that we must assume that there have been
three periods in history—Nature, Fate, and Providence.
All three terms express the same identity, but in different ways. Fate is Providence, too, as recognized in the
world of real things; similarly, Providence is Fate, but
viewed in the ideal world. In the period of Nature,
eternal necessity was identical with and revealed itself as
nature; the opposition between the infinite and the
finite still lay hidden in the common seed of the finite.
Greek religion and poetry had their finest flowering in
this period. Then, seceding from nature, eternal necessity revealed itself as Fate and was brought into conflict
with freedom. This happened at the close of the ancient
world, and, for this reason, its history taken as a whole
may be looked upon as the period of tragedy. The modern world began with a universal "Fall of Man," i.e., a
breaking away from nature. Surrender to nature had not
been sin so long as it was unconscious; this was mankind's Golden Age. With consciousness innocence and
reconciliation with nature were lost; voluntary surrender to it became necessary. From the ensuing struggle
freedom emerged as both the conquered and the con-

queror. Conscious reconciliation with nature, which has supplanted unconscious identity with it and conflict with fate and which restores unity on a higher plane, is expressed in the idea of Providence. It was Christianity that introduced the period of Providence as well as its dominant view of the universe as history and as world ruled by Providence.

Christianity represented a great turning point in human history, and this is why the science of religion in the Christian world is inseparable from history—indeed, why it must be identical with it. But the synthesis of religion with history, without which theology would be inconceivable, presupposes in turn the validity of the Christian view of history.

History is commonly opposed to philosophy, but this opposition holds good only so long as history is conceived of as a sequence of accidental occurrences—the vulgar theory—or as merely empirical necessity—a supposedly superior conception, but actually as narrow as the other. History, too, springs from an eternal unity and has roots in the absolute, just like nature or any other object of cognition. To the common understanding the contingency of events and actions seems to be founded on the contingent nature of individuals. But I ask: What is this or that individual but the very man who carried out this or that particular action? There can be no other definition of the individual. Consequently, if the action was necessary, so was the individual who performed it. Even from a subordinate point of view, what may appear as a free act and hence objective "by accident" seems so merely by the circumstance that the individual supposes to be of his own choice what is predetermined and necessary. At the same time, however, so far as the consequences are concerned and whether for good or for evil, the act was an instrument of absolute necessity.

Empirical necessity is nothing but a device for extending the scope of contingency by making necessity regress indefinitely. If we allow this kind of necessity in nature only on the phenomenal plane, must we not a fortiori do the same where human history is concerned? What intelligent person will persuade himself that events like the development of Christianity, the migrations of peoples, the Crusades, and other great events originated in the empirical causes assigned to them? Even were these in fact the controlling causes, still they have to be regarded as instruments of an eternal order of things.

What is true of history in general is especially true of the history of religion, namely, it is founded upon an eternal necessity, and consequently it is possible to construct it. By means of such a construction history becomes closely bound up with the science of religion.

The historical construction of Christianity can have only one point of departure, namely, the view that the world as a whole, and hence also its history, necessarily shows two different aspects and that the opposition between them, which is that between the modern world and the ancient world, is sufficient to account for Christianity's nature and special characteristics. The ancient world represents the "nature" side of history in the sense that its dominant idea—what gives it unity—is that the infinite exists only in the finite. The end of the ancient world and the beginning of modern times, whose dominant principle is the infinite, could come about only when the true infinite was embodied in the finite—the purpose was not to deify the finite, but to offer it up as a sacrifice to God in His own person and thus to reconcile the two. Hence Christianity's leading idea is God become incarnate, Christ as culmination, the closing out of the ancient world of gods. In Him, as in the ancient gods, the divine principle becomes finite, but the humanity he assumes is not humanity in its highest estate but in its lowest. He stands as the boundary between the two worlds, decreed from all eternity yet a transitory phenomenon in time. He Himself returns to the invisible realm and promises the coming of the Spirit—not the principle which becomes finite to stay finite but the ideal principle which leads the finite back to the infinite and, as such, is the light of the modern world.

All the other leading traits of Christianity are bound up with this basic one. To represent the unity of the infinite and the finite objectively through symbols, as the Greek religion did, is impossible in Christianity because of its ideal orientation. Now symbolism is relegated to the subject; resolution of the contradiction is apprehended internally, not externally, and hence remains a mystery, something hidden. The all-pervasive antinomy between the divine and the natural is transcended within the subject only when both are—in an incomprehensible way—conceived as one. Such a subjective unity is expressed in the term "miracle." In this sense, every idea is a miracle, since it is produced in time without having any relation to time. No idea can come into being in a temporal manner; it is an expression of the absolute—that is, God himself reveals the idea, and this is why the concept of Revelation is absolutely necessary in Christianity.

A religion which exists among men as poetry needs no historical foundation—like nature, it is simply there, open for all to see. But a religion in which the divine principle does not take on any enduring form but makes only fleeting appearances needs some way of recording them, of perpetuating them. In addition to its mysteries, religion requires a mythology—in Christianity mythology is the exoteric aspect, which is founded upon religion; in paganism the opposite is the case: there religion was founded upon mythology.

The ideas of a religion in which the infinite is apprehended in the finite have to be expressed primarily in actually existing things. The ideas of the opposite religion, in which all symbols are subjective, can become objective only in human action. Here the original symbol of God is history. History, however, is endless, immeasurable, and, hence, can be represented only by something infinite yet limited, something that is not real as the state is real but ideal, and that embodies, as immediate presence, the spiritual union of all men without abolishing their individual distinctions. This symbol of God is the Church as a living work of art.

Now, just as the action which expresses the unity of the infinite and the finite may be called symbolic when it is external, the same action, when expressed internally, may be called mystical; more generally, mysticism is a subjective symbolism. Mystical writings have always been frowned upon by the Church, and their authors have occasionally been persecuted because they sought to make the esoteric element in Christianity exoteric—not because the innermost spirit of Christianity is opposed to the spirit of mysticism.

If the actions and customs of the Church are held to be objectively symbolic, on the ground that their significance can only be mystical, at least the Christian ideas symbolized in the dogmas of the Church have retained their full speculative significance, for these symbols have not achieved a life of their own, independent of their meanings, as those of Greek mythology.

The reconciliation of the finite which had seceded from God, a reconciliation effected by God's birth in the finite world, is the basic idea of Christianity; the idea of the Trinity, which expresses the whole Christian view of the world and of its history, is a necessary part of it. Lessing, in his *Education of Mankind*, attempted to develop the philosophical implications of this doctrine, and his observations on this subject are perhaps more profoundly speculative than anything else he wrote. But his interpretation fails to connect this idea closely enough with the history of the world. The true relation is as follows: the eternal Son of God, born of the essence of the Father of all things, is the finite itself, as it exists in God's eternal intuition; this finite manifests itself as a suffering God, subject to the vicissitudes of time, who at the culmination of His career, in the person of Christ, closes the world of the finite and opens the world of the infinite, i.e., the reign of the Spirit.

If it were possible here to go further into the historical construction of Christianity, we should in the same way recognize the necessity of every one of the oppositions between Christianity and paganism, as well as of the dominant Christian ideas and subjective symbols of ideas. It is sufficient for my purpose to have shown the possibility of such a construction. If Christianity as a whole and in its most important forms is historically necessary, and if we recognize that its higher view of history is itself rooted in higher necessity, it becomes possible to understand Christianity historically as a divine and absolute phenomenon, and consequently to arrive at a truly historical science of religion and theology.

9 On the Study of Theology

I find it difficult to speak of the study of theology because I am convinced that the method of that science and the proper perspective in which its truths must be viewed are today lost and forgotten. Its doctrines are interpreted in an empirical sense both by proponents and opponents. Removed from their native soil and planted in the soil of empiricism, they lose all meaning.

According to the theologians, Christianity is a divine revelation, which they represent as an act that God performed in time. Thereby, they themselves take the position that the origin of Christianity can be accounted for in terms of natural causation. You really do not have to know much about the history and culture of the early centuries to arrive at a satisfactory explanation of this type. It is sufficient to read the scholarly books that trace the "germ" of Christianity not just to Judaism but to a single religious community which existed before Christianity. In fact, you do not even have to read those books; Josephus and the surviving fragments of early Christian historians (which have not yet been put to proper use) will supply ample evidence in favor of this theory. In short, Christ as an individual is perfectly intelligible, and it was absolutely inevitable that he would be conceived of as a symbolic person in a higher sense.

As for those who look upon the spread of Christianity as the work of divine Providence, let them study the period of its first conquests; then they will recognize that Christianity was merely a particular manifestation of the spirit of the age. Christianity did not create this spirit; it was only an anticipatory stirring of that spirit, its earliest expression. The Roman empire was ripe for Christianity centuries before Constantine chose to put the Cross on its banner. Widespread dissatisfaction with material things was producing a longing for the spiritual and the invisible; an empire in its decadence, whose power was purely temporal, failure of nerve in the face of the situation, a feeling of unhappiness—these necessarily brought about a collective readiness to embrace a religion which guides men to the ideal world, teaching happiness through renunciation.

Christian religious teachers cannot justify any of their historical assertions without first making their own the higher view of history which is prescribed by both philosophy and Christianity. They have fought unbelief long enough on its own terms, instead of attacking its intellectual foundations. They ought to have said to the Naturalists, "You are perfectly right from the point of view you take, and we believe that in terms of it your conclusions are correct. What we deny is the point of view itself, or at best allow it to be of purely secondary importance. Your position is the same as that of empiricists who prove irrefutably to the philosopher that all knowledge involves external impressions."

The same observations may be made concerning current interpretations of theological dogmas. Clearly, the idea of the Trinity, unless understood speculatively, has no meaning whatever. The dogma of the Incarnation is interpreted in the same empirical manner, namely, that God took on human nature at a given moment of time. This view simply makes no sense for God is eternally outside of time. Consequently, the process of God's becoming man has been going on from all eternity. The culmination of this process is Christ's assuming visible human form, and for this reason it is also its beginning; starting with Christ, it has been going on ever since—all His successors are members of one and the same body of which He is the head. History bears witness that in Christ God first became truly objective, for who before Christ revealed the infinite in this way?

It might be shown that, as far back as historical knowledge goes, two clearly different currents of religion and poetry are distinguishable: the first, the oldest form of idealism, is the intellectual system which has come down to us through the Indian religion; the second represents the realistic view of the world. The first current, after flowing through the whole Orient, found its permanent bed in Christianity and fertilized the barren soil of the Occident to produce the various growths of the modern world. The second current, supplemented by the ideal element of art, brought forth the highest beauty in Greek mythology. And shall we count for nothing the stirrings of the opposite tendency in Greek culture—the mystical elements of a special kind of poetry, the rejection of mythology and banishment of the poets by the philosophers, especially Plato, who anticipated Christianity in an alien and very different world?

The fact that Christianity existed before and apart from its appearance in the world proves the necessity of its idea, and also that here as elsewhere no oppositions are absolute. The Christian missionaries who went to India thought they were bringing unheard-of tidings to the inhabitants when they taught that the God of the Christians had become man. But the Hindus were not surprised; they did not in the least contest the incarnation of God in Christ, and only thought it strange that an event that occurs frequently among them should have occurred only once among the Christians. It is not to be denied that they had a better understanding of their own religion than the Christian missionaries had of theirs.

On account of the universality of its idea, the historical construction of Christianity presupposes the religious construction of history as a whole. Consequently, such a construction has as little in common with the so-called history of religion (which, incidentally, deals with anything rather than religion) as with the special history of the Christian religion and the Christian Church.

By its very nature, such a construction is possible only on the basis of a higher knowledge, one which rises above empirical causality; in other words, it requires philosophy, which is the true organ of theology as science, wherein the highest ideas of the Divine Being, of nature as its instrument, and of history as the revelation of God become objective. Needless to say, no one will confuse the thesis that the principal theological doctrines are speculative in character with the Kantian thesis [in *Religion within the Limits of Reason Alone*]. Kant sought to eliminate all positive and historical elements from Christianity and to transform it into a pure religion of reason. The true religion of reason recognizes the existence of only two forms of religion—the religion of nature, which is necessarily polytheistic in the Greek sense, and the wholly ethical religion which apprehends God in history. Kant does not aim at a speculative but a moral interpretation of these forms of religion. He is not interested in their inherent truth but only in their possible subjective effects on morality, and he does not actually go beyond the empirical point of view.

Like dogmatism in philosophy, dogmatism in theology deals with objects of absolute cognition from the empirical standpoint of the understanding. Kant does not attack the one or the other dogmatism at its root, since he was unable to put anything positive in its place. In particular, to explain the Bible morally in schools, as he proposed, would be merely to use empirical Christianity for purposes which cannot be achieved without misinterpretation and which do not lead to the idea of Christianity.

The earliest books on the history and doctrines of Christianity are merely a particular—and, moreover, imperfect—manifestation of it; its idea is not to be sought in these books whose value is to be measured by the extent to which they express this idea and are in consonance with it. Already for St. Paul, the proselytizer of the Gentiles, Christianity had become something different from what it was for its founder. We must not stop at any arbitrarily chosen point of time; we must have the whole of history and the world that has produced Christianity before our eyes.

One of the operations of the modern pseudo-enlightenment—which, with respect to Christianity, might rather be called a dis-enlightenment—is the attempt to "restore" it, as the saying goes, to its "original" meaning, to its early simplicity, in which form it is sometimes referred to as "primitive" Christianity. One might have thought that Christian teachers would have been grateful to later ages for having extracted so much speculative matter from the meager contents of the earliest religious books and for having drawn it up in a system. To be sure, it may be easier to talk about the scholastic chaos of the old dogmatism, to write popular treatises, and to indulge in hairsplitting and playing with etymologies than to grasp the universal import of Christianity and its teachings. One cannot help thinking that full understanding of it has been hampered by the so-called Biblical literature, which in terms of genuine religious ideas is not even remotely comparable to many other works, old and new, especially the Hindu books.

When the Catholic Church proposed that the people should not be allowed to read the Biblical literature, it was thought that its motives were political. But the proposal might have been advocated on the more cogent grounds that Christianity should remain a living religion, not a thing of the past but an everlasting present. Similarly, it was one of the inconsistencies of Protestantism that, against the teaching of the Church, it maintained that miracles had ceased and restricted them to the past. In reality it has been these early books—no doubt useful to historians as original records but not to the faithful—which time and again have put empirical Christianity in the place of the idea. The idea exists independently of them and is more loudly proclaimed by the history of the modern world than by the history of the ancient world where the idea was still in a rudimentary stage of development.

The spirit of the modern age aims with visible consistency at the destruction of all merely finite forms, and to recognize this is not to go counter to religion. The communal and public status which religion had more or less attained in Christianity could not last since it only partly realized the purposes of the world spirit. Then came Protestantism, which from the first marked a rebirth of the aspiration to the nonsensual. However, this aspiration remained negative; it broke the continuity of Christianity's development without being able to bring about reunification symbolized in a visible Church. Living authority gave way to the authority of books written in dead languages, and as this latter authority, by its very nature, could not be binding, the result was a worse kind of slavery, namely, dependence on symbols founded upon merely human prestige. Inevitably, since it is essentially anti-universal, Protestantism broke up into sects, and unbelief fastened onto particular forms and empirical phenomena, which had become religion's entire content.

Not intellectual giants, yet unbelieving; not pious, yet not witty or frivolous either—like the unhappy souls whom Dante consigned to Limbo, who neither rebelled against God nor were faithful, whom Heaven expelled and Hell rejected (for not even the damned would take them in)—certain scholars (for the most part German) with the aid of a so-called sound exegesis, a rationalistic psychology, and lax morals have stripped Christianity of all speculative elements and even its subjective symbolism. They justified the belief in its divine character by empirical historical arguments; they proved the miracle of the revelation by the existence of other miracles (this was, obviously, to beg the question). Since the divine, by its very nature, is neither empirically knowable nor demonstrable, this "naturalist" school had won the game in advance. The negotiations for surrender to them began the moment the doctrines of theology were made dependent upon the results of investigations into the genuineness of the Christian books when proofs of their divine inspiration were found by interpreting passages out of context. This practice of referring to the letter of a few books inevitably turned theology into philological exegesis. When a so-called science of language comes to be regarded as the sword and buckler of religious orthodoxy, then theology has sunk to its lowest ebb, has reached the farthest pole from concern for its idea. Here a great deal of ingenuity is spent on explaining away as many Biblical miracles as possible—an undertaking no less wretched than its opposite, the attempt to prove the divinity of religion on the basis of these same meager empirical facts. What is the use of getting rid of so many miracles, so long as you cannot get rid of them all? Even one would carry as much weight as a thousand if this kind of proof made any sense whatever.

The philological approach was compounded with the psychological approach; some people have gone to enormous lengths to show that many stories which are obviously Jewish fables suggested to their authors by Old Testament messianic prophecies (this source is indicated by the authors themselves when they say that the events they relate had to take place in fulfillment of what was written) are actually to be accounted for as psychological illusions of the epoch.

Related to this practice is the favorite device of thinning down Biblical texts: on the excuse that a given passage is but an example of Oriental turgidity, it is interpreted in terms of shallow latter-day rationalistic notions. In this way modern morality and religion are read into the original documents of Christianity.

Such a theology, totally divorced from speculative thought, finally spread to public instruction. Teaching, we are told, is supposed to be purely moral in intent, devoid of references to the Idea. And yet morality is not the distinguishing characteristic of Christianity; surely, it is not just for the sake of a few moral maxims, such as "Love thy neighbor," that it became such a turning point in world history? It is not the fault of vulgar rationalism that moral preaching has not sunk still lower and taken up economics. There is no reason why, as the occasion may require, preachers should not provide advice to farmers, physicians, and what not. Why stop at recommending vaccination from the pulpit—why not instruct the faithful on the best method of raising potatoes?

I have had to speak of the present state of theology because I could not hope to say what seems needful concerning the true nature of this science without distinguishing it clearly from the kind prevalent today.

The divine character of Christianity cannot be recognized by any indirect method; it can only be recognized directly in the context of the absolute view of history. This is why the notion (among others) of an indirect revelation, quite apart from its intentional ambiguity, is inadmissible: it is wholly empirical.

Merely empirical matters, such as the critical and philological investigation of the early Christian books, have to be kept entirely distinct from the study of theology proper. The higher ideas can have no influence on exegesis, which—as also in treating secular texts—does not ask whether the things said by an author are rational, historically true, or religious, but only whether or not he actually said them. Whether these books are genuine or not, whether the stories they contain refer to things that actually happened as described or not, whether their content is or is not an adequate expression of the idea of Christianity—such questions have no bearing upon the reality of this idea, for it does not depend on such details, but is universal and absolute. Indeed, if Christianity had not been viewed so exclusively as a mere phenomenon in time, exegesis would have advanced much farther in historical evaluation of these documents, and our knowledge of essentially simple matters would not have got lost along so many learned detours.

The essential thing in the study of theology is to combine the speculative with the historical construction of Christianity and its principal doctrines.

I am aware that to let the esoteric and spiritual elements of Christianity take the place of the exoteric and literal is contrary to what was clearly intended by the earliest teachers and by the Church itself. Both were at all times agreed in opposing doctrines that were not accessible to all men. The fact that the early founders, as well as the subsequent leaders of Christianity, deliberately avoided anything prejudicial to its public character, emphatically denouncing it as heresy, as inimical to its universality, shows that they were clearly conscious of their goals. Among the orthodox leaders and members of the Church, it was the men attached to the letter of the law who acquired the greatest authority, and it was they who created Christianity as a universal religion. Only the Western sense of the letter of the law could give body and outward form to the ideal principle that came from the East—just as the light of the sun can produce its noblest ideas only in the literal substances of the earth.

But the circumstances that brought about early Christianity have repeated themselves: its forms have fallen into decay (as all finite things must) and it has clearly become impossible to maintain Christianity in its exoteric form. The esoteric aspect must therefore come

forward and, throwing off the veils which have sur-
rounded it, shine with its own light. The eternally living
spirit of all culture and creation will clothe it in new
and more enduring forms; there is no lack of matter
waiting to be formed by its opposite, the Idea. The
West and the East have come closer together within one
and the same culture, and wherever two opposites touch,
new life is kindled. In the ruthlessness with which it
allows the most beautiful but finite forms to fall into
decay once their life principle has gone out of them, the
spirit of the modern world has sufficiently revealed its
intention, which is to bring forth the infinite in eternally new forms. It has no less clearly demonstrated that
it wills Christianity not as an individual empirical phenomenon, but as the eternal Idea itself. The lineaments
of Christianity, not confined to the past but extending
over an immeasurable time, can be clearly recognized
in poetry and philosophy. The former requires religion
as the supreme, indeed the only, possibility of renewal;
the latter, with its truly speculative standpoint, has restored the true meaning of religion, has done away with
empiricism and the latter's ally, naturalism, and thereby
has paved the way for a rebirth of esoteric Christianity
and the Gospel of the absolute.*

10 On the Study of History and Jurisprudence

The absolute manifests itself as one and the same in two forms—nature and history. Similarly, theology, the point of indifference of the real sciences, is divided into historical science and natural science. Each of these sciences treats its subject apart from the other and, thereby, apart from the highest unity. However, each of them can reproduce the central identity within itself and thus be related to primordial knowledge.

It is commonly held that in nature everything takes place according to empirical necessity and in history according to freedom. But necessity and freedom are themselves merely forms or modes of existence outside the absolute. History * expresses on the ideal plane what nature expresses on the real plane—it is a higher potency or stage of nature; but for this very reason the essential content is the same in both; they differ only in respect of rank or potency. If we could apprehend the pure being-in-itself in both, we would recognize the same pattern in both—ideal in history and real in nature. Freedom as phenomenon can create nothing; a single universe expresses the two forms of the phenomenal world each for itself, each in its own way. Accordingly, the consummation of history is an ideal nature, i.e., the state conceived of as the external organism of a freely achieved harmony between necessity and freedom. The primary purpose of history is the realization of this community.

The first question that now confronts us, namely, whether or not history in the strict sense can be a science, seems to allow no doubt as to the answer. If history in this sense is opposed to science (as has been assumed in the foregoing), then it is clear that it cannot itself be science. Precisely because the real sciences are syntheses of philosophical and historical elements, neither history nor philosophy can be such a synthesis. History in the strict sense is thus on an equal footing with philosophy.

To see this relation more clearly, we must take into account the different standpoints from which history can be viewed. The highest, which we have mentioned before, is the religious standpoint, from which the whole course of history is conceived as the work of Providence. History in the strict sense cannot be treated from this standpoint because it is not essentially different from the philosophical standpoint. Needless to say, I do not deny the possibility of either the religious or the philosophical construction of history, but the former is part of theology and the latter of philosophy, and in each case the construction is necessarily different from history in the strict sense.

Opposed to the absolute standpoint is the empirical, which in turn has two aspects. First, we have the work of finding out and recording the events of the past; this is the task of the researcher, who represents only one aspect of the historian. This task consists in organizing the empirical data and subsuming them under the rational concepts of the understanding. In other words, because the unity of the understanding cannot be inherent in the events themselves which, at the empirical level, appear accidental and unharmonious, the task consists in ordering the events according to the given historian's didactic or political purpose. This treatment of history, which is intended to achieve a specific purpose, is called "pragmatic," in the sense which ancient writers gave the term. For instance, Polybius says that his historical books are "pragmatic" as his purpose is to concentrate on the technique of warfare. Similarly, Tacitus is pragmatic because his purpose in portraying the gradual decline of Rome is to illustrate the effects of immorality and despotism.

Modern historians are inclined to look upon the pragmatic spirit as the supreme expression of their science and call one another "pragmatic" as though this were the greatest compliment they could bestow. But no sensible person will put the two ancient historians in the first rank for the very reason that they are too subjective. German pragmatic historians can as a rule be characterized by the words Goethe's Faust addresses to Wagner: "What you call the spirit of the age is nothing but the spirit of these gentlemen, in which past times are reflected." In Greece the noblest, maturest minds, richest in experience, wrote history in eternal characters. Herodotus has a truly Homeric brain. In Thucydides the whole culture of the age of Pericles is concentrated in one godlike vision. In Germany, where science is to an ever greater extent confused with busywork, the feeblest brains take up history. What a repulsive sight when great events and figures are portrayed by some shortsighted obtuse writer, especially when he exerts himself to be intelligent and believes he is when he evaluates the greatness of a people or an age on the basis of some pet idea, such as the importance of trade, the beneficial or harmful effects of some invention, etc.—in short, when he measures everything great and noble by the most commonplace standards. Or he may imagine that he is a pragmatic historian when he tries to assert his personality by moralizing or by the lavish use of empty rhetorical phrases like "mankind's steady progress" and "what splendid things *we* have at length achieved!"

Among sacred things nothing is more sacred than history—it is a great mirror of the world spirit, an eternal poem of the divine mind. Nothing should be protected more carefully from the touch of unclean hands.

Pragmatic history, by its very nature, excludes universality and is inevitably confined to a limited object. If the purpose is to instruct, a correct and empirically justified ordering of the events is required. This serves to enlighten the understanding but does not satisfy the reason unless something else is added. Even Kant's *Idea of a Universal History in a Cosmopolitan Sense* aims merely at a rational ordering of the events, which are accounted for in terms of nature's universal necessity; war is supposed to produce peace, in the end even perpetual peace, and after many vicissitudes a world order based on law will finally be realized. But this design of nature is itself only the empirical reflection of true necessity; the real aim of Kant's history is not to formulate it from a "cosmopolitan" point of view but from that of the ordinary citizen, to picture it as the progress of mankind toward peaceful intercourse, industry, and trade, and accordingly to represent these as the most precious fruits of human life and human aspiration.

Clearly, the mere ordering of events according to empirical necessity can never be anything but pragmatic. But history in the highest sense must be freed from every subjective purpose; nor can the empirical standpoint be the highest one.

True history rests on a synthesis of the given and actual with the ideal, but this synthesis is not arrived at through philosophy, for the latter transcends the actual and is wholly ideal, whereas history is wholly actual— though it should at the same time be ideal. This union of actual and ideal, however, is possible only in art, which does not exclude the actual but presents real events and histories (as the stage does) in complete form and unity so that they express the highest Ideas. Thus it is by art that history, a science of the actual, is lifted above the actual to the higher realm of the ideal. Accordingly, the third and absolute standpoint is that of historical art. We must now show the relation of this standpoint to those formulated earlier.

Needless to say, the historian must not for the sake of his art change the content of history whose supreme law is the truth. Nor should the higher type of history fail to show how events are actually interrelated. Rather, it should be like a drama where every action is motivated by what precedes it, and in the end everything follows logically from the original synthesis. The sequence of events, however, must be conceived not empirically but in terms of a higher order of things. History does not satisfy reason until the empirical causes that satisfy the understanding have served to disclose the workings of a higher necessity. Treated in this way, history cannot fail to strike us as the greatest and most marvelous drama, which only an infinite mind could have composed.

We have made history the equal of art. But what art represents is always an identity between necessity and freedom; this identity, especially in tragedy, is the proper object of our admiration. The same identity, however, also defines the philosophical and even the religious view of history, for history recognizes in Providence nothing but the wisdom which in the design of the world unites human freedom with universal necessity, and vice versa. But neither the philosophical nor the religious standpoint is truly historical; accordingly history must represent the identity of freedom and necessity from the standpoint of actuality from which it must never depart. But from this point of view the idenity is blind and wholly objective—it is fate. I do not imply that the historian should invoke fate; but its presence should be made apparent by the objectivity of his presentation, of its own accord, as it were, without his aid. In Herodotus, destiny and nemesis are present as invisible but omniscient gods; in the superior, utterly different style of Thucydides, who by introducing speeches conveys dramatic power, this higher unity is fully expressed in the form.

As for the method of studying history, the following may suffice: the student must look upon history as a kind of epic poem which has no definite beginning and no definite end. He should choose the point that strikes him as the most significant or the most interesting, and starting from it construct and develop the whole in every direction.

So-called universal histories—at least those which have appeared to date—are to be avoided, for they teach nothing. A truly universal history would have to be written in the epic style, i.e., in the spirit Herodotus initiated. What we get today are merely digests in which everything individual and significant is blurred. Even students who are not choosing history as their special field should as far as possible go to the sources and to scholarly monographs—the latter are far more instructive than synthetic histories. Let them learn to love the naive simplicity of the chroniclers, who do not indulge in pretentious descriptions or attempt to provide psychological motivations for events.

However, the student who wants to become a practicing artist of history should keep solely to the great models of the ancients, such as were never again attained after the general decline of public life. Apart from Gibbon, whose work is valuable for its broad conception and for his portrayal of the great turning point of the modern times (although even he is merely an orator, not a historian), there are none but national historians; of these, posterity will remember only Machiavelli and Johannes Müller.*

The heights which must be climbed by anyone who wishes to record history worthily can be seen from the letters Gibbon wrote as a youth. Literally everything—all the sciences and all the arts, plus rich experience in public affairs—all this goes into the formation of a historian. The earliest models for historical style are the great early epic poems and tragedy. Universal history, whose beginnings, like the sources of the Nile, are undiscoverable, loves epic form and richness, whereas special histories have to be focused on some particular point. Needless to say, for the historian tragedy is the true source of great ideas and noble thinking.

We have said that the object of history is the realization of an objective order of freedom, i.e., the state. There is a science of the state, just as there is a science of nature. The Idea of the state cannot be derived from experience, the less so because this Idea must be modeled on other Ideas—the state should be like a work of art.

Jurisprudence, like all the real sciences, is distinguished from philosophy by the historical elements it includes, but only those of its historical elements that express Ideas are truly scientific. Consequently, it should include nothing finite by its nature—for instance, laws dealing merely with the external organization of the state. Now, what is taught in our day as jurisprudence consists almost solely of just such laws, which retain only vestiges of the spirit of public life.

Knowledge of such laws is useful in court trials and in connection with other public affairs. These laws must be treated from an empirical, not a philosophical, point of view; to do the latter would be to desecrate philosophy, which has no part in them. A scientific construction of the state, especially with respect to its inner life, can find no corresponding historical reality in the modern era, save in the sense that even the exact opposite of a thing provides some clues to the nature of that thing. Private life (and with it private law) has become divorced from public life; thus separated, it is no more absolute in character than the existence of individual bodies in nature or their particular relations to one another. Because the public or community spirit withdrew from private life, the latter is left behind without any vitality, as the merely finite aspect of the state, and the Ideas are no longer relevant to the empirical laws governing it. The most that can be done is to apply a mechanical kind of sagacity in bringing forward the empirical grounds of the law in individual cases or in deciding doubtful ones.

The only thing in this science which might be susceptible to a universal-historical approach is the form of public life (including its particular determinations) as it emerges from a comparison between the modern world and the ancient and as it is universally necessary.

The harmony between necessity and freedom expressed in an external objective unity in turn assumes two forms, one real and the other ideal. Complete manifestation of the first is the perfect state whose Idea is attained when the particular and the universal are absolutely one, when everything necessary is at the same time free, and everything free necessary. After the external public life that expressed the objective harmony between necessity and freedom vanished, it was inevitably replaced with a subjective ideal unity, which is the Church. The state as opposed to the Church is the nature aspect of the whole in which the two are one. The state necessarily repressed its opposite (the Church) at the phenomenal level because of its absolute character and because it included the Church within itself. Thus the Greek state knew no Church unless the mysteries are to be looked upon as a Church; these, however, were a branch of public life. Since the mysteries have become exoteric, the state has become esoteric; for although the individual lives in the whole, the whole does not live in the individual. In the actual state unity existed in multiplicity and the two were completely integrated; when the two became antagonistic, all other antagonisms in the state came to the surface. The principle of unity inevitably became dominant not in an absolute but in an abstract form—the monarchy which is essentially bound up with the Church. On the other hand, the multiple or the many, in virtue of its opposition with unity, broke apart into separate individuals and ceased to be the organ of the community. In nature the multiple is the embodiment of the infinite in the finite and, as such, is both unity and multiplicity, which are reintegrated in the absolute; similarly, in the perfect state the multiple, precisely because it was organized as a self-contained world in the servile estate, was absolute, the self-contained real aspect of the state, whereas free men dwelt in the pure ether of an ideal life resembling the life of the Ideas. The modern world is in every respect a mixed world, while the ancient world was one of sharp distinctions and limitations. So-called civil freedom has brought about no more than a muddle of freedom and slavery, neither of which exists as absolute or free. The antithesis between unity and multiplicity in the state made mediators necessary; these, however, caught between the rulers and the ruled, developed no absolute world and existed only within the antithesis, never attaining an independent reality inherently and essentially their own.

The first aim of anyone who desires to master the positive science of law and of the state must be to form, with the aid of philosophy and history, a living conception of the modern world and the necessary forms of its public life. It can scarcely be estimated what a source of culture this science could open up were it pursued for its own sake, without concern for its possible uses.

The essential prerequisite for this is the genuine construction of the state deduced from the Ideas, a task which so far has been carried out only in Plato's *Republic*. Although the differences between the modern world and antiquity must be taken into account, this divine work will forever remain the archetype and model. What can be said concerning the true synthesis of the state in the present context has at least been suggested above and cannot be developed at greater length without reference to existing states. For this reason I shall confine myself to pointing out what has so far been intended and accomplished in treatments of so-called natural rights.*

In this part of philosophy the spirit of formalism and analysis has persisted more stubbornly than anywhere else. The original notions were taken either from Roman law or from whatever current forms were available so that natural right has been bound up with every possible instinct of human nature and the whole of psychology, and given a great variety of formulations. Analysis of these led to a number of formal propositions which, it was hoped, would eventually do away with positive jurisprudence.

Those jurists, especially, who diligently turned the Kantian philosophy into a handmaiden of their science kept busily reforming the system of natural rights. This type of philosophizing is characterized by an indiscriminate chasing after terms, the only requirement being that they be novel. He who manages to fasten on such a term distorts the meaning of all other terms to fit his, thereby giving the impression of having produced a new system. Needless to say, this new system lasts only until the next one comes along.

The first attempt to construct the state as a real organization was Fichte's *Foundations of Natural Law*. When the purely negative side of the form of government which aims only at safeguarding rights is isolated, separated from all positive institutions intended to further the vigor, the regular rhythm, and the beauty of public life, one can hardly conclude differently or arrive at a form of the state different from the one Fichte developed. But emphasis on the finite aspects transforms the organic unity of the state into an endless mechanism in which nothing unconditioned can be found. Generally speaking, all attempts so far made may be criticized for their conditional character: the authors try to conceive an organization of the state which would permit the attainment of a specific end. Whether this end is defined as universal happiness, as satisfaction of the social instincts of human nature, or as something purely formal—such as the freest possible coexistence of free beings—makes no difference here, for in all these theories the state is conceived of as a means, as conditioned and dependent. All true construction is by its nature absolute, whatever its particular form. The aim is not to construct the state as such, but an absolute organism in the form of the state. Consequently, to construct it is not to conceive it as the condition of the possibility of something external to it. However, if the state is the immediate and visible image of absolute life, it will of itself fulfill all other ends. In much the same way, nature does not exist in order that there may be equilibrium of matter, but the equilibrium of matter exists because nature exists.

11 On Natural Science

When we speak of nature in the absolute sense, we refer to the world viewed in itself, without its ideal opposite, and in it we again distinguish two aspects: one in which the Ideas are produced in the real mode and one in which they are produced in the ideal mode. Both result from one and the same absolute productivity and in accordance with the same laws, so that in the world in and for itself there is no dichotomy, but perfect unity.

To grasp nature as universal production of the Ideas, we must go back to the origin and significance of the Ideas themselves. Their origin lies in the eternal law of the absolute, i.e., that it is its own object. In virtue of this law, God's productivity is the process by which the universal essence of the whole is embodied in particular forms. Thereby, these forms, though particular, are at the same time self-contained worlds—what philosophers call Monads or Ideas.

Philosophy shows in detail that the particular things can be in God only through the mediation of the Ideas, and that accordingly there are as many worlds as particular things; and yet, by reason of their identical essence, *one* world is in all. Although in God the Ideas are purely and absolutely ideal, they are not dead but living, the first organisms of divine self-contemplation which, therefore, share all the qualities of His essence; and their particular forms notwithstanding, they participate in undivided and absolute reality.

Through this participation the Ideas are, like God, productive and act according to the same laws and in the same way, embodying their essence in particulars and manifesting it in particular individual things; in and for themselves they are not in time, but from the point of view of the individual things they are in time. The Ideas are the souls of things and the things are the bodies of the Ideas; in this sense, the Ideas are necessarily infinite, the things finite. But the infinite and the finite cannot become one until they have achieved internal and essential equality. Consequently, where the finite, *qua* finite, does not contain and express the whole infinite and is not itself the objective aspect of the infinite, the Idea cannot function as its soul, and the essence is not manifested in itself but through something else, namely, an existent. On the other hand, where the finite as such embodies the whole infinite—as is the case in the perfect living organism—the essence manifests itself as soul, as Idea, and reality is reabsorbed in ideality. This takes place in Reason, which is thus at the core of nature and of the process by which the Ideas become objective.

In the eternal cognitive act, the absolute becomes its own object, thus producing the Ideas. Similarly, the Ideas externally manifest themselves in nature. Fertilized by their divine seed, nature endlessly produces individual things in time.

In the light of the foregoing remarks, it should be clear that there are two distinct approaches to the study of nature. First, nature may be looked upon as the instrument of the Ideas or, more generally, as the real aspect of the absolute and, hence, as absolute itself. Second, nature may be studied in itself, apart from the Ideas, in its relativity. The first approach may be called philosophical, the second empirical. The question to be answered now is: Can the empirical approach lead to a *science* of nature in any sense of the term?

Clearly, the empirical view does not go beyond matter, holding it to be something that exists in itself, whereas in the philosophical view matter is something ideal that has been transformed into something real (through the act by which the subject becomes object). The things are symbols of the Ideas; since the Ideas as such are forms of absolute knowledge, they are manifested in things as forms of objective existence. Similarly, plastic art kills, so to speak, its Ideas, in order to give them objectivity. Empiricism separates objective existence from its symbolic significance so that the world of things appears to be purely finite—the infinite is utterly negated. Modern physics, however, while conceiving of matter as purely corporeal, at the same time conceives the spirit to be absolutely opposed to it. By thus asserting a fundamental dualism, it is not a self-contained system like the atomism of the ancients (especially that of Epicurus). The ancient system is superior because, by annihilating nature itself, it frees the soul from longing and fear. The modern system adopts the notions of dogmatic philosophy and thus helps to perpetuate the dualism out of which it arose.

The system of thought initiated by Descartes marked an essential change in man's attitude to nature. Its conceptions of matter and nature are not higher than those of the atomic theory, and its proponents lack the courage to develop these conceptions into a comprehensive whole; they look upon nature as a sealed book, a secret which by accident or good luck can be partially explored but never comprehended as a whole. But science, by definition, aims at unity, and the idea of the whole is prior, not posterior, to its parts. Clearly, the dualistic theory can never arrive at a true science of nature.

The purely finite conception, by its very nature, excludes any organic view and replaces it with the mechanistic view; similarly, it replaces philosophical construction with explanation. From observed effects, causes are inferred; but even if this kind of inference were admissible, if no phenomena were traceable to an absolute principle, even then it would not be certain that the causes so inferred really account for the effects. For these might result from some other causes. Only if the causes were known in themselves and the effects inferred from them, could the connection between the two have the character of necessity and self-evidence. Not to mention the fact that once you have imagined a cause for the express purpose of inferring a certain effect, the latter will indeed follow from the former.

The inner core of all things, the source of all their living manifestations, is the unity of the real and the ideal, which is in itself absolute repose and which is determined to action only by differentiation from without. Since the ground of all activity in nature is one, omnipresent, conditioned by nothing outside it, and absolute with respect to each thing, the different activities can be distinguished from one another only with respect to form; but no form can be derived from another, for each is in its own way the same as the other. Not the dependence of one phenomenon upon another, but the fact that all flow from a common source constitutes the unity of nature.

Even the hypothesis that everything in nature is mediated by a pre-established harmony and that no one thing changes or affects another save through the medium of the universal substance—even this has been understood in a mechanical sense and transformed into the absurd idea of "action at a distance" (in the sense the term is used by Newton and his successors).

Because matter was conceived of as devoid of an inherent life principle and because of a reluctance to invoke the action of mind on matter as an explanation for the highest phenomena—voluntary motion, etc.—it was assumed that there existed something outside matter, a quasi-matter stripped of the most important attributes of matter (gravity, etc.), an assumption close to the negative concept of mind as immaterial substance —as though the antithesis between the two could be circumvented or at least weakened in this way. If such a thing as an imponderable, weightless, unlimited matter were conceivable, everything in matter would, according to this theory, still be determined by outside action: death would be the principle, and life would be derived from it.

Even if someone succeeded in accounting for all phenomena in mechanistic terms, he would still be in the position of a man who in order to explain Homer or any other author first explains the forms of the written characters, then proceeds to show how they were put together and printed, and finally how the work in question resulted from these processes. Something rather like this actually goes on, particularly in what has been called mathematical constructions in natural science. We have already observed that the mathematical forms in such constructions are used in a purely mechanical way. These forms are not the essential grounds of the phenomena themselves; on the contrary, these grounds are rather sought in something entirely foreign and empirical; for instance, the motions of the celestial bodies are accounted for as the result of a push to one side. It is true that applied mathematics has taught us to determine with precision the distances between planets, the time of their revolutions and their periodic reappearances, but it fails to give us the slightest insight into the essential nature of these motions. The so-called mathematical science of nature has so far been an empty formalism with no trace in it of a true science of nature.

The usual opposition between theory and experience is unacceptable, if only because the concept of theory implies a reference to particular existence and, hence, to experience. Absolute science is not theory, which is itself a mixture of the particular and the universal, such as characterizes ordinary knowledge. Theory differs from experience only in this, that it expresses experience more abstractly, apart from accidental conditions, and in its original form. But to isolate this form, to show in every phenomenon the action of nature, is also the purpose of experimentation; hence, both are equal in importance. Thus there is no reason for regarding the experimental investigation of nature as superior to theory, for only theory guides it; without theory it would not be possible to "put nature to the question" (as experimentation has been described), since nature will give clear answers only to judicious questions. Theory and experiment have this in common, that their starting point is always a specific object, not a universal and absolute insight. Taken in their proper meaning, both can be distinguished from false theorizing, which invents causes ad hoc to account for natural phenomena; for both confine themselves to defining and describing the phenomena themselves and in this respect are like construction, which is not concerned with explanations either. If scientists were clear about their nature, they would use theory and experiment only to reach the center, moving toward it from the periphery, whereas construction proceeds from the center to the periphery. But in either direction the way is endless, and since possession of the center is the first condition of science, the experimental method cannot possibly arrive at science.

Every science must have an exoteric aspect to exist objectively; such an aspect is also present in the science of nature, i.e., in the part of philosophy which constructs nature. This aspect can be found only in experiment and its necessary correlate, theory (in the sense already indicated). But construction is not to be mistaken for the science itself—it is only the real side of science. Here, what is simultaneous in the Idea appears in time and space. Empiricism will not be incorporated in the science of nature until it pursues in its own way the goal of science, i.e., empirical construction; it will not be taught and practiced in accordance with the spirit of the whole until it drops explanations and hypotheses, and aims at a purely objective presentation of the phenomena. It must never seek to express an Idea on any other basis. The misguided attempts of an indigent empiricism to scan the universe or to convert its adversaries to its own views and even to refute self-evident or demonstrable truths—attempts to construct systems on the basis of experiments isolated from a whole it cannot encompass—such attempts to oppose the true science of nature are, to use a well-known simile, like trying to stem a break through of the ocean with a wisp of straw.

The empirical theory of nature, if it is to adopt a systematic procedure directed toward a definite goal instead of wandering aimlessly, must be subordinated to the absolute science of nature, grounded in Ideas. The history of science shows that a construction of phenomena by means of experimentation (in the sense postulated above) has been achieved only in isolated cases, as though by instinct; if this method of exploring nature is to become universally valid, it must take as its model the kind of construction that characterizes an absolute science. What I mean by an absolute science I have already dealt with at sufficient length.

The science of nature, like any science, goes beyond individual phenomena and investigates their common source, the Idea, in which they are one. Even empiricism, no matter how unclearly, views nature as a whole, every individual element in it determining and being determined by all the others. It is of small value to know an individual part if we do not know the whole. But it is precisely the identity of the particular and the universal that is the object of philosophical knowledge, or, to be more precise, philosophy is knowledge of this identity.

The primary purpose of philosophy is to show that all things originate in God or the absolute. Insofar as nature is the real aspect of the eternal act by which the subject becomes its own object, the philosophy of nature is the real aspect of philosophy as a whole.

The principle of philosophy is absolutely ideal, i.e., the subject as such. But the subject would remain forever unknowable, wrapped in itself, were it not for the act by which it becomes objective; finite, visible nature is the symbol of this transformation. Philosophy as a whole is absolute idealism because that act is contained in divine knowledge, but the philosophy of nature is not the opposite of absolute idealism. It is the opposite of relative idealism, which takes in only the ideal aspect of the absolute. The essence of the absolute, by being embodied in the particular and becoming identical with it, produces in God the Ideas. As distinct, independent entities, they are real; insofar as they are in the absolute, they are ideal—their ideality and reality being two aspects of what is essentially one and the same. According to this view, nature is one, not only in its essence, where it is the total absolute act by which the subject becomes object, but also at the phenomenal level where it represents the relative-ideal or objective aspect of that act. Nature is thus inherently one; there is one life in all things, all equally endowed with existence by the Ideas. Nothing in nature is purely material; everywhere soul is symbolically transformed into body, though one or the other may be preponderant at the phenomenal level. For the same reason the science of nature is one, and the parts into which it is divided by the understanding are branches of one absolute knowledge.

Philosophical construction is representation of the real in the ideal, of the particular in the universal or Idea. Every particular thing as such is form; but the eternal and absolute form is the source and origin of all forms. The act by which the subject becomes object pervades all things and is reproduced in the particular forms, which, being merely different modes of manifestation of the universal and absolute, are themselves absolute within the absolute form.

Since, further, the inner pattern of all things, by reason of their common source, must be one—and this can be grasped with logical necessity—the construction which is founded on this unity has the same character of necessity. Consequently, it does not need the confirmation of experience; * it is self-sufficient and can be carried on where experience runs into insurmountable obstacles—for instance, it can penetrate the hidden springs of organic life and of universal motion.

Not only in relation to action is there such a thing as fate; knowledge too is confronted with unconditional necessity, namely, the essence of the universe and nature. An ancient writer said that a brave man's struggle against fate is a spectacle in which even the gods take pleasure; the mind's arduous efforts to gain insight into primordial nature and the eternal inner essence of its phenomena is no less sublime a spectacle. In tragedy the conflict is truly resolved neither by the defeat of fate nor by the defeat of freedom, but only when the one rises to perfect equality with the other. Similarly, mind is reconciled with nature only when nature has become for it perfectly identical with itself, when it has been transfigured into the ideal.

The unquenchable thirst for knowledge no doubt creates conflict—conflict such as the poet [Goethe], in the most German of all poems,* has utilized as vehicle of his own invention to open up an eternally fresh spring of inspiration, sufficient of itself to rejuvenate the science of the day, to breathe new and fragrant life into it. Let all who would penetrate the temple of nature drink in this music of a higher sphere, absorb while young the strength that emanates from this poem, whose dazzling radiance lights up the very heart of the world.

12 On the Study of Physics and Chemistry

The various phenomena and forms known by experience necessarily presuppose that of which they are manifestations, i.e., matter or substance. Empiricism knows the latter only as bodies, that is, matter with variable forms, and conceives of even primal matter—when it refers to it at all—merely as an indefinable aggregate of corpuscles of unchangeable form, which for this reason are called atoms. In other words, empiricism has no knowledge of the original sources from which everything in nature comes and into which everything returns.

To penetrate to the essence of matter, we must abstract from its particular forms (for instance, so-called organic or inorganic matter) for matter in itself is only the common seed of these forms. Taken in the absolute sense, it is the objective or real aspect of the eternal act by which the absolute becomes its own object. To discover this essence of matter and to show how the particular things and phenomena are produced by it are exclusively philosophical tasks.

The first of these tasks has been sufficiently dealt with

in the preceding lectures; I shall now confine myself to the second. Every Idea is inherently *one,* and the one Idea can produce an infinite number of things of the same kind—its infinite potentiality is not exhausted by any actuality. Since the absolute is indivisible, the particularity of each Idea cannot consist in a negation of other Ideas, but only in this, that all are embodied in each in a manner compatible with its particular form. This order in the world of Ideas must be our model for the cognition of the visible world. In this world, too, the primary forms will be unities that contain all other forms as particulars and produce them; for this reason, they themselves appear as universals. The way in which they become extensional and fill space must be deduced from the way in which the one is eternally embodied in the many. In the Ideas, as has been shown, the one is identical with the many, but at the phenomenal level they are distinguishable and distinct. The primary universal pattern of spatial extension is necessary because the sensible unities flow from a common central point at the phenomenal level, just as the Ideas flow from the absolute as their center. In other words, since each Idea is itself productive and can be a center, the particular things are produced from common central points and, like their archetypes, are in some respects dependent and in others independent.

Next to the construction of matter, the cosmos and its laws are the first and noblest object of physical knowledge. As is well known, after Kepler's divine genius formulated these laws, the mathematical theory of nature has attempted to construct them on entirely empirical foundations. Now, we can accept as a general rule that whatever in an alleged construction is not pure universal form can have neither scientific value nor truth.

Mathematical theory deduces the centrifugal motion of the celestial bodies not from a universal form, but from an empirical fact. From the point of view of reason, which conceives all things in terms of the absolute, the Newtonian force of attraction is meaningless; though it may be a necessary assumption from the reflective point of view, this force cannot serve in philosophical construction. It is possible to understand Kepler's laws without any empirical aids, on the basis of the doctrine of the Ideas and the two unities which in themselves are one unity and in virtue of which every being, though it is absolute in itself, is at the same time in the absolute, and vice versa.

Physical astronomy, the science of the particular qualities of the celestial bodies and their relations to one another, is entirely based upon broader conceptions and, particularly in respect to the planetary system, upon the correspondence which exists between this system and the products of the earth.

The celestial body resembles the Idea of which it is a copy; like the Idea it is productive and brings forth all the forms of the universe. Matter, the body of the universe at the phenomenal level, is itself differentiated into soul and body. The body of matter is made up of individual bodies; in it unity is wholly lost in multiplicity and extension, and for this reason the individual material bodies appear as inorganic.

The inorganic forms are the objects of a separate branch of knowledge, which is purely descriptive and correctly refrains from any reference to internal qualities. Now that the specific differences of matter have been reduced to quantitative differences—so that it has become possible to view matter as the metamorphosis of one and the same substance, a process of mere changes of form—the way is paved for an historical construction of the system of material bodies. Henrik Steffens * has made a decisive beginning along these lines.

Geology should do the same thing for the earth as a whole. It must not exclude any of the earth's products; it should demonstrate the genesis of all in their historical continuity and interrelations. The real aspect of any science can only be historical (because, apart from science, only history aims directly at truth), and geology, when it has been fully developed, will be the history of nature, the earth merely its starting point. As such it would be the truly integrated and objective science of nature—experimental physics can be no more than a means to this end.

Just as physical things are the body of matter, so light is its soul, its ideal aspect. In being thus related to matter, it becomes finite itself and, subsumed under extension, manifests itself as an ideal element which delineates space without filling it. In other words, it is the ideal element at the phenomenal level, but not the *whole* ideal aspect of the act by which the subject becomes object (since part of it remains in the material element); it is only relatively ideal.*

Knowledge of light is like knowledge of matter; indeed, it is one with it, for each can be truly grasped only as the opposite of the other, as the subjective and the objective aspect of one and the same reality. Since the spirit of nature, i.e., light, withdrew from physics, life in all the divisions of this science has been extinguished, because it can no longer make the transition to organic nature. Newtonian optics shows clearly how a whole structure of false conclusions can be built up on an experimental foundation. The truth is that the purpose of experiments and the sequence in which they are carried out are determined by a previously existing theory. The experimenter discovers the natural order only in rare cases, when he happens to hit on it instinctively or is guided by a construction. And yet experimentation, which may disclose details but can never give a complete view, is still looked upon as the infallible principle of our knowledge of nature.

The earth is a seed that only light can bring to germination. For only after matter has been particularized and become form, is the universal essence of light disclosed.

The universal form in which bodies are particularized is that which makes them internally cohesive, identical with themselves. In it, unity is embodied in difference, and all specific differences of matter can be understood on the basis of their relations to this universal form. All things, as they emerge from identity, strive to return to unity; this striving is their ideal aspect, that which makes them appear animated.

The noblest goal of physics, even in the ordinary narrow sense, as divorced from organic nature, is to formulate an all-inclusive view of the living manifestations of bodies. These manifestations of the activity inherent in bodies have been called "dynamic" and the sum total of their various forms, "the dynamic process."

These forms are necessarily parts of a cycle and follow a common pattern. Only by determining this pattern can we be sure that no important link has been omitted and that we have not ascribed manifestations of a single principle to different causes. Ordinary experimental physics is in the greatest uncertainty on this score; it assumes a new principle to account for every newly discovered phenomenon and is at a loss to say which is derived from which.

Evaluated by the standard previously defined, the current theories and the way these phenomena are accounted for are found wanting; nowhere in them is any form conceived of as universal and necessary, but only as contingent. There is no logical need to assume the existence of certain imponderable fluids to account for magnetic and electrical phenomena; the fact that these fluids are so constituted that their homogeneous elements repel each other and their heterogeneous elements attract each other is wholly accidental from the logical point of view. If we imagine that the world is made up of such hypothetical elements, we get the following picture. In the pores of the coarser kinds of matter there is air; in the pores of the air there is phlogiston; in the pores of the latter, the electric fluid, which in turn contains in its pores the magnetic fluid, which in turn contains ether. At the same time, these different fluids, contained one within another, do not disturb one another, and each manifests itself in its own way at the physicist's pleasure and never fails to go back to its own place, never getting lost. Clearly, this explanation, apart from its having no scientific value, cannot even be visualized.

The Kantian construction of matter first led to a higher view directed against the materialistic approach, but all its positive elements remained at too low a level. The forces of attraction and repulsion, as Kant defined them, are merely formal factors deduced analytically from the concepts of the understanding; they give no idea of the life and essence of matter. Moreover, it is impossible, on the basis of relations between these forces which Kant conceived in quantitative terms, to account for the qualitative differences in matter. The followers of Kant, and the physicists who attempted to apply his theories, retained only the negative elements of the dynamic conception. Similarly, they thought they had formulated a higher theory of light when they described it as nonmaterial. This theory, by the way, is compatible with other mechanical hypotheses—Euler's, for example.

The error underlying all these views is the conception of matter as purely real. The subjective-objective character of all things, and especially of matter, had to be established scientifically before the phenomena which express its inner life could be understood.

The ground of the living manifestations of matter has been stated earlier: every individual thing exists in the universal soul and when separated from the One, strives to return to it. The particular forms of activity are not accidental but the original, inborn, necessary forms of matter. Just as the unity of the Idea unfolds into three dimensions at the level of existence, so life and activity, following the same pattern, are expressed in three forms which, like the three dimensions, are inherent in the essence of matter. By means of this construction we have not only established with certainty that the living manifestations of matter have only these three forms, we have also discovered the universal law that governs all their special determinations and shows them to be necessary.*

Here I shall confine myself to the chemical process, because the science of its phenomena has developed into a separate branch of the study of nature. In recent times, physics has become almost entirely subordinated to chemistry. The key to the explanation of natural phenomena, even the higher forms, such as magnetism, electricity, etc., is supposed to be found in chemistry; and the more all explanation of nature has been reduced to chemistry, the more difficult chemists have found it to account for chemical phenomena. From the period of its youth, when perception of the inner unity of all things came more naturally to the human mind, chemistry has inherited a number of figurative terms, such as affinity, for example, which, far from guiding this science toward an Idea, have provided a sanctuary for ignorance. What can be determined by weighing things has gradually come to be regarded as the supreme principle and extreme limit of knowledge. The "inborn spirits" that held sway in nature and produced the indestructible qualities have themselves become bits of matter which can be caught and imprisoned in test tubes and retorts.

I do not deny that modern chemistry has enriched us with many facts, although it is regrettable that the new world was not opened up to us from the outset by a superior insight. It is ridiculous to imagine that a theory has been established by stringing facts together, linked only by meaningless terms, such as matter, attraction, etc., at a time when such concepts as quality, chemical synthesis, analysis, etc., had not begun to be grasped.

It may be advantageous to separate chemistry from physics, but then chemistry must be looked upon as a merely experimental art with no pretension to science. The construction of chemical phenomena is not the task of a special science, but of the science of nature as a whole, which does not treat these phenomena as subject to laws of their own outside the context of the whole, but as particular manifestations of the universal life of nature.

The universal dynamic process, insofar as it affects the earth as a whole and the cosmic system, is the object of meteorology in the broadest sense, which is part of physical astronomy, for the variations of the earth as a whole can be fully understood only if they are related to the cosmic system.

As for mechanics, which has largely become a part of physics, it belongs to applied mathematics, but its fundamental forms, which are the forms of the dynamic process expressed as purely objective, as though lifeless, are taken from physics.

Physics in the usual sense of an independent discipline is confined to the sphere of the general opposition between light and matter or gravity. The absolute science of nature deals both with the physical phenomena in the above sense and the higher phenomena of the organic world in whose products the entire process by which the subject becomes object is manifested simultaneously in its two aspects.

13 On the Study of Medicine and the Theory of Organic Nature

According to the most ancient view, the organism is a microcosm in which the whole of nature is reflected. Similarly, the science of organism is the focal point in which all rays of our knowledge of nature are brought together. In nearly all periods, knowledge of physics has been looked upon as a necessary preliminary before one entered the temple of organic life. But the theory of organic nature could not take as its scientific model a physics which, lacking a universal conception of nature, could only clutter up and deform the theory with its own hypotheses—as has happened often enough since the artificial barriers that separated universal from organic nature had more or less broken down.

The modern rage for chemistry made it, among other things, the cognitive ground of organic phenomena and reduced life to a chemical process. Theorists who account for the formation of living matter by elective attraction or crystallization and for organic motion (including so-called sensory activity) by changes in chemical composition enjoy great vogue, but so far no one has told us what chemical affinity and composition *are*, a question which I suppose these theorists think they can answer.

This question cannot be answered by merely extending and applying one part of natural science to another. Each part is absolute in itself, no part can be derived from another, and all can become truly one only when the absolute laws governing them have been recognized and the particular has been derived from the universal.

For some time it has been recognized that medicine, more than any other discipline dealing with natural phenomena, should become the comprehensive science of organic nature, so that the parts now separated from it would be merely branches of it, and that in order to achieve that status, its fundamental principles must not be empirical or hypothetical but self-evident and philosophical. However, here as elsewhere, philosophy should for the time being be concerned solely with bringing external formal unity into the existing diversity and with restoring to physicians a good name long denied them by poets and philosophers. If the only merits of Brown's theory * were its freedom from empirical explanations and hypotheses, its recognition and thorough application of the great principle of purely quantitative difference, and its consistent adherence to a single basic principle and the scientific method, its originator would still be unique in the history of medicine, the creator of a new world in this field of knowledge. To be sure, he stops at the concept of excitability and has no scientific insight into it, but at the same time he rejects all empirical explanations and warns against unphilosophical searching into causes. Doubtless he did not thereby deny the existence of a higher sphere of knowledge in which excitability could be deduced from a higher concept, just as he derived forms of disease from excitability.

The concept of excitability is merely reflective; it applies to individual organic things but not to the essence of the organism. The absolutely ideal, which is fully manifested in the organism both objectively and subjectively—as body and soul—is in itself outside all determination. The individual organic body, however, is determinable and necessarily determined from the outside. Now, since the absolutely ideal safeguards the unity of form and essence in the organism—for it is in virtue of this unity that the organism symbolizes the absolutely ideal—every outside determination which disturbs this unity induces the organism to act in order to restore the unity. Consequently, the individual organism is only indirectly determined—that is, by changes in the external conditions of life, never in itself.

The organism is the expression of the entire act by which the subject becomes object, because in it matter (which at a lower stage was opposed to light and manifested itself as substance) combines with light (thus combined, the two can only be *attributes* of one substance) to become a mere accident or unessential characteristic of the organism and, hence, pure form. In the eternal transformation of subjectivity into objectivity, objectivity or matter can be only an accident, the opposite of which is subjectivity as the essence or substance. Substance, however, loses its absolute character in this opposition and manifests itself as the relatively ideal (i.e., as light). Hence, it is the *organism* that shows substance and accident in perfect unity, integrated, as they are in the absolute act by which the subject becomes object.

This basic transformation of matter into form gives us insight not only into the essence of organism but also into its individual functions. They must fall into the same patterns as the universal one of living motions, with the difference that in the organism the forms, as noted before, are completely integrated with matter. If we review all the empirical attempts to account for these functions and their specific determinations, nowhere do we find so much as a hint that they are universal, necessary forms. Once again the assumption of imponderable fluids, dependent on similarly assumed affinities, compositions, and decompositions in the constitution of the organism, is the dreary last refuge of ignorance. Such assumptions fail to account for any organic movement —for muscular contractions, for example—they fail to make it intelligible even in mechanical terms. It is true that an analogy between these phenomena and those of electricity was noticed at a very early date, but since the latter were known only as particular, not general, forms, and there was no idea of potencies or levels in nature, the organic phenomena, instead of being placed on the same plane as the phenomena of electricity (let alone a higher one), were deduced from electricity as mere effects of it. Even though electricity was recognized as a principle of activity, this required additional hypotheses to account for the peculiar pattern of contractions.

At the level of inorganic nature, magnetism, electricity, and the chemical process appear in the guise of accidents or modifications of matter (as their substratum or substance). At the organic level these reappear in a higher guise—as forms identical with the essence of matter.

The concept of a physical body includes only the body itself; the infinite potentiality of all other things exists outside them as light. The concept of organism directly involves other things; here light is present in varying

degrees in the thing itself, and matter, which was previously posited as substance, now becomes accident.

The following levels of organic life may be distinguished: (1) The ideal principle [light] is bound to
matter only for the first dimension; here matter is per-
meated with form and at one with it only *qua* the dimension of being-in-itself; the organism contains the
infinite potentiality only of its own self, as individual or
species. (2) The ideal principle is bound to gravity, so
that matter is posited as accident for the second dimension, too, which is that of being-in-other-things; then
the organism contains the infinite potentiality of other
things outside it. The first level is that of the reproduc-
tive function; here potentiality and actuality are confined to the individual, and thereby both are one. The
second level is that of independent motion: the individual passes beyond itself to other things; here potentiality and actuality cannot coincide because the other
things are posited expressly as other, as being outside the
individual. (3) When the two preceding levels are combined in a higher one and the infinite potentiality of
other things is nevertheless actuality within the individual, the highest function of the organism is posited.
Matter has now become wholly accident of the essence—
of the ideal principle—which is productive in itself, but
here, bound up with the finite organism, is productive
at the sensory level only, as sense perception.*

Next to insight into the organic functions and the universality and necessity of their forms, of basic importance
is insight into the laws which rule the interrelations
among the functions and forms in the individual organism and in the organic world as a whole.

The individual is confined within certain limits which
cannot be transgressed without making its existence im-

possible; hence, he is subject to disease. The construction of this condition is a necessary part of the general theory of organic nature and inseparable from what is called physiology. In the most general terms, it may be deduced entirely from the opposition between potentiality and reality in the organism and from the disturbance of their balance. But the special forms and manifestations of disease can be recognized only by changes in the three basic organic functions. We may distinguish two aspects in the organism—the "natural" and the "divine." Insofar as the organism expresses a quantitative balance of vital functions, it stands in a certain relation to nature and external things. Insofar as the organism is a more or less complete image of the universe, it is an expression of the absolute. Brown was concerned only with the natural aspect, which is the one that matters in medicine. He did not explicitly deny the importance of the other aspect in the physician's task of determining the principal cause of the morbid imbalance nor in the task of selecting the proper treatment. The "specific" effects of the remedies and the nature of the symptoms cannot be fully understood unless this other aspect is taken into account.

I would merely be repeating what worthy men have said if I were to show that the science of medicine in this sense presupposes a general philosophical culture and must itself be based on philosophical principles. If additional arguments were needed to convince experts of this truth, we might mention the following: (1) Experimentation, the only possible basis for empirical construction, is impossible in medicine; (2) medical experience, by its very nature, is uncertain; whether a theory based on such experience is true or false can never be ascertained, for it is always possible that it has been wrongly applied in a given case; and (3) in this branch of knowledge, more than in any other, experience has no meaning unless it is related to a theory. Thus, Brown's theory of excitability made all previous experience appear in an entirely new light. One might also mention in this context the physicians who, without any scientific knowledge of first principles, merely drifting with the current of the times, teach the new theory in books and lectures although they are incapable of understanding it. They make themselves ridiculous even to their pupils by trying to combine this theory with teachings that are incompatible with it; they treat scientific matters as if they were historical matters and in lieu of proof give us stories. One is reminded of what Galen said of the majority of physicians in his day: "They are untrained and uncultured, and yet arrogant and quick to furnish proofs, although they do not know what proof is; why should we bother with such unreasonable creatures and waste time over their nonsense?"

The laws that govern the metamorphoses of disease also govern the universal transformations that nature effects in producing the different species. For in the species, too, we have a single fundamental pattern repeated with continual quantitative variations, and clearly medicine will not be integrated in the universal organic theory of nature until it construes the species of disease —which are, so to speak, "ideal organisms"—as unmistakably as natural history construes the species of real organisms. Then the correspondence between the two will be apparent.

What can guide the historical construction of organism, which retraces the meanderings of the creative mind, if not their external forms? In virtue of the eternal law by which the subject becomes object, all nature is the outward visible sign of its inner essence and undergoes the same regular and necessary transformations.

The history of organically creative nature is thus recorded in the visible forms of living structures from plants to the summit of the animal kingdom. The branch of knowledge dealing with these forms has been called, somewhat narrowly, comparative anatomy. It is doubtless true that in this kind of knowledge comparison is the leading principle—this does not mean comparison with empirical models, least of all with the human structure, which, because it marks the terminal point in the series, stands at the limit of the organic world. Formerly, the human body was the sole object of anatomy because that science was primarily intended to serve medicine. However, this was no advantage to anatomy. The human organism is so complex that the science of anatomy could not have attained even its present development without resorting to comparisons between the human and other structures. The fact that it was taken as the starting point distorted our perspective and made it harder to arrive at basic universal insights. The resulting impossibility of accounting for such a complicated structure led to separation between anatomy and physiology—which should be treated as two correlative disciplines, one dealing with the internal and the other with the external aspects of the organism—and to the mechanical method of exposition which is followed by most textbooks and lecture courses.

An anatomist who aspires to be a student of nature and to treat anatomy in the spirit of the whole must first of all recognize that he cannot arrive even at a historical view of the real forms unless he rises above ordinary conceptions. He must grasp the symbolic nature of forms and see that the individual always expresses a universal form, as the external form always expresses an inner pattern. He need not ask what is the use of this or that organ, but rather, how it did originate, and then show the laws governing its formation. The more general the view from which derives the genesis of forms and the less closely modeled on particular cases, the sooner will he grasp the extraordinary simplicity of so many natural structures. Above all he should avoid—in the name of admiration for God's wisdom and reason—a public exhibition of his own unwisdom and unreason.

He must constantly be guided by the idea of the unity and inner affinity of all organisms, the fact that they all originate in one archetype whose objective aspect alone changes and whose subjective aspect is unchangeable. Above all he must try to discover the law governing these changes; then he will recognize that, while the archetype always remains the same, that which expresses it can be changeable only in form and, hence, that an equal amount of reality goes into all organisms, but it is variously distributed. When one form is less developed, another is more developed at the expense of the first. Guided by reason and experience, he will draw up a table of the internal and external dimensions embodying the productive impulse. He will thus obtain a visual prototype of all organisms, unchangeable in over-all outline but capable of wide modification in detail.

A truly historical construction of organic nature would give us the real, objective aspect of the universal science of nature, a perfect expression of the science in terms of the Ideas.

14 The Science of Art

The science of art may first of all denote the historical construction of art. In this sense, its material pre-requisite is direct contact with existing works of art. Since this can easily be done in the case of poetry, the science dealing with this art is explicitly included among the subjects of academic study as philology. However, this is not philology as we defined it earlier. Philology in our sense is rarely taught at universities—which should not surprise us, considering it is no less an art than poetry. The true philologist, like the true poet, is born, not made.

Still less can we expect to find historical construction of the fine arts in universities, for they lack the facilities for viewing the works. Even where, as a matter of prestige, lectures on this subject are attempted with the aid of richly endowed libraries, they are necessarily confined to a scholarly treatment of the history of art.

Universities are not art schools. Nor can they teach the science of art with a view to practical or technical application.

There remains, therefore, the purely speculative view,

which is concerned solely with the intellectual conception of art. But this presupposes a philosophical construction of art, concerning which serious doubts arise
both from the philosophical and the artistic points of
view.

Philosophers aim at the truth via intellectual intuition, and what they call truth is accessible only to the
mind's eye, not to the eye of sense. What, then, can they
have to do with art, whose sole purpose is to produce
visible beauty and whose products are either merely
deceptive images of truth or wholly sensual? Most people, indeed, think of art as a delight to the senses, as a
recreation or relaxation for minds tired by more serious
occupations, as an agreeable stimulation superior to
others only by the subtler means it employs. In the eyes
of the philosopher, art shares in the corrupting effects of
civilization, which is a further reason for condemning
it. Indeed, in this sense, art is no worthy concern of the
philosopher.

I speak of art in a more sacred sense—of the art which,
in the words of the ancients, is an instrument of the
gods, herald of divine mysteries, unveiler of the Ideas.
It is that preternatural beauty whose inviolate light
illumines only pure souls, which is as hidden and inaccessible to the sensible eye as pure truth itself. The philosopher is not interested in what the vulgar call art. To
him, art is a direct and necessary expression of the absolute, and only insofar as this can be demonstrated has it
any reality to him.

"But did not the divine Plato himself condemn imi-
tative art in his *Republic*?" someone might say. "Did he
not banish the poets as useless, even harmful, to his
state? Could there be more convincing proof that art and

philosophy are incompatible than this judgment by the king of philosophers?"

To understand Plato's condemnation of poetry, we must confront it with directly opposed statements he made on the same subject. Here, as elsewhere, unless we determine clearly from what standpoint he speaks, we will never be able to grasp his richly nuanced thought—this is true of Plato more than of any other philosopher. To begin with, we must recall that Greek culture was essentially hostile to speculative philosophy and particularly to Plato's, which was incompatible not only with the sensual character of the Greek religion but also with the objective, real forms of the Greek state. Now, the state depicted in Plato's *Republic* is entirely ideal—spiritualized, so to speak. Are not the restrictions he imposes on poetry necessary in the state he depicts? A detailed answer to this question would take us too far afield. The hostile attitude toward philosophy in Greek culture was inevitably reflected in philosophy itself. Plato, in this respect, is neither the earliest nor the only example. From Pythagoras (and even farther back) down to Plato, philosophers felt that they were an exotic growth on Greek soil. The feeling is expressed, for example, in the fact that all those who were initiated into higher doctrines, either by the wisdom of the early philosophers or by the mysteries, instinctively turned to the East, the motherland of the Ideas.

But even granting the existence of this merely historical, not philosophical, antagonism, what is Plato's rejection of the art of poetry—especially when compared with his praise of "enthusiastic" poetry in other works —what is it but a polemic against poetic realism, an anticipation of the spirit and, especially, of the poetry of a later age? Plato's condemnation simply does not apply to

Christian poetry, which as a whole expresses the infinite as unmistakably as ancient poetry expressed the finite. We can define the character of ancient poetry more exactly than Plato could; he was unaware of any antithesis. We can arrive at a more comprehensive view of poetry than he. What according to him justified a condemnation of the poetry of his time, we recognize as a limitation not unrelated to its beauty, because we have had a longer historical experience. The anticipation implicit in Plato's criticism we see fulfilled today. The Christian religion, and with it the longing for spirituality which ancient poetry could not fully gratify or express, has created its own poetry and art. Thereby it has become possible to formulate a complete objective theory of art.

It is clear from the foregoing that the construction of art is a worthy subject for the philosopher and, especially, for the Christian philosopher. One of his tasks is to survey and delineate the world of art.

But passing from the philosophic to the artistic point of view, a question arises: Can the philosopher penetrate the essence of art and convey a true idea of it?

"Who can speak authoritatively of the divine principle which inspires the artist, the spiritual breath which animates his work," it will be asked, "unless it be a man who is himself seized with the divine fire? Is it possible to make an a priori construction of something as unfathomable in its origin, as marvelous in its effects? Can we define and subject to laws something that by its very nature recognizes no law but its own? Is it not just as impossible to imprison genius in a definition as to create it by fiat? Who will venture to go farther, to reach out for what is obviously the freest, the most absolute thing in the whole universe—to try to extend his field of vision beyond its outermost boundaries in order to set new boundaries there?"

Such might be the language of a certain kind of enthusiasm which sees only the effects of art and knows neither what art really is nor the place assigned to philosophy in the universe. For even granting that art cannot be derived from something *superior* to art, the law of the universe knows no exceptions. Everything contained in this world has its archetype or counterpart in another. So absolute is the universal opposition between the real and the ideal that even at the ultimate frontier of the infinite and the finite, where the phenomenal oppositions are resolved in the purest absolute, the same relationship asserts itself, this time at the highest level: the relationship between philosophy and art.

Art, although entirely absolute, although the real and the ideal are perfectly united in it, is to philosophy what the real is to the ideal. In philosophy the opposition between the two is ultimately resolved in pure identity; nonetheless, philosophy is ideal in relation to art. The two meet at the summit, and because both are absolute, each can be the archetype of the other. This is why philosophy enables us to gain the deepest insights into art; indeed, the philosopher can form a clearer idea of the essence of art than the artist himself. Because the ideal is always a higher reflection of the real, what is real in the artist is, in the philosopher, a higher ideal reflection of it. This shows not only that art can become an object of philosophical knowledge, but also that nothing about art can be known absolutely save in and by philosophy.

The same principle is present in the philosopher as a subjective reflection and in the artist as an objective reality; this is why the artist's attitude toward it is not subjective or conscious—not that he cannot become conscious of it, but if he does, he is not conscious of it in his capacity as artist. As an artist he is driven by this principle and, for this very reason, cannot be said to possess it; when he conceives of it ideally, he attains to a higher stage as an artist, but even then his attitude remains objective, and whatever has been subjective in him becomes again objective. The opposite takes place in the philosopher; that is, in him the objective is reabsorbed in the subjective. This is why philosophy, for all its inner identity with art, remains always and necessarily science—i.e., ideal—while art remains always and necessarily art—i.e., real.

If the philosopher remained on the plane of reality, he would never be able to investigate art closely enough to discover its secret source, to penetrate into the very workshop of its creations. Philosophy can do this only by rising to the same height in the realm of the ideal as art does in the realm of the real. The rules of art that genius throws overboard are rules prescribed by a merely mechanical understanding; the artist of genius is autonomous—not in the sense that he is subject to no law, but in the sense that he is subject to no law but his own. He is a genius insofar as he expresses the highest law, and it is precisely this absolute law that philosophy recognizes in him, for philosophy is not only autonomous itself but also seeks to penetrate to the very *principle* of autonomy. This is why true artists in every epoch have been serene, simple, great, and, like nature herself, acting in obedience to inner necessity. The kind of enthusiasm that sees in the artist nothing but genius exempt from all rules—the purely negative aspect of genius—is itself a product of reflective thinking. This is enthusiasm at second hand, not the kind that inspires the artist and is at the same time, in its godlike freedom, the purest and highest necessity.

Now, granting that no one can understand the mystery of art, its absolute element, better than the philosopher, it may be asked whether the philosopher is equally capable of understanding its rational elements, of formulating the laws governing them. I refer to the technical aspect of art: can philosophy lower itself to consider empirical details of execution and the conditions under which the work is made?

Since philosophy is concerned solely with the Ideas, its task with respect to the empirical aspect of art is confined to formulating general laws of the phenomena, and these only to the extent that they express ideal forms. The forms of art are the forms of the things-in-themselves as they are in the archetypes. Consequently, the philosophy of art deals with these forms only insofar as they are universal and can be grasped in and for themselves, not insofar as they pertain to rules of execution or practice. What deals directly with the particular or with empirical means designed to achieve a given end is not philosophy but merely theory; philosophy is unconditioned, an end in itself. The objection might be raised that because the technical aspect of art includes the means by which an illusion of truth is created, the philosopher should deal with it. However, the truth the philosopher recognizes in art is of a higher kind, is identical with absolute beauty, the truth of the Ideas.

In view of the inconsistencies and dissensions—even on the meaning of fundamental terms—which inevitably characterize art criticism in an age intent upon revivifying sources that have gone dry, it is especially imperative that we should investigate the absolute view of art as well as the forms through which it is expressed. For, so long as this is not done, there is no basis in judgment for criticizing vulgar and commonplace works, passing fads, etc.

Construction of art in all its particular forms leads of itself to relating them to the epochs that produced them and thus passes over into historical construction. There is little doubt that such a construction is entirely possible and can be extended to the whole history of art, since the dualism between ancient and modern art has already been studied by critics and demonstrated by poets. Construction always resolves oppositions; those within art arise out of its dependence upon time, and they are as inessential and purely formal as time itself. Scientific construction, therefore, will aim at demonstrating their common source and unity in order to arrive at a more comprehensive view.

Such a construction of art is, of course, unlike anything which up to this time has existed under the name of aesthetics, theory of the fine arts and sciences, etc. The originator of the term "aesthetics," at least, had some intimation of the beautiful as a manifestation of the archetype in the concrete world which is its copy. Since then, however, the idea of beauty has been made increasingly dependent on the moral and the useful. Similarly, in psychological theories beauty has been explained away as a ghost story or some other kind of superstition. Kantian formalism introduced a new and higher conception, but at the same time it gave rise to a great many hollow theories.

The seeds of a genuine science of art, sown by keen minds since Kant, have not yet fulfilled their promise. The philosopher who sees in art the inner essence of his own science as in a magic and symbolic mirror will inevitably make the philosophy of art one of his goals. To him it is a science important in itself, as the construction of the most admirable of all things in the world—as complete and self-contained as nature herself. From such a construction the enthusiastic student of nature learns the true archetypes of the forms which in nature he finds confused and obscure; he learns to recognize these forms in works of art as sensuous images which have their origin in nature and which are her symbols.

The intimate bond between art and religion, the total impossibility of creating a fresh poetic world outside of religion or without its help, and the impossibility, on the other hand, of giving religion adequate objective embodiment without the help of art—these considerations make a truly scientific insight into art a necessity in religion.

In closing, let me say that it is a disgrace in those who have a direct or indirect part in governing the state not to have familiarity with or receptivity to art. Nothing honors princes and those in authority more than respect and appreciation of the arts and encouragement to artists. It is a sad and shameful spectacle when those who have the means to promote art's finest flowering waste their money on tasteless, barbarous, vulgar displays. Even though the public at large may find it hard to grasp that art is a necessary, integral part of a state founded on Ideas, we should at least recall the example of antiquity, when festivals, public monuments, dramatic performances, and other communal activities together made up a single, universal, objective, and living work of art.

Editorial Notes

PAGE 7 *(tending toward unity)*

In Germany at the turn of the eighteenth century the term *Entzwei-ung* (cleavage, disunity, divorce) was as popular as the term "alienation" is today. Poets, artists, and philosophers complained of the intolerable cleavages between God and the world, spirit and nature, morality and happiness, etc. The epoch's most urgent need, they felt, was restoration of unity.

Madame de Staël who visited Germany in 1803 and 1807/8 notes this tendency *(De l'Allemagne,* III, 7): "I don't see why the idea of a single principle of philosophy, whether material or intellectual, is regarded as more truly philosophical. One principle does not make the world more easily comprehensible than two, and systems which recognize the physical and moral worlds as distinct are more congenial to our feelings."

In a surviving fragment of a lecture dating from 1803 *(Werke,* V, viii), Schelling says: "Kant posits as many different Reasons as he wrote Critiques. There is a well known epigram in which an observer listening to several art critics discussing various tastes cries out, 'But where is the taste of all the tastes?' Similarly Kant might be asked, 'Where is the Reason of all your Reasons?'"

PAGE 7 *(birth to a new world)*

The apocalyptic sentiment expressed here is characteristic of Schelling's philosophy which implies a desire to change the world, although Schelling himself scarcely ever offers any practical suggestions to achieve this metamorphosis here below. In his writings prophetic utterances about impending universal renewal occur constantly. For instance, as late as 1827 he assured his listeners that the moment was approaching "when at last the 4,000-year-old instability of human knowledge will end, and the ancient misunderstandings of mankind will be resolved." In 1841 he still expected the millennium.

PAGE 10   *(reality and substance of things)*

In other words, Schelling maintains in opposition to Kant that "the thing-in-itself" is accessible to reason.

PAGE 12   *(Action! action!)*

The words "Action! action! This is what we are for" are found in the concluding paragraph of Fichte's *Lectures on the Vocation of the Scholar* (first delivered at Jena in 1794). The whole passage seems to be a veiled attack on Fichte's emphasis upon "practical reason."

In 1804 Schelling wrote *(Werke,* VI, 540 f.): "The difference usually made between action and knowledge is nonessential. . . . The essence of the soul is one. There are no faculties—these are assumed by a false psychological abstraction. Whatever springs from the essence of the soul, whether knowledge or action, is absolute, is true, and both free and necessary.

"Abstraction (i.e., isolation of things from the whole), which is the source of all errors, of all one-sided and false systems, leads to the death of all true action. . . .

"The idea that knowledge is one thing and action another first led to the false belief that freedom can be independent of necessity. . . . If truthfulness (the ground of all virtues) is unity of action and knowledge, the separation between the two is the first lie. Our morality is merely this lie continued, namely, the belief in a virtue that does not spring from the essence of human nature."

PAGE 24   *(Lichtenberg)*

Lichtenberg, Georg Christoph (1742–1799) was a physicist by profession. His occasional writings (among them, *Letters from England* and *Aphorisms*) are celebrated for their wit and humor.

PAGE 27   *(the student's eyes)*

Schelling's portrait of the ideal teacher is suspiciously like himself. His tendency in his early period to present his ideas before they had fully matured had the saving grace of making him an exciting lecturer. Various contemporary sources confirm his popularity as a teacher. In his diaries, Henry Crabb Robinson, after describing the dullness of other professors, notes:

"I shall at the close of this lecture instantly proceed to Schelling and purify my fancy polluted by the inspection of rotten carcasses and smoked skeletons, by hearing the modern Plato read for a whole hour

his new metaphysical theory of Aesthetics or the Philosophy of the Arts:
I shall, in spite of the obscurity of a philosophy compounded of the
most profound abstraction and enthusiastic mysticism, be interested by
particular ingenious remarks and amused by extravagant novelties. . . .
I shall be a little touched perhaps by the contemptuous treatment of
our English critics and hear something like his abuse of [Erasmus]
Darwin last Wednesday. . . . I shall hear again Burke and Horne and
the 'thick-skinned' Johnson and the 'shallow' Priestley briefly dis-
patched and hear it intimated that it is absurd to expect the science
of beauty in a country that values the mathematics only as it helps to
make spinning jennies and stocking-weaving machines and beauty only
as it recommends their manufactories abroad. I shall sigh and say too
true! . . . At 4 I shall again return to Schelling and hear his grand
lecture on speculative philosophy. I shall be animated if I happen to be
in an enthusiastic frame, at the sight of more than 130 enquiring
young men listening with attentive ears to the exposition of a philosophy in its pretensions more glorious than any publicly maintained
since the days of Plato and his commentators: a philosophy equally
inimical to Locke's empiricism, Hume's scepticism and Kant's criticism,
which has been but the ladder of the new and rising sect."

(*Crabb Robinson in Germany, 1801–1805.* Oxford University Press,
1929. pp. 117 f.)

PAGE 40 *(Goethe's poem)*

The reference is to "Apotheosis of the Artist" where the pupil, told
to study the book of nature, replies:
    The pages are too colossal,
      And the characters strangely abbreviated.

PAGE 40 *(Wolf)*

Wolf, Friedrich August (1759–1824), founder of the science of philology, was a champion of classical studies. His *Prolegomena ad
Homerum* (1795) advanced the theory that the *Iliad* and the *Odyssey*
were based on songs composed by earlier rhapsodists—a view which
reflects romantic exaltation of nature as opposed to art.

PAGE 50 *(in the Idea)*

According to Kant, every intuition is "sensuous," i.e., involves a
sensory impression, and an intellectual intuition would be a contradiction in terms. To Schelling, intellectual intuition is identical with
Spinoza's third (and highest) kind of knowledge: in it, the observer "is"
the thing observed, subject is identical with object, infinite with finite,
universal with particular. To the philosopher it is what the creative
imagination is to the poet, the faculty that enables us to rise above

the finite world of change and apprehend the eternal archetypes, the Ideas. This faculty is no more mystical or mysterious than our intuition of pure space, which makes empirical intuition possible. Not all men possess it, however, any more than all men possess the poetic faculty.

Hegel had no place for intellectual intuition; according to him we know Ideas through "concepts" as distinguished from mere abstractions. The concept and its objective existence, he says, are two aspects of one and the same thing; the unity of actual existence and the concept is the Idea. Schelling apparently felt that Hegel's "concept" was not essentially different from his own "intellectual intuition." In the letter (Nov. 1807) he wrote to Hegel after reading the Preface to the *Phenomenology* (the last in the correspondence between the two philosophers), he says: "I am still unable to understand in what sense you oppose 'concept' to 'intuition.' Surely, your 'concept' denotes what you and I used to call 'the Idea,' whose very nature is to have one aspect as concept and another as intuition."

PAGE 53   *(slavery in new forms)*

Like so many young men of the time Schelling began as an enthusiastic supporter of the French Revolution and became disillusioned with the Terror, an attitude which Napoleon's dictatorship reinforced. In 1804, in his famous memorial essay on Kant, Schelling noted that the decline of Kantianism (i.e., the rise of the new idealism) and the ebb of the French Revolution coincide. To quote him, "What the two have in common is the merely negative and inadequate resolution of the conflict between reality and abstraction, which the Kantian system could not master speculatively any more than the Revolution could overcome on the practical plane."

PAGE 53   *(expression of Ideas)*

Schelling developed this point more fully in an essay entitled *Über das Verhältniss der Naturphilosophie sur Philosophie überhaupt* (1802). Morality, he says, liberates the soul from alien material elements, and "the same purification of the soul is prerequisite to philosophy." The moral and intellectual viewpoints coincide: both are governed by pure universal reason. The moral point of view that excludes the intellectual ceases to be moral, and vice versa; neither has precedence over the other, although at the empirical level, the moral principle seems to come first. Innate knowledge is a reflection of the infinite and the universal in our natures; the moral imperative spontaneously aims at incorporating our particularity in the universal and infinite. "True knowledge turns away from mere reflections of the infinite in the finite, toward being-in-itself or primordial knowledge, requiring complete resolution of the particular in the universal, i.e., moral purity of the soul. Conversely, there is no true (not merely negative) morality without the soul's being at home in the world of Ideas. The kind of morality divorced from intellectuality is necessarily empty, for only the latter provides it with the matter of its actions. A man who has not purified his soul to the point of participating in primal knowledge has not attained moral perfection: the pure universal appears as something outside himself."

PAGE 54 *(First Citizens)*

The allusion is to Frederick the Great.

PAGE 58 *(pertain to its forms)*

Schelling's attitude here is illustrated by an anecdote told by Henry Crabb Robinson, who had supper with Schelling on Dec. 2, 1802. The guests "did not quit the table or rather the room till near one. The chat was half convivial, half philosophical, but it was rather the conviviality of philosophers than the philosophy of *bons vivants*. The more learned disputed about the reality of Paradise, of Homer, Orpheus, etc. On which occasion Schelling asserted that the Serpent was a much higher personage than Jesus. A gentleman present had a ring from England in the form of a serpent. 'What?' said Schelling to me. 'Is the Serpent the emblem of English philosophy?' 'O no,' I said, 'but in England they use it as the symbol of German philosophy which changes its coat every year.' 'A proof,' he replied, 'that Englishmen do not look deeper than the coat.'" (*Crabb Robinson in Germany, 1801–1805*. Oxford University Press, 1929, p. 119 f.)

As for the reference to the Serpent: In his Lectures on the Philosophy of Art (winter 1802), Schelling observes that Lucifer is far more individualized and realistic than the other angels, in Christian mythology.

PAGE 74 *(incapable of understanding)*

A passage in Hegel's *Phenomenology* which deals at length with the inadequacy of feeling in philosophy and the need for disciplined thinking, is often quoted in disparagement of Schelling.

PAGE 78 *(in every part)*

Schelling often illustrates "the basic pattern of the universe" with the help of the bar magnet. In the act of self-cognition the absolute constitutes itself as object (the real world) and as subject (the ideal world). Between the two is "the point of indifference." In the bar magnet represented as the line

A	C	B

A and B indicate the positive and negative poles (= ideal and real) and C the neutral area (= point of indifference). No matter at what point the magnet is broken, the same pattern will be repeated in each fragment.

PAGE 81   *(only with medicine)*

The place accorded to medicine by Schelling reflects the actual situation at that time. Medicine was almost the only "natural science" taught at the university.

PAGE 102   *(the Gospel of the absolute)*

In the essay quoted above (note to p. 53) Schelling summarizes these same views as follows. Every religion is essentially a deification of the finite or a direct intuition of God in the finite. "This is the only possible antithesis in religion, and for this reason there are only two religions, paganism and Christianity. The former sees the natural principle directly in divine and spiritual archetypes; the latter sees *through* nature conceived of as the infinite body of God, and penetrates to its innermost core, to God's very spirit. In both, nature is the ground and source of the intuition of the infinite."

Christianity, Schelling goes on to say, arose out of the feeling of a divorce between God and the world; it aimed at reconciliation with God, not by raising the finite to infinity, but by God's becoming man. Viewed historically, Greek religion and poetry began with the finite and ended with the infinite. Christianity proceeds in the opposite sense, and is not yet completed. Once its goal—the absorption of the infinite in the finite—has been achieved, once it has been transfigured and attains the beauty of Greek religion, "the kingdom of Heaven will be reconquered and the absolute Gospel proclaimed." Schelling concludes: "Whether the present epoch, so remarkable a turning point in culture, science, and works of man, will also prove a turning point in religion, and whether the time has come for the true Gospel of reconciliation between God and the world . . . is a question that must be answered individually by those who scan the future."

Schelling's dream of a philosophical religion reconciling "the ancient conflict" has yet to be realized.

PAGE 103   *(History)*

The term "history" can denote (1) the events themselves, and (2) the historian's account of them. Schelling most often uses two different words: *Geschichte* for history in the first sense, and *Historie* for history in the second sense. We translate the second (wherever ambiguity might arise) as "history in the strict sense." However, Schelling is not himself perfectly consistent in his usage.

PAGE 109　*(Müller)*

Müller, Johannes von (1752–1809), Swiss historian, wrote a universal history among other works.

PAGE 113　*(natural rights)*

Schelling's contribution to the topic of so-called natural rights is an essay entitled "New Deduction of Natural Right," published in 1796. In it he reduces the concept to absurdity: "Natural right inevitably destroys itself," for ultimately it entrusts the preservation of right to brute force. The real philosophical problem, he says, is how to make the physical power of the individual identical with the moral power of law, or how to create conditions in which brute force is always on the side of right.

PAGE 124　*(confirmation of experience)*

This passage must not be interpreted as a rejection of the role of experience in natural science. Perhaps the clearest statement of Schelling's views on this subject is found in the *Introduction to the Draft of a Philosophy of Nature* (1799): "Everything we know, we know originally through experience, and in this sense all our knowledge consists of experiential propositions. These become a priori propositions when we realize that they are necessary, and any proposition, whatever its content, can be raised to the dignity of an a priori. . . . It is nature itself that is a priori, i.e., every thing in it is determined in advance by the whole. And since nature is a priori, it must be possible to recognize it as something that is a priori, and this is the true sense of our assertion."

In the essay *On the True Idea of the Philosophy of Nature* (1801), Schelling notes on the subject of "construction": "Nature is her own legislator. . . . In my Philosophy of Nature I consider nature as self-constructed. To understand this, one must rise to intellectual intuition of nature. The empiricists do not rise so high, and for this very reason all their explanations are their own [not Nature's] 'constructions.'"

PAGE 124　*(the most German of all poems)*

The reference is to the *Faust Fragment* of 1790.

PAGE 128　*(Steffens)*

Steffens, Henrik (1773–1845), Norwegian-born German scientist, was an enthusiastic but not slavish adherent of Schelling's philosophy of nature. In addition to works on geology and anthropology, he wrote poems and an interesting autobiography.

PAGE 128   *(relatively ideal)*

In his early treatment of nature Schelling's method is often inductive. Some of his formulations foreshadow dialectical materialism, for example: being is prior to thought; nature is process at the core of which is conflict, and the highest development of which is the human mind; nature's so-called products are precarious moments of balance, and the scientist's task is to account not for the eternal creative process but for the possibility of moments of stasis. Schelling also rejects the theory of creation out of nothing in favor of the Spinozistic view (he called his philosophy of nature "the Spinozism of nature"): "Nature is not the product of some unintelligible creation, but this creation itself; not merely the manifestation of the eternal, but this eternal itself" (*Abhandlungen z. Erl. des Idealismus der Wissenschaftslehre*, 1796).

Later formulations, however, show a different spirit. Schelling resorts to poetic analogies which reflect his Gnostic preoccupations. For example, apropos of gravity and light, he says: "Gravity is merely the *ground* of reality in things . . . it is eternal night, an abyss of eternal stillness and seclusion in which things have no life of their own. But the infinite substance, insofar as it reaffirms its affirmation, is not merely ground but *cause* of reality. As such it manifests itself in light. Light is the affirmation of all things *qua* particular life; it is the eternal *word* of nature. . . . Gravity is Nature's eternal inhalation, light Nature's exhalation. . . . Gravity is the maternal principle of all things in nature, light the paternal. Made pregnant by light, gravity gives birth to the particular forms of things. . . ."

"In the true universe there are no suns and no planets, there is only one infinite omnipresent sun, light itself, and only one infinite planet, which is gravity. The things we commonly call suns and planets are individual images or copies of the absolute identity of gravity and light, some of which are more accomplished than others; in an organic body, the instruments of motion, the muscles, for example, are in a sense the planets, while the sense organs, especially the eyes, are the suns; the soul, omnipresent, feels and contemplates herself in each organ."

"The earth, and not only the earth, every part of matter *is* already plant and animal, it can *become* it because it already *is* it. Petrified fossils are not imprints of actual organisms, they express the awakening of the organic pattern in the earth itself, they are abortive organisms which were frustrated by gravity and sank back into rigidity . . ."

"So-called dead matter is merely a slumbering plant and animal world, drunk with finiteness as it were, which still awaits its resurrection or has missed it." (*Phil. Propedeutik* and *System der ges. Phil.*, etc., 1804; *Werke*, VI, 266, 360, 389, 390.)

PAGE 131 *(to be necessary)*

In 1806, Schelling drew up the following diagram illustrative of the organization of the universe:

God
the All

Relative-real totality		*Relative-ideal totality*
Gravity, matter		Truth, Science
Light, motion		the Good, Religion
Life, organism		Beauty, art
The Cosmos	Reason	History
Man	Philosophy	The State

Schelling adds: "We warn against misuse of this diagram by persons unable to breathe life into it" (*Werke*, VII, 184).

PAGE 135 *(Brown's theory)*

Brown, John (1735–1788), Scottish physician, advanced the theory (in his *Elementa medicinae*, 1779) that all life processes, including disease, can be accounted for by "excitability," i.e., the organism's responses to external or internal stimuli. Diseases are either "sthenic" or "asthenic," that is, marked by an excess or deficiency of "excitability," and accordingly must be treated either by sedatives or stimulants. The book caused a great stir in Scotland, even leading to riots there; Germany was especially receptive to such a single unifying, all-encompassing system. Historically, John Brown's theory marked an advance over the older theory according to which most diseases are inflammations of impure fluids in the body and must be treated by purges or blood-letting.

PAGE 138 *(as sense perception)*

Perhaps some light is thrown on this obscure passage by the following excerpts (*Werke*, VI, 398 f.; 1804):

"The first dimension is that of selfhood, self-continuation (e.g., magnetism). . . . Corresponding to the first dimension is reproduction in the broadest sense of the term, for by reproduction the organism is capable of indefinitely extending its own existence as . . . individual (growth) or as species (begetting other organisms like it). . . . This dimension is represented chiefly by plants."

"The second dimension is the one whereby a thing is in other things . . . it corresponds to living motion or irritability, . . . by which the organism comes into contact with things outside itself. . . . This dimension is represented by animal life."

"The third dimension is the synthesis of the other two. Here the organism is productive of other things . . . but in such a way that these are within itself. . . . This dimension represents sensibility or perceptivity."

Index